GIFTS
of the
SPIRIT

GIFTS
of the
SPIRIT

RONALD E. BAXTER

KREGEL PUBLICATIONS
Grand Rapids, Michigan 49501

Gifts of the Spirit Copyright © 1983 by Ronald E. Baxter. Published by Kregel Publications, a division of Kregel, Inc. All rights reserved.

Library of Congress Cataloging in Publication Data

Baxter, Ronald E., 1983-
  Gifts of the Spirit.

  Bibliography: p.
  1. Gifts, Spiritual.   I. Title.
BT767.3.B34   1983   234'.13   83-14963
ISBN 0-8254-2243-4 (pbk.)

Printed in the United States of America

To my wife Glenys

who is richly endowed with the "quiet gifts" of exhortation and helps. Through all the years of my ministry, she has been a faithful helper and encourager in every undertaking for God's glory, both in the home and in the pastorate. This book is largely the result of her proper exercise of these gifts in relationship to her husband.

CONTENTS

CONCLUSION

IMPORTANT!

The numbers in parentheses following a quotation refer to the Bibliography list beginning on page 251 together with the page number of the book cited. Example: (79:3) refers to Bibliography book number 79, page 3.

PREFACE

"GIFT THEOLOGY" so called, is exploding upon the market place. Whereas prior to 1965 very little was written on "The Gifts of the Spirit," today the situation has reversed. One writer indicates that approximately 80% of his books on the subject were written after 1970 (72:20).

In saying that there has come a flood of books on this previously forgotten subject, I am not suggesting that one could vouch for the "gift theology" being expounded. Perhaps in the push to publish, theology has been relegated to a position of minor importance. Whatever the reason, much of what is being written has a "feeling" orientation. Scripture tends to be subordinated to "experience."

Because of this, there has arisen a "non-theology," which reads the Scriptures but lives by "the gifts." There can even be a seeming emphasis on Scripture, which merely gives a facade to the individualized experience as being biblical. Thus we are bombarded by such double jargon as this, coming out of "Jesus 79," and quoted in *Christianity Today:*

> Episcopalian Maureen Gross, of New York City, expressed gratefulness for the charismatic movement. The organized ecumenical movement, she observed, pushes aside biblical doctrines in its attempts to recreate unity. "Today," she said, "we experience the unity of a solid scriptural basis" (91:43).

This claim to "a solid scriptural base" was made in spite of the fact that a major contributor to the "togetherness" was Cardinal Suenens, who has been charged by the Vatican with oversight of the charismatic renewal movement within Roman Catholicism. What, pray tell, is the difference between the older ecumenical movement and this newer version, if the Bible has nothing to say to such doctrinally divergent participants? Can both be on the same "solid Scriptural base"?

Surely, in view of this present situation, there is ample room for a fresh look at the gifts, in the sane light of the Word of God. So many theological myths have sprung from the fertile ground of experience, that we need to seriously consider the gifts—not in some new light—but in the old light of the Holy Scriptures.

To that end this work is written. It is a call back to the Word of God as the foundation and building material for all theology. May God use it to breathe sanity into the present chaos, in order that searching souls will be able to divide between experiential myth and biblical truth.

INTRODUCTION

1

LET'S DEMYTHOLOGIZE THE GIFTS

A MYTH is "a fictitious narrative usually involving supernatural persons or events." A number of years ago in Canada, three church groups went together to produce Sunday School material called, "The New Curriculum." However, such a furor resulted over the attempt to "demythologize" the first eleven chapters of the Bible that one group never did use the material.

For one to interpret any portion of the Bible as a myth would be totally unacceptable to evangelical Christians. To us the Bible is the Word of God, inerrant and infallible. It is not a collection of evolutionary thought about God, the world, man and sin. We believe the Bible to be literally true from Genesis to Revelation and of final authority on all matters of faith and practice.

Then why does an avowed evangelical, indeed an avowed fundamentalist, speak of "demythologizing the gifts"? Am I implying that 1 Corinthians chapters 12, 13 and 14, Rom. 12:6-8 and Eph. 4:7-11 are myth? Or am I implying that these passages of God's Word are not to be taken literally? Am I saying that the gifts, as they are found in the Scriptures, are myths?

To answer these important questions, we must face a matter even more fundamental. What is our basis for believing in the gifts? In what light are we to interpret them? Can we agree that we have an objective source from which we can unerringly discover God's revelation about the gifts of the Holy Spirit?

Fortunately we do not have to wallow in either indecision or uncertainty, in facing these matters. In closing off His revelation of Himself to mankind, God has written to us the injunction of Rev. 22:18-19. But what do these verses have to do with "demythologizing the gifts"?

The importance of these verses is seen, on the one hand, in relationship to such groups as the liberal theologians which we already mentioned. They would "take away from" the writings of the Bible. Their destructive "criticism" would remove the supernatural, strip Jesus Christ of His deity and reduce the Scriptures to a collection of human ponderings. Thus God's warning is:

> And if any man shall take away from the words of the book of this prophecy, God shall take away his part out of the book of life, and out of the holy city, and from the things which are written in this book (Rev. 22:19).

But there is another side to God's final warning to mankind regarding the completion of His revealed Word. We are not to "add to" the teaching of the Book. It is not to be the Bible plus Church tradition, as Roman Catholicism proclaims. The Book of Mormon is not to be added to the Scriptures as Joseph Smith and his adherents teach. When the Scriptures ended, the canon of holy revelation was complete. God Himself says so in Rev. 22:19, as quoted previously.

The fact is that it is just as important not to bring myth to the Scriptures, as it is not to call any Bible passage a myth. Our appeal must always be to the Scriptures alone. This was the watchword of the sixteenth-century Reformation—*sola Scriptura,* or "Scripture alone!" This ought to be the method of all who hold to a high view of Scripture. As the great expositor, W. Graham Scroggie wrote:

> The only test of what is, or is not of God, is the Scriptures, and not the doctrines of men, neither our experiences, save in so far as they demonstrate the truth of Scripture (79:3).

If a position held is not in accordance with the Scriptures, therefore, it is not only right to disagree with it but also to expose its error on biblical grounds.

Well, what does all this have to do with our thinking on the gifts of the Spirit? Just this, we need to be absolutely sure that what we teach and believe about the gifts is according to *sola Scriptura.* Ours must be an objective belief that is grounded upon the rock of the Holy Scriptures. We must be absolutely sure that we are not superimposing our "myths" on the teaching of the Word of God. As John F. Walvoord states:

> The final test must always be what the Scriptures actually teach. Experience may serve as a partial test of the conclusions, but, in itself, the Bible must be taken as the final authority. Experience ever possesses two fatal grounds for error: (1) a misapprehension of the experience itself and its content and divine origin, (2) a faulty conclusion as to the doctrinal meaning of the experience. Hence, on the one hand, an experience supposedly of divine origin may be purely psychological, or worse, a deceiving device of Satan himself. On the other hand, a genuine experience may be misunderstood and mislabeled, as the common denomination of the work of the filling of the Spirit, as the baptism of the Spirit. The Christian seeking the truth must come in all humility and dependence on the Spirit, to the Word of God, relying on its teachings implicitly, avoiding even by undue emphasis any warping of the truth (73:174).

Now just here is the problem with much that is written, believed and taught about the gifts. There is so much subjectivism (i.e., teaching and belief founded upon experience), that many can get along quite well without any real contact with the Scriptures.

> And when we speak of experience over the Word, we are saying that the meaning of the Bible is subordinated to the meaning which man imposes on the Word (89:21).

Thus each one is left to "do his own thing," which does not necessarily have any relationship to God's revealed will in the Bible.

You see, there is a so-called "Gift Theology"[1] abroad that, carried to its logical conclusion, so downgrades objective understanding of the Scriptures, as to make the Bible second to one's own subjective position. For example, when dealing

---

[1] C. Peter Wagner uses this term to describe his philosophy of gifts. In as much as he is an associate professor at Fuller Theological Seminary, and a part of the Fuller Evangelistic Association, teaching "church growth" to over 3000 pastors yearly; and in as much as he specifically teaches many seminars on "the gifts of the Spirit" across America, we can expect to see the development of this term in the days ahead.

with the number of gifts, C. Peter Wagner opts for an "open-ended approach." And what does he mean by that? Let him explain:

> Because none of the three primary lists is complete, and the three lists together are not complete, it is reasonable to conclude that the list of all the gifts mentioned in the Bible (and we have counted 25 of them) may not be complete either.
> This is what I mean by an open-ended approach to the gifts. I do not doubt that there are even more than 27 of them. Some might want to add the gift of music and make it 28 or craftsmanship and make it 29. I ran into another gift recently which might be called the "gift of names" (72:73).

Do you see the possibilities? Some may decide they have the gift of "mountaineering," others of "garbage collecting," and so on!

The emphasis is no longer on the Word of God, but on the individual. The Scriptures become subservient to the person, rather than being the authoritative rule and guide in his life. It was this same subjective "theology" which plunged our world into "situational ethics" a few years back. The ultimate end is, "whatever is right for you, is right."

Because of this, Wagner tells churches not to be concerned about their position on the gifts. They are not to worry about examining them in the light of the Scriptures, but simply to continue whatever their "gift-mix" might be. To him it really does not matter whether or not that "gift-mix" is according to the Scriptures. Such an approach is the logical outgrowth of pure subjective "theology" as opposed to objective truth. The emphasis is on "experience" rather than Scripture (72:81ff).

The attitude is well illustrated by this account from a two-day Charismatic Renewal Conference that took place in Londonderry, Ireland, in February 1977. As an informal discussion progressed, non-charismatic Rev. James McClelland asked the lady with whom he was speaking if she had her Bible, so that together they could discuss the Scriptures concerning the gifts of the Spirit. She confessed that she did not bring a Bible with her to the conference, whereupon a bystander came to her defense with the statement, "You don't need to have a Bible at this meeting, the preacher has one" (87:3).

The point is, "as long as you have the experience," subjectivism strongly argues, "you do not really need the Bible." Thus the basis for belief is shifted from the Scriptures to the individual. And just at this point we are back to the basic problem; *if the Bible does not have absolute authority in our belief and practice, then absolute authority must be placed in man.* When we reach that position, the opinion of each person is as valid as the opinion of every other person.

Harold Lindsell aptly illustrates this point:

> Writing about the meeting of 12,000 Roman Catholic charismatics at Notre Dame last June, Willmar Thorkelson of the Minneapolis *Star* quoted Vinson Synan, author of a very competent history entitled, The Pentecostal Holiness Movement, as saying that he rejoiced "at the growth of Catholic Pentecostalism" and that "the Spirit of God told me it was real." But suppose someone else says it is counterfeit. Whose word shall we then take? The Old Testament abounds with evidences both of true and false prophets. Jeremiah was a true prophet, Hananiah a false one. The test of a true prophet is whether what he prophesied comes to pass. Hananiah failed this test. The test of the tongues-speaker is not that he has spoken in tongues, for even pagans do this, but how he receives and accepts the propositional revelation of God in Holy Scripture. It is a matter of what he believes, not simply of an experience he has had (85:10).

The Word of God must be our sole court of appeal in dealing with experience. Only then can we be saved from the confusion of the present-day subjectivism.

When speaking to a young man about his involvement in the Charismatic Movement, I was confronted with this subjective statement as a final argument, "Well, you can't deny my experience!" The fact is that I was not trying to deny his experience, but I was denying that it was Scriptural. Objective truth is the test of experience, and that is found only in the Bible.

Well says Geoffrey J. Paxton on this matter:

> Evangelism needs to beware. The miraculous, the unusual, the pragmatically "helpful" may govern our approach to the Word so that what we find is only the confirmation of our

experiences. The slogan, "The man with an experience is never at the mercy of the man with an argument," is highly dangerous and can be positively pagan! (89:30).

If experience (subjectivism) closes the door to a search of the Scriptures (objectivism), then we deny the authority of God's Word upon our lives. Thereby, no matter what the experience, Jesus is not Lord (Luke 6:46).

John F. MacArthur puts the choices clearly when he states:

> There are only two basic approaches to biblical truth: (1) the historical objective approach, which emphasizes God's action toward man as recorded in Scripture, (2) the personal subjective approach, which emphasizes man's experience of God. If we had our choice, how would we build a theology? Would we go to the Bible or to the experiences of thousands of people? If we go to the people, we will have as many views as there are individuals to give those views.
>
> Objective historic theology is Reformation theology. It is historical evangelicalism. It is historical orthodoxy. We begin with God's Word and anybody's thoughts, ideas, or experiences are validated or invalidated on the basis of how they compare with that Word (32:61).

If we are to stand with those who historically lived by and died for the Word of God, we must choose the objective approach to faith and practice and found our entire theology upon the Scriptures.

This was the methodology of the early church, and in view of this, those experience-oriented charismatics of our day need to take a long, hard look at the Church in Berea. We read of them:

> These were more noble than those in Thessalonica, in that they received the word with all readiness of mind, and searched the Scriptures daily whether those things were so (Acts 17:11).

Those who search the Scriptures for objective truth will always be "more noble" than those whose foundation is the shifting sand of experience.

When Paul wrote his first letter to the Thessalonica Church, he ended with this triumvirate of admonitions.

> Quench not the Spirit, despise not prophesyings, prove all things; hold fast that which is good (1 Thess. 5:19-21).

Note well the order and the advice. The ultimate of faith in relation to the Holy Spirit comes when everything we hear and see is "proven" by the Word of God, as to whether it is indeed biblically so. Far from "quenching the Spirit," such a procedure recognizes the work of the Spirit in Divine revelation and is commended by God Himself.

Peter tells us that we got our Bible, when "holy men of God spake as they were moved by the Holy Ghost" (2 Peter 1:21). Then, immediately he plunges into a warning about teachers and about teaching that is not according to the truth of the revealed Scripture. He says:

> But there were false prophets also among the people, even as there shall be false prophets among you . . . and many shall follow their pernicious ways; by reason of whom the way of truth shall be evil spoken of (2 Peter 2:1-2).

How do we ensure that the Bible—"the way of truth" written under inspiration of the Holy Ghost—does not "be evil spoken of?" By examining all teaching and experience in the objective light of heaven's standard of truth, the Word of God, and by submitting ourselves to its meaning.

To the people of His day, who were rejecting Him as Messiah and Savior, Jesus said:

> Search the scriptures; for in them ye think ye have eternal life: and they are they which testify of me (John 5:39).

Our Lord Himself appealed to people to let the objective truth of Scripture be their final court of appeal in relation to His ministry. Indeed, later He went even farther in saying:

> He that rejecteth me, and receiveth not my words, hath one that judgeth him: the word that I have spoken, the same shall judge him in the last day. For I have not spoken of myself; but the Father which sent me, he gave me a commandment, what I should say, and what I should speak (John 12:48-49).

To Jesus the Word of God was the standard for judging and being judged on the beliefs and practices we embrace.

To sum up, what we believe and teach about the gifts of the Holy Spirit must not take away from nor add to the teaching of the Word of God. It would be wrong for us to follow the course of the so-called "higher critics" of the Scriptures, and remove or reject passages of the Bible because of the supernatural involved in them. On the other hand, it would be equally wrong to build our personal myths around certain passages and thereby "add to" the teaching of the Word of God.

My present concern deals with the latter. It seems to me that the pendulum has swung so far that the gifts have been unintentionally mythologized. Much of that which is being taught and believed is in addition to, and not because of, the Word of God. A whole extra-biblical "tradition" has sprung up which is fast becoming (if it has not already become) as authoritative among Charismatics as is the Word of God. My plea to demythologize the gifts is, therefore, a call back to God's own standard given to us in Rev. 22:18-19.

PART 1
MYTHS BASED IN TERMS

2

THE GIFT AND THE GIFTS

IN DEMYTHOLOGIZING the gifts of the Spirit, one must differentiate clearly on a number of fronts. As the gifts are seen in contrast to other components of the doctrine of the Holy Spirit, they can be divided from the whole and examined in their individual parts. Without such a procedure, much mythical teaching and belief is given fertile ground in which to be sown and grow.

A. THE GIFT OF THE HOLY SPIRIT

Some of the last words Jesus spoke to His disciples are recorded in John 14:16-17. They speak of a gift which the Father would bestow in the name of the Lord Jesus (John 15:26). These are the words:

> And I will pray the Father, and he shall give you another Comforter, that he may abide with you for ever; even the Spirit of truth; whom the world cannot receive, because it seeth him not, neither knoweth him: but ye know him; for he dwelleth with you, and shall be in you (John 14:16-17).

The same promise was repeated just before Christ's ascension but this time in terms of a "baptism." In Acts 1:4-5 we read that:

> He commanded them that they should not depart from Jerusalem, but wait for the promise of the Father, which, saith He, ye have heard of me. For John truly baptized with water; but ye shall be baptized with the Holy Ghost not many days hence.

This "promise" was the one heard from Christ in John 14:16-17 and was to be fulfilled "not many days hence."

Some ten days later, after the gift of the Holy Spirit had been given on Pentecost, the concept of "the gift" was crystallized in New Testament preaching. Peter said to those concerned about salvation:

> Repent, and be baptized every one of you in the name of Jesus Christ for the remission of sins, and ye shall receive the gift of the Holy Ghost. For the promise is unto you, and to your children, and to all that are afar off, even as many as the Lord our God shall call (Acts 2:38-39).

The "gift of the Holy Ghost" was now regarded as received in salvation.

Later, in Acts 19, where Paul seeks to discover the spiritual condition of "certain disciples" at Ephesus, the crucial question asked is that of verse 2. By an unfortunate translation however, the King James version gives an entirely wrong impression of Paul's statement.[1] *The New International Version* (along with many other modern translations) renders the text more correctly with the words: "Did you receive the Holy Spirit when you believed?" (99). What Paul was seeking to determine was whether or not these people were truly saved (Rom. 8:9). If they had received "the gift" they were saved; if they had not, they were not saved.

Merrill F. Unger correctly deals with this matter when he says:

> The term "gift of the Spirit," therefore, does not refer to some experience subsequent to salvation but to salvation itself. Nor does the phrase refer to a gift to be received today. It was received over nineteen centuries ago at Pentecost and has been the permanent deposit of the church ever since and the heritage of each believer, the moment he trusts Christ and experiences salvation (65:135).

Each and every "born again" person has received the gift of the Holy Spirit, or else he is not truly born again.

We are now ready to consider the second term:

B. THE GIFTS OF THE HOLY SPIRIT

There is a clear difference between the "gift" and the "gifts" in the Scriptures. The gift of the Holy Spirit is related to the

---

[1] Marvin R. Vincent explains that: "The two verbs are in the aorist tense, and therefore denote instantaneous acts. The A.V. therefore gives an entirely wrong idea, as there is no question about what happened after believing; but the question relates to what occurred when they believed" (66:551).

note

saving work of Christ in the heart and soul of the lost. The gifts of the Holy Spirit on the other hand deal with the service of that saved individual within the local church.

W. A. Criswell relates the gift to doctrines such as the indwelling of the Holy Spirit, stating that this occurs at conversion. The Holy Spirit thereby resides forever in the life of the regenerate soul. At the same time:

> The "gifts" (plural) are imparted to the saved by the Holy Spirit for service in the Church. The child of God is to stir up, to kindle his gift and not to neglect it (2 Tim. 1:6) (7:146).

In his view also, the gifts (plural) flow from the gift (singular) of the Holy Spirit.

It is obvious, therefore, that if one has not received "the gift," he cannot have "the gifts." The Holy Spirit in one's life marks the difference between mere religious profession and a genuine possession of the new birth. Since this is true, Bryant remarks, "He is the source of all other gifts" (5:68). Therefore, "the gift" of the Holy Spirit is again stated to be foundational to the reception of "the gifts."

note

C. DEFINING "THE GIFTS"

But what are spiritual gifts? Various definitions have been given to specify what the term signifies:

Merrett: The gifts were divine in origin, miraculous in manifestation, and supernatural in operation (36:172).

Walvoord: Spiritual gifts are divinely given capacities to perform useful functions for God, especially in the area of service (74:38).

Clemens: By definition a spiritual gift is the ability given by God for a special type of service. It is not a place of service, nor is it a ministry to a particular age group. It is, rather, the ability itself, such as teaching or pastoring (6:314).

Owen: . . . they are that without which the church cannot subsist in the world, nor can believers be useful unto one another and the rest of mankind, unto the glory of Christ, as they ought to be. They are the "powers of the world to come;" those effectual operations of the power of Christ whereby his kingdom was erected and is preserved (42:832).

When we come to the Word of God, we discover that there are two main words used of the gifts in 1 Corinthians chapter 12. First of all:

1. The Gifts are Ta Pneumatika

In 1 Cor. 12:1 we read: "Now concerning spiritual gifts, brethren I would not have you ignorant." In the original, "gifts" is not found. These are literally "the spirituals" (*ton pneumatikōn*), and are defined in verse 7 as "the manifestation of the Spirit [which] is given to every man to profit withal."

Vine gives an excellent review of the use of the parent word *pneumatikos* in the New Testament, telling us that the word:

> always connotes the ideas of invisibility and of power. It does not occur in the Septuagint nor in the Gospels; it is in fact an after-Pentecost word (71:64).

He tells us that it applies to angels as "spiritual hosts;" to things having their origin and harmony in God, to the purposes of God, to songs of the Church, to people who walk so as to please God, to blessings accruing to Christians, and to all that is produced and maintained among regenerate men by the Spirit of God.

Among its many uses is that which describes the gifts of the Spirit. They are "spiritual" gifts. Thus, they are gifts which are not of man, neither by man, but of God. They are produced in man by the Holy Spirit's sovereign distribution (1 Cor. 12:11).

The derivative *ta pneumatika* therefore, denotes the things of the Spirit. Walvoord says, "The word directs attention to the source, the Holy Spirit, and the realm of these gifts" (73:164). Thus these gifts were entirely separate from what we might call "talents," or "natural abilities."

J. Oswald Sanders corroborates this thought. When speaking of the significance of spiritual gifts, he calls attention to G. Campbell Morgan's translation of the term by the word "spiritualities." Then he states, "The Corinthian Church was plagued with carnalities and needed to return to the spiritualities, that which has its source in the Spirit"

(49:109). The gifts are, therefore, set forth in the Scriptures as the endowment of the Spirit of God.

There is a second word used of the gifts.

2. The Gifts are Ta Charismata

This is the expression used in 1 Corinthians chapter 12 verses 4, 9, 28, 30 and 31. Let verse 4 suffice to illustrate its use, "Now there are diversities of gifts, but the same Spirit." This also serves to press home the spiritual nature of the gifts—whether *ta pneumatika,* or *ta charismata.*

In the singular the word is *charisma* (gift) and the Greek scholar, J. H. Thayer, interprets it to mean:

> the extraordinary powers, distinguishing certain Christians and enabling them to serve the church of Christ, the reception of which is due to the power of divine grace operating in their souls by the Holy Spirit (62:667).

The word clearly shows the nature of spiritual gifts and the method of their reception. As Walvoord states:

> This word brings out the ground and nature of spiritual gifts. They are bestowed in grace, are entirely undeserved, and their power and operation is due to God alone (73:164).

While the word *charisma* is used extensively in the New Testament, Vine finds that it is always used in connection with "grace (*charis*) on the part of God as the Donor" (69:147). He gives many instances of this. These include the bestowal of salvation upon a sinner by *charis,* the deliverances received by God's children in answer to prayer, and a variety of endowments upon believers by the operation of the Holy Spirit in the churches. All of these uses emphasize God's grace in relation to spiritual gifts. They are God's undeserved gifts to His children, that they may be able to serve Him acceptably.

In conclusion, the gifts are not only spiritual but also undeserved. They are grace gifts bestowed at conversion. Tying together the gift and the gifts, Unger says:

> In reality all saved people are a deposit of the gift of the Spirit, are baptized by the Spirit into Christ, and are recipients of the

varied gifts of the Spirit for service in the church, the body of Christ (65:135).

Without the gift there are no gifts. However, when one has received "the gift," he has also received "the gifts" which God in sovereign grace gives to enable us to serve Him.

3

THE GIFTS AND THE GIFTED

To AVOID the mythological in our beliefs about the gifts of the Holy Spirit, there is another difference to be noted. This distinction has to do with the gifts and gifted men. Such a separation of terms will save us from much misunderstanding concerning offices and officers within the churches.

While making this division we need to be aware of what we mean by "the gifts and the gifted," as well as understanding their two different sources and their different functions. Think with me about:

A. THE MEANING OF THE GIFTS AND THE GIFTED

As a person reads the various lists of gifts recorded in the New Testament, he becomes aware that some are "personified" and some are not. Some refer to "gifts" and some refer to "gifted men." In broad terms, 1 Corinthians 12 speaks in terms of "gifts" and Ephesians 4 speaks in terms of "gifted men."

Let us consider the two lists with this in mind. The first passage dealing with gifts in 1 Corinthians 12 is found in verses 8 to 10. Then near the end of the chapter another list is presented in verse 28. Putting these two together we come up with these gifts:

1 Corinthians 12:8-10	*1 Corinthians 12:28*
1. The word of wisdom	1. Apostles
2. The word of knowledge	2. Prophets
3. Faith	3. Teachers
4. Gifts of healing	4. Miracles
5. Working of miracles	5. Healings
6. Prophecy	6. Helps
7. Discerning of spirits	7. Governments
8. Tongues	8. Tongues
9. Interpretation of tongues	9. Interpretation

It is clear that there is duplication in the lists. Furthermore, it is evident that even in 1 Corinthians 12, there is some personification,[1] but the majority are gifts bestowed upon individuals. However, when we come to Eph. 4:11 a simple glance at the list reveals that there is total humanization of the gifts mentioned:

1. Apostles   3. Evangelists
2. Prophets   4. Pastors-Teachers

These are not gifts apart from the men, but are rather the men themselves. The list is one of "gifted men." As Bryant observes:

> This personalization points to a two-pronged emphasis on gifts in the New Testament. They are spiritual abilities within men, and they are men of spiritual ability. The ability is God's spiritual gift to the man. The gifted man is God's spiritual gift to the church. The effect of this two-pronged emphasis is to remove the matter of spiritual gifts from the realm of personal edification and place those gifts plainly into the realm of the edification of the whole church (5:66).

Seeing this distinction saves the Bible student from confusion. Clearly, as Walvoord states:

> Spiritual gifts has reference to the supernatural powers possessed by individuals, while gifted men has reference to the sovereign placing of gifted men in the church for the purpose of ministering to the body (73:164).

We must keep this difference well defined in our thinking, for it removes theological thinking which can easily grow into an unscriptural myth.

There is a second concern which we must face in differentiating between these two terms. This deals with:

B. THE SOURCE OF THE GIFTS AND THE GIFTED

You will recall that in dealing with the gifts mentioned in 1 Corinthians 12, we discovered that each and every one

---

[1] This is obvious in the gifts listed as "apostles," "prophets," and "teachers." The function of these gifted men may be a fulfillment of some of the gifts in the earlier list.

mentioned was the sovereign work of the Spirit of God. After listing the gifts, Paul declares:

> But all these worketh that one and the selfsame Spirit, dividing to every man severally as he will (1 Cor. 12:11).

Thus our terminology is formed, "the gifts of the Spirit."

However, when we look at the list enumerated in Eph. 4:11 and ask ourselves, "From whence come these gifted men?" the answer is different. You see the focus of Ephesians 4 is our Lord Jesus Christ and His ministry to the church. Thus, when Paul is recording the source of these gifted men of verse 11, he says:

> But unto every one of us is given grace according to the measure of the gift of Christ. Wherefore he saith, When he ascended up on high, he led captivity captive, and gave gifts unto men (Eph. 4:7-8).

They are "the gift of Christ." They are His ascension "gifts unto men."

It would seem, therefore, that "the gifted men" precede "the gifts" in their placement in the church. The very last thing Christ did was to give "gifted men." The very first thing the Holy Ghost did was to make men "gifted!" This is not to say that the gifted existed without the gifts but it is to say that the gifts could exist in other than the gifted. The fact is that gifted men were often empowered by a superabundance of the gifts, for some of them (as we shall see later) held extraordinary offices. Therefore, the two terms are not entirely separated as 1 Cor. 12:28 confirms.

The third aspect of difference concerns:

C. THE FUNCTION OF THE GIFTS AND THE GIFTED

It is quite apparent that the Corinthian believers had lost sight of why they received the gifts of the Spirit. They had become selfish and sensual (1 Cor. 5:1). Carnality had so gripped them that they were factionalized into a variety of spiritual cliques (1 Cor. 1:12).

Such egocentric living carried over into the church services. The big thing was not the exalting of Christ and the benefitting of others, but the glorification of self. Compounding the tragedy was the fact that the gifts were being used to promote such sorry worship.

Now unto this church Paul wrote 1 Corinthians 14. It was like a bombshell! All that they were so piously doing in their selfish worship services caused Paul to explode. The grand purpose for which the gifts were given was "outward" and not "inward." They were not for selfish ends but for edifying ends—and that of the entire church.

So, the use of the gifts—all of the gifts—in 1 Corinthians 12 was to be tempered by three basic questions: (1) "Does it bring glory to God?" (1 Cor. 14:23, 33, 40), (2) "Does it edify the entire church?" (1 Cor. 14:1-4, 26), and (3) "Does it lead the lost to Christ?" (1 Cor. 14:23-25).

On the other hand, when Paul expounds in Eph. 4:12-16 on the function of the gifted men, he views matters from a leadership standpoint rather than from a congregational setting. Says Green, "The purpose of these primary gifts to the church is 'to equip the saints for work of service in building up of the body of Christ' " (20:67).

What are the functions of the gifted men? In this passage they are:

1. The "perfecting," or maturing of the believers (v. 12).
2. The "work of the ministry," or serving is involved (v. 12).
3. Edifying, or the spiritual upbuilding of the members is a part (v. 12).
4. Promoting "unity" among the membership through "faith" and the "knowledge" of Christ (v. 13).
5. Teaching the members, so that they know right from wrong in doctrine (v. 14).
6. Exhorting that all speak in love and in truth, as together the people grow in Christ (v. 15).
7. Encouragement of the members to use their gifts for the edifying of the total body (v. 16).

You will notice that the ministry of the gifted is totally given over to others. It is to be unselfish, spiritual, morally sound, and encouraging. In the same manner, the gifts given by the Holy Spirit are to be developed for the greater good of all within the local church.

An obvious conclusion to this understanding of the gifts is the knowledge that they are not solely for the gifted today. In some quarters there has been an erroneous view that only in evangelists, or pastors, or teachers do the gifts reside. Nothing could be farther from the truth. As they always were, so they are now; today's gifts are the deposit of the Holy Spirit within "the body of Christ" and "members in particular."

Gifted men may indeed be endowed with an abundance of the gifts by virtue of God's sovereign purpose and call upon their lives. However, gifted men need members who are gifted to contribute to church growth that glorifies God, edifies the members, and reaches the lost. As Hollis Green states, "Each individual Christian has been chosen to exercise a specific responsibility. Some are in positions of leadership, yet each has a contribution that he alone can make to the church" (20:67).

4

GIFTS, TALENTS AND FRUIT

DIFFERENTIATING between the gifts of the Holy Spirit and that with which they are mistakenly joined is important. Without isolating the gifts, one cannot examine them in the light of Scripture. Yet the searchlight of the Word is precisely that which demythologizes the gifts.

With this in mind, let us consider two more distinctions from the gifts. The first of these concerns the natural, the second concerns the spiritual. First of all, we must be aware that:

A. THE GIFTS DIFFER FROM NATURAL TALENTS

When Peter wrote to the Christians who had been "scattered" abroad during the days of intense persecution, he addressed them as "strangers." That is how they felt, and that is what they were. They were exiles from home!

However, the gift God had bestowed upon each of them went with him wherever he was driven. Hence, Peter wrote the following words to encourage these Christians in service:

> As every man hath received the gift, even so minister the same one to another, as good stewards of the manifold grace of God. If any man speak, let him speak as the oracles of God; if any man minister, let him do it as of the ability which God giveth: that God in all things may be glorified through Jesus Christ, to whom be praise and dominion for ever and ever. Amen (1 Peter 4:10-11).

In spite of all that was against them, they were empowered to be God's representatives in speech and ministry.

What is it that enables ordinary people to excel in service for Christ? A. B. Simpson answers:

It is not splendid talent, it is not deep culture, that constitute efficiency in the body of Christ, it is simply and absolutely the power of the Holy Spirit. It is a divine ministry and must have a divine equipment (53:123).

Gifts of the Spirit alone can enable a man to "speak as the oracles of God." Only as God endows the "ability" can a person "minister" properly.

Distinguishing between "natural" and "spiritual" gifts is important for a clear understanding of the gifts of the Spirit. Bryant does so in writing:

Some men seem to be born with natural endowments which fit them for a special service. On the other hand, some men who have little natural ability have been endowed spiritually with abilities so far beyond their natural inclinations that they become spiritual giants. There is a difference between natural gifts and spiritual gifts. Spiritual gifts are related to a man's spiritual nature. Since this nature is dead before salvation, spiritual gifts are bestowed upon men only after they are saved. They need not be naturally gifted to receive spiritual gifts, but they must have been saved. These gifts may be referred to as "grace gifts" (*charismata*) which are in no way deserved. They are given in grace according to the sovereign will and purpose of God. Hence, the apparently most qualified people do not necessarily receive the best gifts (5:65).

It is not always the most brilliant orator who is the great preacher. Only as a man has received the gift can he minister the same with power. This is the distinction Paul is making in 1 Thess. 1:5. "For our gospel came not unto you in word only, but also in power, and in the Holy Ghost, and in much assurance." It is the power and not the speech that brings the blessing.

Some seem to feel that natural talents and spiritual gifts are one and the same. John Stott seems to border on this when he philosophizes:

Is it not apriori unlikely that God will give a spiritual gift of teaching to a believer who in pre-conversion days could not teach for taffy? (58:93).

How different from Paul's argument in 1 Cor. 1:26-29.

For ye see your calling, brethren, how that not many wise men after the flesh, not many mighty, not many noble, are called:

But God hath chosen the foolish things of the world to confound the wise; and God hath chosen the weak things of the world to confound the things which are mighty; And base things of the world, and things which are despised, hath God chosen, yea, and things which are not, to bring to nought things that are: That no flesh should glory in his presence.

Paul obviously argues that the totality of spiritual ability is from God. None of us has wherein we may boast. Spiritual pride and arrogance are entirely out of place, therefore, in relation to our gifts. We are absolutely dependent upon God for all that we are and have. Therefore, it is the gift of the Spirit and not his native talent that gives a person spiritual ability for service. As Harry Ironside observes:

> "Natural brilliancy or ability" is not to be confounded with a divinely-bestowed gift. If there be, for instance, ability of speech and readiness of utterance, these alone do not constitute a man a preacher. If there be aptness in didactic instruction, this is not in itself to be confounded with the gift of the teacher. It is the divine unction that makes the ready speaker a true gospel preacher, or the thoughtful exponent of deeper truths a real teacher. The tongue like as of fire, though now unseen, rests still upon the head of the God-anointed servants to the Church (24:61).

There is a further cogent argument on this point in 1 Cor. 2:12-14. Paul is teaching these believers that the ministry that is really effective must be "in demonstration of the Spirit and of power." But for such a ministry there needs to be a divine intervention of the Holy Spirit in a person's life. Hence his statement:

> Now we have received, not the spirit of the world, but the spirit which is of God; that we might know the things that are freely given to us of God: which things also we speak, not in the words which man's wisdom teacheth, but which the Holy Ghost teacheth; comparing spiritual things with spiritual. But the natural man receiveth not the things of the Spirit of God: for they are foolishness unto him: neither can he know them, because they are spiritually discerned (1 Cor. 2:12-14).

Again we learn that the "natural" is not enough.

Realizing this, J. Dwight Pentecost also differentiates between the natural and the spiritual, with this thought:

We recognize that there are men who are naturally gifted, or talented; who by birth have a higher intelligence quotient and abilities, which put them head and shoulders above other men. But when we speak of the gifts of the Spirit, we are not speaking about the native talents with which certain individuals have been endowed by natural birth. We are speaking of a supernatural endowment (44:165).

The gifts are not "natural" abilities, but the supernatural capabilities given by God, the Holy Spirit. You see "the foolishness of God is wiser than men; and the weakness of God is stronger than men" (1 Cor. 1:25).

Surprisingly, in spite of the biblical evidence there are some who seem to feel that natural ability somehow evolves into the spiritually endowed gift. For example, David R. Mains makes this remarkable statement:

> In those areas where I have natural abilities, such as a facility for public speaking, the difference between their being talents or gifts of the Holy Spirit is found in my attitude. If I recognize the talent as from God, and in prayer and continual dedication commit it to Him to be used in ministry in a special way, it becomes a gift of the Holy Spirit with supernatural expression. The proof of this is seen in the gradual way God increases this gift for His service (34:62).

To him the difference seems to be psychological, rather than spiritual. Thus if one's attitude is correct, the natural becomes the supernatural!

Pentecost quotes Charles Ryrie, who amazingly seems to say almost the same thing:

> To covet the better gifts is not a matter of sitting down and conjuring up enough faith to be able to receive them out of the blue. It is a matter of diligent self-preparation. For instance, if one covets the gift of teaching, he will undoubtedly have to spend many years developing that gift. The Holy Spirit is sovereign in the giving of gifts, but in the development of them He works through human beings with their desires, limitations, ambitions, and the like (45:28).

Although Ryrie throws in that "the Holy Spirit is sovereign in the giving of gifts," he seems to make this secondary to "self-preparation" and the spending of "years developing that gift." Such a process reduces the supernatural gift, to a naturally developed power.

Even John F. Walvoord seems to believe that a certain amount of natural "capacity" must be there before God can give the gift of teaching, for example. He writes that, although the gift of teaching does not necessarily require superior knowledge, it:

> does require the capacity for successful communication and application of the truth to the individual. No doubt the gift of teaching natural truth is similar to that of teaching spiritual truth, but the spiritual gift is especially adaptable to teaching the Word of God. Hence a person might be quite gifted in teaching natural truth who would not be effective in teaching the Word of God (74:39).

To him, the gift seems merely to be an adaptation of natural talent and ability. Certainly the adaptation is a gift, but this is only part of the "gift of teaching" as found in the Scriptures.

It would appear to me that if God could use a man like Moses—who had to plead, "O my Lord, I am not eloquent, neither heretofore, nor since thou hast spoken unto thy servant: but I am slow of speech, and of a slow tongue" (Exod. 4:10)—, He can by supernatural gift make the most unlikely man a teacher. God's answer to Moses' inability is as illustrative of empowerment by His gifts of the Spirit as one could hope for. We read that God said to him, "Who hath made man's mouth? or who maketh the dumb, or deaf, or the seeing, or the blind? have not I the Lord? Now therefore go, and I will be with thy mouth, and teach thee what thou shalt say" (Exod. 4:11-12). The totality of Moses' ability to speak would be by God's sovereign bestowal.

Is it not time for another sober-minded John Owen to arise and remind our world that:

> As these gifts were not any of them to be bought, no more are they absolutely to be attained by the natural abilities and industry of any; whereby an image of them is attempted to be set up by some, but deformed and useless. They will do those things in the church by their own abilities which can never be acceptably discharged but by virtue of those free gifts (42:835).

No amount of manufacturing can possibly duplicate the gifts before God. There may indeed be the "form," but "the power thereof" will be missing. "A sounding brass" and "a tinkling cymbal" will be the result. The gifts of the Holy Spirit are neither of man, nor by man. They come, as the term clearly denotes, from God.

There is a second major difference to be noted, for:

B. THE GIFTS DIFFER FROM SPIRITUAL FRUIT

The most famous passage on the fruit of the Spirit is Gal. 5:22-23. There we read: "But the fruit of the Spirit is love, joy, peace, longsuffering, gentleness, goodness, faith, meekness, temperance: against such there is no law." Other lists of fruit also appear throughout the New Testament although they are not so-called.[1]

Spiritual fruit is the outgrowth of the work of God's Spirit in the believer's life. Its growth follows horticultural lines. Says John W. Sanderson:

> The fruit of the Spirit does not initially take the form of outward deeds, or even of habits of life. Perhaps it will be well to borrow a word from older theologies and speak of "habitudes." More modern synonyms might be "abilities," "sets of mind," "seeds." The fruit of the Spirit is a cluster of seeds which grow and appear at their appointed time (50:38).

To a great extent then, the producing of fruit in the Christian's life is the "secret" work of the Holy Spirit over an extended period of time.

The depth and nature of this inward work of the Spirit is stated by Paul when he warns us to, "work out your own salvation with fear and trembling. For it is God which worketh in you both to will and to do of his good pleasure" (Phil. 2:12b-13). God the Holy Spirit works into our souls what we must work out in our lives.

Now precisely because of this relationship between "the fruit of the Spirit" and the life of the believer, there is seen a great difference between "the gifts" and "the fruit" of the Spirit. J. Oswald Sanders puts it well in stating:

> A gift may be imparted from without, and may remain separate and distinct. Fruit, however, is not an extraneous addition to a

---

[1] Consider Rom. 5:3-5; 1 Tim. 6:11; 2 Tim. 3:10; 2 Peter 1:5-7; and, stated in negative terms, 1 Cor. 13:4-8.

tree, but the issue of its life, and is produced from within (49:10).

Fruit growing is the outcome of the Spirit's work *within.* As fruit on a tree comes from the very life of that tree, so the fruit of the Spirit is produced by the Holy Spirit's life within us working its way out into our lives.

On the other hand, the *gifts* by their very nature are from *without.* It is this fact that leads John Owen to differentiate between the grace of God at work in the inner life of the believer and the gifts of the Spirit exercised without. He observes:

> The gifts change not the heart with power, although they may reform the life by the efficacy of light. And although God doth not ordinarily bestow them on flagitious[2] persons, nor continue them with such as after the reception of them become flagitious, yet they may be in those who are unrenewed, and have nothing in them to preserve men absolutely from the worst of sins . . . They may and do, in those who are possessed of them in and under their exercise, make great impression on their own affections, but they change not the heart, they renew not the mind, they transform not the soul into the image of God (42:849).

One can readily see that the gifts of the Spirit differ radically from "the fruit" in the product of life. I shall deal with this again later.

Even the use of the word "fruit," is clearly a differentiation from "gifts" in the Spirit's work. Using the physical analogy, Eric Fife says:

> Fruit is not something that can be artificially produced; we cannot go into a workshop and make a grapefruit. Fruit is a product of life, and it is only as the life-giving power of the Holy Spirit lives fully in us that genuine fruit will appear in our lives. This process of fruit-bearing also takes time. A spiritual gift may make its presence known immediately, but fruit-bearing cannot be hurried. To be sure, we can buy artificial fruit, but its artificial nature is easily detectable even before we try to eat it (12:118).

---

[2] "Flagitious person" refers to one with a deeply wicked life; one whose life is characterized by shameful acts, or deeds.

There is no short-cut to fruit-bearing. There is no "several distribution" of fruit as there is of the gifts. Fruit must grow within and be produced through the believer's life by the work of the Holy Spirit. Therefore, Fife rightly concludes in his distinguishing statement:

> Gifts of the Spirit do not necessarily prove that a man is Spirit-filled; in addition we have to look for evidence of spiritual fruit, for that cannot be falsified for any period of time (12:120).

To the Corinthian believers Paul wrote, "ye come behind in no gift" (1 Cor. 1:7). Could he have also written, "ye come behind in no fruit?" Even the most charitable would have to admit that the greatest lack in that church was "the fruit of the Spirit." The presence of such fruit would have evidenced spirituality, but the lives of the believers evidenced carnality (1 Cor. 3:1-3).

This point is illustrated in the life of John Sung, a Chinese evangelist. He had been wonderfully saved and became a clearly gifted evangelist. However, he also had an ungovernable temper and was known to dismiss as many as three interpreters in one meeting. "The gift was great, but the fruit was scarce" (12:119).

The presence of spiritual fruit is far more reliable evidence of spirituality than are the gifts. Our Lord's infallible test for spirituality is, "by their fruits ye shall know them" (Matt. 7:16). As Sanders says, "Satan can counterfeit and imitate spiritual gifts, but he is baffled in trying to imitate the fruit of the Spirit" (49:109).

Unlike the "fruit," "the gifts of the Spirit" are no guarantee of spirituality. The gifts at Corinth did not seem to affect the moral or spiritual life of the Church. The fact is that there is a clear emphasis on the *charis* (grace) of the bestowal of the gifts. They were undeserved, just as salvation is undeserved (Eph. 2:8-9). They were a "treasure in earthen vessels" and sometimes those vessels were very "earthy." As William J. Sweeting points out, "The gifts of the Spirit did not guarantee spiritual depth. Many of these Corinthians possessed gifts, but how woefully carnal, immature and sinful they were" (60:124). This same insight caused Pentecostalist, Donald Gee, to lament of modern Charismatics:

Who make a big outward show of the gifts of the Spirit but seem to have very little of the fruit, very little holiness; their lives are not showing the grace of our Lord Jesus Christ. These are the people who do more harm to the Pentecostal testimony than all the writers and preachers who have written and spoken against it put together (17:27).

Then he states pointedly, "There is something radically wrong with the experience that gives you gifts and doesn't give you holiness" (17:27). Even a Baptist could say, "Amen," to that!

Now it is precisely here that traditional Pentecostals face difficulties with the modern charismatic movement. They see much emphasis on the gifts (and with that they are happy), but they see little emphasis on the life (and with that they are puzzled). Harold Lindsell sympathetically states their quandary like this:

Traditional Pentecostals hold that the baptism of the Spirit produces a change of life-style. Their beliefs have always caused them to eschew alcohol and tobacco. They are genuinely puzzled by Catholic Charismatics whose Spirit baptism has not kept them from smoking cigarettes and drinking cocktails. They firmly believe that the body of the Christian is the temple of the Holy Spirit and is not to be defiled. At a time when the surgeon-general of the United States warns that tobacco is hazardous and when cigarette-induced lung cancer is at an all-time high, they do not think it amiss to ask: How can a person baptized in the Spirit so defile his body? They feel the same way about alcohol, especially in light of the alcohol addiction of millions of Americans. It is, of course, easier to focus on items like these than it is to deal with such sins as greed, selfishness, racism, gossip, and lack of love; but traditional Pentecostalism teaches that Spirit baptism makes these things inconsistent with the Christian life too (85:10).

Can it be that what Pentecostals hailed originally as "later rain" has, in reality, become a spiritual "wash-out"?

In discussing "the gifts of the Spirit," George Shaw speaks of the emphasis placed on "signs and wonders" in some quarters today and then adds:

But it is wrong for the Church to think that the gifts are the all-important thing. The holiness of life is the greatest of the power of the Christian religion. The sanctified man is the greatest product and the greatest evidence of the power of the gospel. Much greater than the wonder-worker. The Spirit cleansing and dwelling in the heart of man is essential to man, but not the gifts of the Spirit (52:329).

And is not this the overwhelming emphasis of Scripture? Certainly its importance is so great that we are expressly told, "Follow . . . holiness, without which no man shall see the Lord" (Heb. 12:14).

In summation, "the gifts" and "the fruit" of the Spirit are not synonymous terms. They differ, and nowhere greater than in the life of a believer. The person who has "the gifts" without "the fruit" is one who is in imminent danger of spiritual collapse. Better by far would it be to live without any gift but with the fruit of the Spirit evident in one's life, than to possess the gifts in abundant measure without corresponding spirituality. Surely that is the thesis of 1 Corinthians 13, a subject for another chapter.

5

THE GIFTS THEMSELVES

THUS FAR we have been discussing myths that have sprung up around the gifts of the Spirit, yet the gifts themselves have not been analyzed! It is a part of the present dilemma that one must clear away enough mythical debris; so that in coming to a closer examination of the gifts, he does not merely replace these with his own myths. This is especially important for the subject on hand.

A. WHERE THE GIFTS ARE FOUND

There are three main passages in the New Testament which present us with lists of spiritual gifts. The earliest of these is in 1 Corinthians. In chapter 12, two lists are presented, and these somewhat overlap as the following indicates.

Verses 8-10	Verses 28-30
1. The word of wisdom	1. Apostles
2. The word of knowledge	2. Prophets
3. Faith	3. Teachers
4. Healings	4. Miracles
5. Miracles	5. Healings
6. Prophecy	6. Helps
7. Discerning of spirits	7. Governments
8. Tongues	8. Tongues
9. Interpretation of tongues	9. Interpretation of tongues

One can readily see that there are five overlapping gifts mentioned. These are healings, miracles, prophecy, tongues and interpretation of tongues. With this in mind the 18 gifts can be reduced to 13 as follows:

1. Apostles	5. The word of knowledge
2. Prophets	6. Discerning of spirits
3. Teachers	7. Faith
4. The word of wisdom	8. Healings

9. Miracles
10. Helps
11. Governments

12. Tongues
13. Interpretation of tongues

These 13 are the core gifts of 1 Corinthians 12.

The second list of spiritual gifts is found in Rom. 12:6-8. In this passage they are delineated as:

1. Prophecy
2. Ministry
3. Teaching
4. Exhorting

5. Giving
6. Ruling
7. Mercy

When we check this list against that in 1 Corinthians 12, we discover two overlapping, namely, prophecy and teaching. Thus our list of new gifts mentioned in Romans 12 becomes:

1. Ministry
2. Exhorting
3. Giving

4. Ruling
5. Mercy

If we add these to the streamlined list of 1 Corinthians 12, we now find a total of 18 gifts.

Eph. 4:11 holds the third list of spiritual gifts. This Epistle was written earlier than either of the other two books. The group of gifts is now personified as:

1. Apostles
2. Prophets

3. Evangelists
4. Pastors-Teachers

Since the first two have already been mentioned, we drop them from the list. This leaves us with two further gifts:

1. Evangelists

2. Pastors-Teachers

Adding these two gifts to the list already mentioned gives us a grand total of 20 gifts of the Spirit.

B. HOW THE GIFTS ARE VIEWED

Some of these undoubtedly complement each other, if they do not altogether overlap. However, such a procedure does give a starting point for determining the number of gifts of the Spirit. From this foundation we can begin to categorize them.

Various authors have formed their own methodology in this. Criswell lists a number of "typical groupings" (7:154ff), and demonstrates well the ingenuity of men to systematize what they study. Two examples to add to Criswell's list might be the following by J. Oswald Sanders and Gerald L. Stover.

The gifts of the Spirit may be classified roughly as follows: (a) Gifts which qualify their possessors for the ministry of the Word: apostleship, prophecy, teaching, shepherding, evangelism, knowledge and wisdom, kinds of tongues, interpretation of tongues, discerning of spirits.
(b) Gifts which equip their possessors to render services of a practical nature: miracles, healing, administration, ruling, helps (49:110).

It is said that in dispensing the gifts, there are such that meet the needs of the soul (wisdom, knowledge, faith) in verses 8, 9. There are those gifts that meet the need of the body (healing, miracles) in verses 9, 10. Finally, there are those gifts that meet the needs of the spirit (prophecy, spiritual discernment, tongues and the interpretation of tongues) in verse 10 (59:49).

My own preference in the light of what the Bible teaches about the gift, is to first divide the total between those which were clearly first-century gifts and those which are also present-day gifts, and from there to deal with the area of life for which they equip an individual.[1]

Of course, there are those who agree with the standard Pentecostal doctrine on this matter. R. E. McAlister, (former General Secretary-Treasurer of the Pentecostal Assemblies of Canada), writing in *The Pentecostal Testimony* about the effects of "the baptism of the Holy Spirit," says:

The baptism of the Holy Spirit in the believer makes the work of Christ continuous and perpetual upon earth. This is clearly taught in the Word of God. That is why you hear about so many miraculous cases of healing in connection with those who stand for the baptism of the Holy Spirit. They are no different than other people, but the Holy Ghost is indwelling them and perpetuating the ministry of Christ upon earth (86:9).

Note well the words, "continuous and perpetual," for they sum up traditional, mainstream, Pentecostal doctrine on the permanancy of the gifts.

---

[1] See chapters 9 through 16 for a full treatment of the gifts using this method.

Another viewpoint is stated by J. Dwight Pentecost when he writes the following warning:

> The Word of God recognized two kinds of gifts: permanent and temporary. Some gifts were designed to operate as long as the church has its existence upon the earth; other gifts were designed to be temporary in duration. If one puts emphasis upon that which was divinely designed to be temporary, and seeks to make those temporary gifts the norm for spirituality in a day when they do not operate, he will be led into disillusionment or to some fleshly excess which manifests a pseudo-spirituality (44:166).

His position is that some gifts were "signs to substantiate and corroborate a message that has been given" (44:167). He mentions "tongues" as among such gifts (1 Cor. 14:22). On the other hand the permanent gifts were for the building up of the body of Christ throughout the church age, and are of necessity perpetual.

Rather than arguing the point, we shall allow the treatment of the individual gifts to present the biblical reasons for the position personally taken. Sufficient to say for now that, by their very nature, some gifts were destined to end. As 1 Cor. 13:8 puts it, "Charity never faileth: but whether there be prophecies, they shall fail, whether there be tongues, they shall cease; whether there be knowledge, it shall vanish away." Note clearly that the three gifts mentioned are said to have an ending.[2]

C. THE ORDER OF IMPORTANCE

Perhaps this is also the time to consider the order of the gifts as we find them in the lists mentioned. One treatment in particular, that of 1 Cor. 12:28, indicates numerically that the Apostle has some kind of sequence in mind. Yet, as with other aspects of these lists, different writers have chosen differing interpretations.

Charles Hummel, for example, believes that:

> Paul consistently selects and orders gifts randomly in order to illustrate diversity, rather than to indicate rank. Where there

---

[2] I shall deal with this in more detail as these gifts arise in chapter 9.

appears to be a logical order, it must be understood in the context of the passage and not made an absolute for all occasions (23:246).

J. H. Pickford on the other hand believes:

> There is a sequence, but it is a time sequence, in which such gifts appeared in the church in accordance with the divine purpose; and one gift gives place to another as that purpose is fulfilled. It was apostles, prophets and inspired teachers each in his time, each fulfilling his function with each office being replaced in the development of the church, so that none of these offices exists today (90:6).

Others, of course, disagree with both of these men.

The fact of the matter is that the Scriptures indicate that all of the gifts are not of equal value. Paul clearly states this in 1 Cor. 14:5; "Greater is he that prophesieth than he that speaketh with tongues." There can be little doubt, therefore, that Paul's order in 1 Cor. 12:28 is not "random," nor mere "time sequence." It is a list from the "best" to the "least" of the gifts of the Holy Spirit. As J. Oswald Sanders aptly warns, "Let us be careful not to put first what God has put last" (49:112).

D. THE TIME GIFTS ARE RECEIVED

When does a person receive these gifts? Since it is by the Spirit's baptism that we are placed in "the body of Christ," it would seem reasonable to hold that the Spirit equips us to function in that body at the moment of our baptism in the Spirit. As water baptism initiates us into and unites us with the local "body of Christ" (1 Cor. 12:27), so this spiritual baptism makes us a part of all the gifts, rights and blessings of the spiritual body. However, we do well to heed Harry A. Ironside's observation, "The gifts are never cited as the proofs of the baptism of the Holy Spirit" (24:57).

This baptism of the Holy Spirit occurs at the moment of conversion. As surely as salvation is our entering into that historic atonement forever completed on Calvary's center cross, so the baptism of the Spirit is our entering into that which was forever completed on that historic Pentecost when the church was born. It is not a second, or a thirty-second blessing! Rather, it is the initiation of the regenerated soul into "the body of Christ" (1 Cor. 12:13). All Christians have been baptized into that body, or they do not belong to Christ (Rom. 8:9).[3]

A believer, therefore, receives his spiritual gifts at the moment of conversion. These gifts may not show up immediately, but they are as latently within us as are natural gifts at our physical birth. Says Walvoord:

> In the analogy of natural gifts as seen in the natural man, it is clear that all the factors of ability and natural gift are latent in the newborn babe. So, also, it may be true for spiritual gifts in the one born again. In both the natural and spiritual spheres, it is a matter of proper use and development of gifts rather than any additional gifts being bestowed (73:166).

These gifts belong to the Christian from that "birth" moment by the sovereign act of the Spirit of God.

It may be objected on the basis of Romans 1:11 that gifts were "imparted" after conversion in Bible times. Such an interpretation of Paul's statement is based on a faulty understanding of the word "impart." The word does not mean "give" as we understand that word, but rather "share . . . as distinct from giving" (69:149). Therefore, James Denney correctly interprets the text by saying:

> No doubt, in substance, Paul imparts his spiritual gift through this epistle: what he wished to do for the Romans was to further their comprehension of the purpose of God in Jesus Christ—a purpose the breadth and bearings of which were yet but imperfectly understood (8:588).

Rather than giving them some new gift, Paul wanted to share with them for their edification from among the gifts he personally had as an apostle.

In conclusion, these gifts are ours forever. They are irrevocably given. As eternal as everlasting life, so are the gifts of the Spirit. "God's gifts and His calling are irrevocable" ([Rom. 11:29] 99). According to Vincent this means "not subject to recall" (67:130). This refers not to the gifts given to the church at Pentecost but to the believer when he was converted. The believer, therefore, never needs to

---

[3] See Chapter 9, "Divers Kinds of Tongues" (The Receiving of, etc.) for a fuller treatment of this subject (pages 147-162).

pray, or agonize, or plead for his gifts. They are already given and all that is necessary is to use them. Therefore, do not be mistaken about the gifts. Though some were temporarily given to the early church, the permanent gifts with which God has endowed you are yours for the totality of your life on earth.

PART 2
MYTHS BASED IN TEMPERAMENT

6

AN ATTITUDE OF SUPERIORITY

MYTHICAL BELIEF in the gifts of the Holy Spirit provides fertile ground for the growth of pride and arrogance. Pentecostalist David J. du Plessis is an ecumenical, charismatic leader. When flush with initial successes, he stood before a Presbyterian congregation in September, 1967, and proclaimed, "A Pentecostalist is a person who thinks he's arrived because he speaks in tongues" (84:39). Some today would echo the sentiment with regard to the Charismatic Movement.

The myth of superiority is one of the most persistent. Yet when we come to the Word of God, we discover it to be without foundation. For example, we find that:

A. THE GIFTS ARE SOVEREIGNLY GIVEN

After listing nine gifts, Paul told the Corinthians, "But all these worketh that one and the selfsame Spirit, dividing to every man severally as he will" (1 Cor. 12:11). He goes on to describe their local assembly as "the body of Christ," with each member a spiritually equipped part. Then he explains how that body came together, "But now hath God set the members every one of them in the body, as it hath pleased him" (1 Cor. 12:18). Finally, after again emphasizing their corporate nature as "the body of Christ and members in particular," he returns to his list of gifts saying, "And God hath set some in the church, first apostles, secondarily prophets, thirdly teachers, after that miracles, then gifts of healings, helps, governments, diversities of tongues" (1 Cor. 12:28). "It is God alone, through the Spirit, who by virtue of His sovereignty, decides upon the qualification of which we stand in need for a ministry which He alone foresees" (43:181).

It is clear, therefore, from the expressions of sovereignty used by Paul (i.e., "as He will," "hath God set," "as it hath pleased Him," and "God hath set"), that the individuals had nothing to do with determining their "gift," or "gifts." "Spiritual gifts are received, not achieved" (72:45), said Wagner. All of them were sovereignly endowed by the Holy Spirit, according to His will. To Him the entire administration of the church has been committed during this present church age. Therefore, the following warning by Pentecost is well taken.

> Spiritual gifts are not to be sought by men. A man does not receive a spiritual gift because he prayed for it, because he sought it, coveted it, trained for it. Spiritual gifts are a sovereign bestowal apart from the will or the inclination of the individual. The recognition of that fact immediately dispels a great deal of the excess and abuse attached to false teaching on spiritual gifts (44:169).

Notice how this administration of the Spirit radiates from Him in 1 Cor. 12:4-6 and 11. A. J. Gordon sees this in terms of a striking series of concentric circles with a single fixed center which holds each circumference in a definite relationship to itself, and continues:

> So here we see all the "diversities of administrations" determined by the one Administrator, the Holy Ghost. "Varieties of gifts, but the same Spirit"; "diversities of working, but the same God"; different words "according to the same Spirit"; "gifts of faith in the same Spirit"; "gifts of healing in the one Spirit"; miracles, prophecies, tongues, interpretations, "but all these worketh the one and the same Spirit, dividing to each one severally as he will." Whether the authority of this one, ruling, sovereign Holy Ghost be recognized or ignored determines whether the church shall be an anarchy or a unity, a synagogue of lawless ones or the temple of the living God (19:129).

Obviously, in Corinth the problem was the former, for things were indecent and disorderly.

The verb used for "given" in 1 Cor. 12:7, 8 and 24, reinforces the sovereign nature of the giving. It "denotes a free gift, stressing its gratuitous character," and it is "always used in the New Testament of a spiritual or supernatural gift." Hence in Eph. 4:7 and 11 it is used of the "gifts" given by the ascended Christ. John L. Benson emphasizes the sovereign character of the bestowal of God's gifts by stating:

> Regardless of how many emotional overtones are associated with discrimination, God discriminates between each of us according to His divine will (1 Cor. 4:7). Theologians are in the habit of calling it "discriminating grace." In harmony with God's sovereign purpose and choice, He has given to some and withheld from others (1 Cor. 12:11). The gifts of the Spirit are a matter which God determines and dispenses without paying any respect to human qualifications (2:41).

What discord there would be, without the Divine Conductor of the life of the church. What discordant notes would be heard.

> Every joint supplieth according to the effectual working in the measure of every part (Eph. 4:16).

> The eye cannot say unto the hand, I have no need of thee: nor again the head to the feet, I have no need of you. Nay, much more those members of the body, which seem to be more feeble, are necessary (1 Cor. 12:21-22).

Bishop Webb, an Anglican of another era, brings this out beautifully when he writes of the Divine Providence that gives to one and withholds from another. He points out that God is working according to His master plan and each singular gift is a part of the great whole. Each one is necessary in his appointed place and the picture would be imperfect without any one of us. Then he switches to the analogy of a great Musician and comments:

> He is the Author of our various gifts; playing, like a great Master, upon the various instruments with which He has to deal: Isaiah, Jeremiah, Moses, the sweet Psalmist of Israel,— each has his own tone of distinct utterance. The Holy Spirit is the Musician, drawing out strains from each heart, to swell the melody "of Moses and of the Lamb." One presents one strain, and another presents another. Because your special part does not sound exactly like that of some saint or ideal person, whom you revere, you must not suppose that you are not wanted, to furnish some part of the harmony in the great orchestra (76:28).

The gifts were sovereignly given. They are according to the will of the Holy Spirit. If we grasp this fact it will save us from numerous myths about the receiving of the gifts. As J. Oswald Sanders puts it, "The lesson to be mastered is that we cannot dictate to the Spirit in His administrations" (49:112).

This obviously leads to important implications, the main thought being:

B. THERE IS NO ROOM FOR SPIRITUAL PRIDE

Notice how Paul reasons in 1 Cor. 12:14-17:

> For the body is not one member, but many. If the foot shall say, Because I am not the hand, I am not of the body; is it therefore not of the body?
> And if the ear shall say, Because I am not the eye, I am not of the body; is it therefore not of the body?
> If the whole body were an eye, where were the hearing? If the whole were hearing, where were the smelling?

For the body to function properly, each part needs to fulfill its function. Envy and pride would argue for a ridiculous "body"—the whole "an eye," or the entire system "an ear." "And if they were all one member, where were the body?" (1 Cor. 12:19). Such bodies would be caricatures of the real thing.

Thus Paul continues by stressing the necessity of each "member," each "part" of the body of Christ, the local Church at Corinth. Verses 20-23 are relevant:

> But now are they many members, yet but one body. And the eye cannot say unto the hand, I have no need of thee: nor again the head to the feet, I have no need of you. Nay, much more those members of the body, which seem to be more feeble, are necessary: And those members of the body, which we think to be less honorable, upon these we bestow more abundant honor; and our uncomely parts have more abundant comeliness.

Every member needs every other member. United they stand, divided they fall. None is an island unto himself, for each is a part—and that a necessary part—of every other member.

Therefore, though the body has "many members," none can survive without the rest. Hear Paul's concluding argument:

> For our comely parts have no need: but God hath tempered the body together, having given more abundant honor to that part which lacked: That there should be no schism in the body; but that the members should have the same care one for another. And whether one member suffer, all the members suffer with it; or one member be honored, all the members rejoice with it (1 Cor. 12:24-26).

Did you catch it? Because the body is one regardless of the different functional gifts given, "the members should have the same care one for another." The honor of one is the honor of all, and the dishonoring of one dishonors "all the members."

So, when the Spirit chooses (i.e., wills) to give any believer a certain gift he should be humbled rather than exalted thereby. Paul wrote of the need of this humility in 1 Cor. 4:7, "For who maketh thee to differ from another and what hast thou that thou didst not receive? now if thou didst receive it, why dost thou glory, as if thou hadst not received it?" Says Criswell on this same point:

> All that we have in the kingdom and patience of Jesus is given us by His gracious love. There is no room for personal boasting. The gifts are not even bestowed as rewards. They are not indications of spiritual excellence or superiority. They are meted out to us "as the Spirit will." They are not bestowed because we have sought them. They are not to be vaingloriously sought by men. Although we can ask in prayer, we do not receive them because we prayed for them or coveted them. They are sovereignly bestowed . . . We can ask, we can pray, we can covet a gift (1 Cor. 14:39) but the decision lies beyond us. The power of choice is not ours and does not function at our behest. That is why envy, boasting, superiority, contumely are so out of place in the churches of our Lord (7:151, 150).

It was the Lord Jesus Himself who said of the ministry of the Holy Spirit, "He shall glorify me: for he shall receive of mine, and shall shew it unto you" (John 16:14). There is a sense in which the gifts are the things of Christ (Eph. 4:8). Can we not say, then, that the principle reason for them is to glorify Christ? In using the analogy of a tool in a worker's hand, A. B. Simpson reminds us that the worker and not the tool is recognized and praised. Then he adds:

As Richard Baxter has put it so wisely, "Each of us is just a pen in the hand of God, and what honor is there in a pen?" While we recognize this we shall be saved from all self-consciousness, egotism, and elation, and we shall lie in the dust at His blessed feet, hidden and empty vessels, in the place where He can use us best (53:124).

Oh, that the charismatic winds of today would carry that message world-wide!

With characteristic freshness, Spurgeon also pricks the bubble of pride and arrogance exhibited by many in "their" gifts. In a sermon entitled, "Grace Preferred to Gifts," and based on 1 Cor. 12:31, he gives this formula for remaining humble even when one is the recipient of the choicest gifts:

Recollect, also, dear friends, that some may receive gifts, yet those gifts will not be tokens of God's love to them at all, for he may only have given them with a view to other people. Possibly, you hand to a porter at your door a parcel of valuables to carry, but that is no proof of your love to him; it is a very handsome present that you are sending to a friend upon his birthday. The love-token is to the person who gets it, not to the porter who carries it. I may come here to-night, and be nothing but God's porter to bring precious treasures to your souls; and in the case of many a minister, or many a Sunday-school teacher, it may be no token of love that God gives them his messages to carry. They are only the go-betweens, the porters; the love-token is to those who receive it . . .

Recollect also, dear friends, that though you covet gifts, and receive them, you will lose them one day. All the wisdom that a man has acquired he may lose in an instant by a crack from a stone on his skull . . .

Remember, yet again, that gifts cannot comfort a man when he is in deep depression of spirit, when he is sick, and especially when he is near to death. Many a man, lying on a sick-bed, has found comfort in the grace which God has given him; but there never was one who found comfort in his gifts . . . Ah! we may live for fifty years or more, and gather a great church, and do much good; but there is not a speck of the small dust of comfort in it all, for we recollect that God may have simply used us as builders used their scaffolds as long as they want them; and when the house is built, they take the scaffold down, and put the material away. God may use us in the same way if we have gifts without grace; but if we have grace, it will not be so with us. Grace unites us to Christ; it makes us living stones in the building of which he is the foundation. When we come to be sick, grace brings us the promises. Grace looks to Christ, grace gives us hope, grace gives us the foretaste and pledge of glory, and especially is it so with that sweet and blessed grace of love. The man who is full of grace, though he has not a solitary talent, and is all unknown, yet is a happy and blessed man; in poverty and in obscurity, in sickness and in death, he is blessed because his soul is full of the majestic grace of love divine (57:467, 468).

To summarize: the myth of superiority in possession of the gifts of the Holy Spirit is patently false. Were they not *ta charismata* (the gifts of grace), we might have wherein to boast. But they are neither earned, nor deserved. They are the sovereign choosings of God, to fulfill His eternal purposes in the Church. Therefore all boasting is vain.

7

AN ATTITUDE OF INFERIORITY

AS WRONG AS the elitist superiority shown by some Charismatics, is the devastating inferiority felt by some noncharismatics. Neither is biblical and neither pleases God. Both are myths to be destroyed.

When Paul wrote to the Roman believers about the gifts of the Spirit, he said:

> For I say, through the grace given unto me, to every man that is among you, not to think of himself more highly than he ought to think; but to think soberly, according as God hath dealt to every man the measure of faith (Rom. 12:3).

You will notice that this verse is a part of his introduction to the gifts mentioned in verses 6 through 8. What is being said here is vitally connected to a biblical understanding of these gifts "which God hath dealt to every man," and also, thereby, to our perception of ourselves.

What are we told in this verse concerning self-perception? We are warned against superiority thinking. But notice we are told that each of us has a level at which he "ought to think" concerning himself. That level has its center in "the measure of faith" which "God has dealt" to us. It tells us that to think down upon, or feel inferior about our gifts is false humility. Indeed it is involuted pride! Well says René Pache, "In the body, there are no useless members or organs. In the Body of Christ, each believer receives a gift to carry out the function allotted to him" (43:182).

Peter takes up the same thought when he writes, "As every man hath received the gift, even so minister the same one to another, as good stewards of the manifold grace of God" (1 Peter 4:11). Can God be glorified by one who is moping around with a mistaken, inferiority complex about the gift which the Spirit has sovereignly selected and given? Surely each one of us needs to understand with A. B. Simpson that:

> this blessed enduement is not for apostles, prophets, miracle workers, teachers, special officials, merely, but for every member of the church of God. Every part of the body is necessary and important, and, as the apostle reasons very beautifully from human physiology, the weakest and humblest members of the human frame are often most highly honored; so also, in the church of Christ, God uses and honors the weakest and the lowliest, filling them with His own enabling, and thus glorifying His own grace (53:123).

An inferiority complex about your gift, or gifts, is the devil's tool to destroy your effectiveness for God. Indeed such thinking dishonors the Giver! You and I are by faith to think of ourselves at the level at which we "ought to think." We are what we are "by the grace of God" (1 Cor. 15:10). We are to rejoice in and gratefully use the equipment with which God has endowed us for service.

If this is to be accomplished:

A. YOU MUST DISCOVER YOUR GIFTS

Several years ago I sat among a group of pastors and listened to a "new wave" speaker teach on the gifts of the Spirit. As I sat and listened, I became increasingly alarmed that what I was hearing seemed more psychological than spiritual. The gifts of the Spirit seemed to be reduced to mere "personality profiles." I felt that, had the material been presented to a secular audience, one could have conceivably applied the explanation of "the gifts" to all present.

What are the gifts of the Spirit? Are they the same as native abilities? Is a person born with "the gifts?" Are they conferred at conversion, or at a "second" dealing of God with the individual? Are native personality traits merely given life at the time gifts are conferred, or are the gifts a brand new phenomenon in the individual's life? These and many other questions crowd a person's mind in beginning to think about finding his personal gift, or gifts.

No matter how the above questions are answered, all of us need to beware of opportunists who pontificate about the gifts, as if they were the ones to bestow them and not the

Spirit of God. Thomas F. Torrance has this very necessary warning in an article entitled, "Protestant Sacerdotalism,"[1] concerning this approach:

> Protestant Churches are full of "psychological priests" and more and more they evolve a psychological cult and develop a form of psychological counselling which displaces the truly pastoral ministry of Christ (92:34).

Such would seem to be the atmosphere of many of today's "gift seminars."

So strongly have some pastors reacted against this psychological "gift theology," that they have changed their entire position on the seeking of spiritual gifts. Among these is Gene Getz, a professor at Dallas Theological Seminary and the founding pastor of Fellowship Bible Church, a dynamic, growing assembly in Dallas. For years Getz taught that Christians should seek to discover their gifts. Now he has totally reversed that position,[2] and has written a book in which he rejects gift-seeking because of the confusion caused among Christians; the rationalizations being made from gift theology for not fulfilling normal, biblical role-functions; and self-deception by which people only think they have spiritual gifts, which they do not possess.[3]

Having been warned of, and recognizing the dangers inherent in such an approach, it still is wise for us to learn to use the gifts, which God has entrusted to us as His stewards. Someday He will hold us responsible for these gifts (Matt. 25:14-30). Does it not make sense for us to use our endowments to the maximum, that we may please God in all that we do? Only then can we hope to hear that final:

---

[1] Sacerdotalism: "Of priests or priesthood; ascribing supernatural powers to priests." Torrance claims that in today's world many Protestants are laying claims to such as Roman Catholic clergy alone erroneously claimed in years gone by.

[2] In his church, Getz now emphasizes "body maturity," stressing faith, hope and love, together with the leadership qualities listed in 1 Timothy 3 and Titus 1, instead of the gifts. He says "it suddenly dawned" upon him that, in none of the three gift chapters (1 Corinthians 12, Romans 12, or Ephesians 4), "can we find any exhortation for individual Christians to 'look for' or 'try to discover' their spiritual gift or gifts" (18:9).

[3] See Wagner, C. Peter, *Your Spiritual Gifts Can Help Your Church Grow.* Glendale, Cal.: Regal Books Division, G/L Publications, 1979, pp. 45ff. for a fuller sympathetic analysis of Getz' position from one who disagrees.

Well done, good and faithful servant; thou hast been faithful over a few things, I will make thee ruler over many things: enter thou into the joy of thy lord (Matt. 25:23).

Recognizing our spiritual gifts can also make service for God a real blessing instead of a burden. Let me illustrate by using a fable attributed to Charles Swindoll, pastor of the Evangelical Free Church of Fullerton, California.

A group of animals decided to improve their general welfare by starting a school. The curriculum included swimming, running, climbing and flying. The duck, an excellent swimmer, was deficient in other areas, so he majored in climbing, running and flying, much to the detriment of his swimming. The rabbit, a superior runner, was forced to spend so much of his time in other classes that he soon lost much of his famed speed. The squirrel, who had been rated "A" as a climber dropped to a "C" because his instructors spent hours trying to teach him to swim and fly. And the eagle was disciplined for soaring to the treetop when he had been told to learn how to climb, even though flying was most natural for him (72:107).

What is the point? It is simple. God has endowed us with certain gifts. All gifts are not the same. They do not even fit us all to do the same work (1 Cor. 12:17), but they are all necessary within the church (1 Cor. 12:20-23). When each of us exercises his particular gifts within the local church the way God intends, then the body moves forward with the precision, vitality and efficiency of a trained athlete. But, when we ignore our personal gifts and try to be what we are not, then our total service quotient drops. As J. Dwight Pentecost states:

Joy in our Christian experience and profit in our Christian ministry, depends on each individual recognizing his gift and using it. There may not be edification to the body if you try to exercise my gift; nor will there be edification to the body if I try to exercise your gift. But joy and blessing and success will depend on your knowing what your gift is and using that gift (44:171).

"God has given each new Christian a gift, and the entire Christian community stands in need of that gift!" (50:29). To discover your gift is to discover what God has endowed you to be capable of doing. The gifts of the Spirit not only are intended to enable you to do those things but, rightly understood, to also enjoy doing them. You can excel in service for God in the area of your gifts. That was God's sovereign plan, when he gave them to you.

However, it is one thing to say that a person must discover God's gift to him but quite another thing for a person actually to discover that gift. Let me say at once:

B. YOU CAN DISCOVER YOUR GIFTS

God has not given you a gift to keep you in ignorance. "All is arranged by Him. Each has some gift; the HOLY SPIRIT can teach you what are the special gifts that He has given to you, and desires to develop in you,—to bring out through you" (76:32). It is God's plan for your life that you be aware of His gift to you.

But how does a person go about discovering his gift? To begin with:

1. Put the Lord First in Your Life

As with every "material" gift God gives to you in life (Matt. 6:25, 31-32), so it is with "spiritual" gifts. There is an abiding principle in God's Word that stretches from Genesis to Revelation. It is simply this, "Put God first in everything, and He will take care of all the rest." To put it in biblical language, "But seek ye first the kingdom of God, and his righteousness; and all these things shall be added unto you" (Matt. 6:33). So, if you would know your spiritual gift, does it not seem logical that this is where you must begin?

The gifts are not revealed to satisfy a curiosity you have developed over the years. They are not there to give you an emotional "high." No gift is revealed that you may be able to get along without the Lord. The gifts are given to glorify Him.

Greatest among tragedies is that which keeps unsaved men from Christ. Jesus said, "Ye will not come to me, that ye might have life" (John 5:40). Those who have tasted and have seen "that the Lord is good" (Ps. 34:8), marvel that human nature is so stubbornly opposed to Christ.

But at least as great is the tragedy of God's people refusing to put Him first in their lives. How it robs them of temporal and spiritual blessing. All "these things" with which God desires to bless their lives are lost. They are robbers of their own selves!

So, my friend, if you would know the gifts which God has added unto you, "seek ye first the kingdom of God, and his righteousness; and all these things shall be added unto you" (Matt. 6:33). It may not sound as exciting as some charismatic flash of insight but it is biblical, and it is no "myth." Begin your search by putting the Lord first in your life.

In the next place, you must:

2. Put Emphasis on God's Will for Your Life

In seeking to discover your gift, remember that God's will for your life always coincides with your gift. John Owen explains it this way:

> Thus God chooseth some men unto some office in the church, or unto some work in the world. As this includeth a preferring them before or above others, or the using them when others are not used, we call it election; and in itself it is their fitting for and separation unto their office or work. And this temporary election is the cause and rule of the dispensation of gifts. So He chose Saul to be king over His people, and gave him thereon "another heart," or gifts fitting him for rule and government. So our Lord Jesus Christ chose and called at the first, twelve to be His apostles, and gave unto them all alike miraculous gifts. His temporary choice of them was the ground of His communication of gifts unto them (42:842).

Thus, in seeking your gift, the emphasis must be put on "the will of God" for your life. What God wills that you do, He equips you to do. Therefore, the job or place God has for you will automatically reveal the gift you have been given.

Often people put the emphasis on the gift when God puts the emphasis on the place of service. This service emphasis is well illustrated in Acts 13:1-4. Is it not logical to assume that what God called them to do, he had equipped them to do? The fact is that even before conversion God had a plan for

Saul (Acts 9:15-16), and for that plan God had equipment to match the service Paul would perform.

Hence, your gift is as the service to which and for which you are called (1 Peter 4:10). This is brought out clearly by Oswald J. Smith when he asks:

> What was the evidence to Elisha that he had received a double portion of Elijah's spirit? Was it some ecstatic feeling, some special manifestation? It was not. The evidence was that Elisha now had Elijah's power, so that when he, too, smote the waters of the Jordan with Elijah's mantle, they divided as they had for Elijah. The evidence comes in service (54:66).

So, the confirmation of your gift comes in doing the task God has called you to do. Your service for Christ reveals the Spirit's gift to you.

But then how does one know the will of God for his life? Do not miss the fact that Rom. 12:1-2 is an introduction to Paul's teaching on the gifts in succeeding verses.

> I beseech you therefore, brethren, by the mercies of God, that ye present your bodies a living sacrifice, holy, acceptable unto God, which is your reasonable service. And be not conformed to this world: but be ye transformed by the renewing of your mind, that ye may prove what is that good, and acceptable, and perfect, will of God (Rom. 12:1-2).

A surrendered body and a renewed mind form the unerring pathway to knowing the will of God for your life.[4]

If you would know God's gift, learn God's will. What God calls you to do He has already equipped you to do.

> Indeed no Christian is entitled to ask, "Am I qualified?" but only, "Is it the will of God?" If it is the will of God the Holy Spirit will be our qualification (12:113).

God's gifts are revealed to those who are ready to do God's will and God's will is revealed to those who sacrificially

---

[4] Some, like C. Peter Wagner, react strongly against what they call "consecration theology," preferring instead a "gift theology." To them the gift shows the will of God for a person's life. However, the very logical order in which Paul deals with the totality of Romans would lead us to the assurance that he is not haphazardly throwing verses at us in Romans 12. Therefore, we are justified in stating that without Rom. 12:1-2 being worked out in our lives, we will have a difficult time knowing God's will and thereby God's gifts to accomplish that will.

surrender their bodies and conscientiously seek renewal of their minds, so that they do not conform to this world.

In the next place it is important to:

3. Know the Scriptures

Do not fall into the mythological maze of today's subjective wanderings. All authority for faith and practice in your life rests in the Word of God. On the peril of your life do not translate that authority to your feelings, experiences, or ecstasies. Let neither the mundane, nor the miraculous, pry you loose from this central conviction, "I must have biblical authority for all that I do. I must search the Scriptures as to whether these things are really true."

It seems to me that in this "throw away" generation, when so much is made to be discarded and so little is made to last, many are building their spiritual houses with that same philosophy. Jesus said:

> Whosoever cometh to me, and heareth my sayings, and doeth them, I will shew you to whom he is like: He is like a man which built an house, and digged deep, and laid the foundation on a rock: and when the flood arose, the stream beat vehemently upon that house, and could not shake it: for it was founded upon a rock. But he that heareth, and doeth not, is like a man that without a foundation built an house upon the earth; against which the stream did beat vehemently, and immediately it fell; and the ruin of that house was great (Luke 6:47-49).

Because many today refuse to dig deep into the Word of God to lay a solid foundation for their beliefs and practices, we are seeing the spiritual houses of their lives crumbling. Meanwhile they are running around without true spiritual understanding crying out, "Jesus is Lord," while at the same time our Lord calls back, "And why call ye me, Lord, Lord, and do not the things which I say?" (Luke 6:46).

Study the Scriptures for an overview of the gifts. Know what they are and how they were used. Do a word study, so that you might know the actual meaning of the gifts mentioned. Find out if they related primarily to the first century, before the Scriptures were complete as God's perfect revelation of Himself to mankind. Learn if any were to pass away or to cease. See if there were any gifts that seemed not to outlast the apostles but seemed to have diminished during their lifetime. Practice bringing everything people say about them under an intense scrutiny of the Word of God.

Remember that "the gifts of the Spirit" are not the invention of the charismatic movement, or of any other group or of a particular church (though at times the interpretation of them might be!), but that they are the gracious revelation of God's Word concerning equipment for service. Therefore, "study to shew thyself approved unto God, a workman that needeth not to be ashamed, rightly dividing the word of truth" (2 Tim. 2:15). If you are "approved of God" in your study and understanding of the Word of God, you need not fear that your gifts will remain a mystery to you, or be misinterpreted by you.

Furthermore, I suggest that you:

4. Ask God to Reveal His Particular Gifts to You

In teaching about prayer in the Sermon on the Mount, our Lord Jesus said:

> Ask, and it shall be given you; seek, and ye shall find; knock, and it shall be opened unto you: For every one that asketh receiveth; and he that seeketh findeth; and to him that knocketh it shall be opened. Or what man is there of you, whom if his son ask bread, will he give him a stone? Or if he ask a fish, will he give him a serpent? If ye then, being evil, know how to give good gifts unto your children, how much more shall your Father which is in heaven give good things to them that ask him? (Matt. 7:7-11).

Now I make no attempt to link these "good gifts" to the gifts of the Spirit, but I do believe with all my heart in the principle of "ask and ye shall receive." Surely we will receive from God the revelation of our gifts, if we ask Him.

Much later, shortly before He was crucified, Jesus challenged His disciples with these words, "Verily, verily, I say unto you, Whatsoever ye shall ask the Father in my name, he will give it you. Hitherto have ye asked nothing in my name: ask, and ye shall receive, that your joy may be full" (John 16:23-24). The principle had not changed through the years of His ministry. Not only did Christ restate the principle, but He further added His desire that they would put it into operation in their lives. He "asks" them to "ask and ye shall receive." God desires us to receive an answer to the prayers we bring to Him—even about our gifts. Prayer is invariably, therefore, an integral part of knowing God's spiritual gifts to us.

Remember that what you are asking from God is information on a gift you have already received. You are not asking God to give you the gift. That was given at conversion. What you need from God is wisdom to determine with which of the gifts He has equipped you to serve Him. This wisdom is yours by prayer, for, "If any of you lack wisdom, let him ask of God, that giveth to all men liberally, and upbraideth not; and it shall be given him" (James 1:5). To know your gift you must, therefore, pray.

In the next place, in seeking to discover your gift:

5. Expect Confirmation from Others

Wilbert Welch relates the following incident which occurred during a minister's hour at a conference in Grand Rapids, Michigan. Dr. Howard Sugden was one of the guest speakers. During a question and answer period someone asked, "Dr. Sugden, do you feel that you are as filled with the Holy Spirit as some of the saints of other days?" Characteristically, Sugden gave a quiet yet pointed answer. He said, "My young man, this is not an easy question to answer. I would remind you that when the Holy Spirit came on the day of Pentecost, and cloven tongues like as fire rested on each one, it was not possible for him to see what was resting upon him but evident only to those who were around him" (93). So it is also with the gifts. The evidence of the gifts in your life will be recognized by others—perhaps even before you recognize the gifts yourself.

This is stated and illustrated by Dr. J. Dwight Pentecost in these words:

> If you feel that you have a gift and you try to exercise it and nobody in the assembly indicates that you have that gift, then it is quite evident that that is not your gift. There should be the public recognition. I had been in my first pastorate just a matter of months when some people came to me and said, "You

are a teacher. You ought to be in a theological seminary." I laughed, yet that is where I am today. Somehow, they seemed to recognize that I had a gift that I had no idea that I possessed, and it was the public recognition that authenticated the fact of the gift (44:176).

The corroboration of the local church is, therefore, important as a check on your personal assessment of just which gifts you possess. This will help dispel confusion, as well as save you from making a mistake. Not only will there be the inner witness of the Spirit that God has gifted you in this way, but an outer evidence will follow also. Others seeing that gift being used will confirm the witness of the Spirit to your own heart.

It was a surprised George W. Truett who was told by the Whitewright Baptist Church that he was to be ordained to the gospel ministry. The young man replied, "But I have sought to be a lawyer." The Church answered, "But God has called you to be a preacher." And they thereupon proceeded to ordain him! Others will know of your gift (7:152).

This incident recorded by W. A. Criswell may seem rather extreme, but it does illustrate the point of outer corroboration very well. If God has given you a gift, He has also revealed that fact to others.

There is one last point to be considered. In learning your spiritual gifts:

6. Be Prepared to Face Responsibility

When God reveals your gift or gifts, you are immediately under obligation to use them for His glory. Paul wrote, "For though I preach the gospel, I have nothing to glory of: for necessity is laid upon me; yea, woe is unto me, if I preach not the gospel! For if I do this thing willingly, I have a reward; but if against my will, a dispensation of the gospel is committed unto me" (1 Cor. 9:16-17). When Paul received his gifts for service, a great responsibility came to rest upon him. The burden of the gift pressured him to preach. The stewardship of the gift necessitated that he preach. But the joy of the gift inspired him to preach!

Elizabeth O'Connor has written concerning the responsibility laid upon us by virtue of God's gifts of His Spirit, in these words:

The identifying of gifts brings to the fore . . . the issue of commitment. Somehow if I name my gift and it is confirmed, I cannot "hang loose" in the same way. I would rather be committed to God in the abstract than be committed to him at the point of my gifts . . . Commitment at the point of my gifts means that I must give up being a straddler. Somewhere in the depths of me I know this. Life will not be the smorgasbord I have made it, sampling and tasting here and there. My commitment will give me an identity (41:42).

Are you willing for such responsibilities? They are the outcome of knowing your gifts.

To conclude, please do not feel inferior! There is no need to. God has given you spiritual gifts. You must discover those gifts. More than this you can know your gifts. Find them, and use them to the glory of God and to the building up of all around you. If you do, you will never feel spiritually inferior again.

8

AN ATTITUDE OF UNDERSTANDING

WHAT IS THE purpose of the gifts? The 20th century myth seems to be that they are given for "a spiritual high." To people who believe this, the gifts allow for an emotional binge. Once the "baptism" produces the "gifts," the problems of life are solved!

But why are the gifts given? It was stalwart, old John Owen who wrote:

> By his work of saving grace . . . he makes all the elect living stones; and by his communication of spiritual gifts, he fashions and builds those stones into a temple for the living God to dwell in (42:832).

The gifts are the equipment to enable us to be spiritual builders for Christ.

Now how do we accomplish this work of temple building? We do it by using the gifts we are given to glorify Christ, to edify others, to equip the Church and to arm soldiers.

First of all:

A. THE GIFTS ARE GIVEN TO GLORIFY CHRIST

Before Jesus ascended to heaven, He prepared His disciples for the day of His departure. One of the greatest chapters on these final instructions to His own is found in John 16. There Jesus is telling of the coming of the Holy Spirit. In doing so He speaks of the ministry of the Spirit to convict the unsaved "of sin, and of righteousness and of judgment" (John 16:8-11).

Then the ministry of the Holy Spirit among believers is set forth. The Spirit is to guide into "all truth," to reveal "things to come" and especially, "He shall glorify me: for he shall receive of mine, and shall shew it unto you" (John 16:14).

This glorification of Christ is the hallmark of all true ministry of the Spirit in our midst. So it is with the gifts. Contrary to much that is taught, sung, believed, preached and written, the gifts do not glorify and magnify the Holy Spirit.

The story is told of a man who heard Joseph Parker and Charles H. Spurgeon on two consecutive Sundays. Afterwards he spoke concerning his assessment of these men, saying, "Dr. Parker is a great preacher; but Mr. Spurgeon has a great Savior!" In one, the gift was magnified; in the other, the Savior was magnified. They are given, and the Holy Spirit sovereignly administers them that the Lord Jesus may be glorified.

The list of gifts mentioned in 1 Cor. 12:28 begins, "And God hath set some in the church, first apostles, secondarily prophets, . . ." That "hath set" is an interesting expression in the original. It is in the "middle voice" and it therefore implies, "for His own use." The primary reason for gifts in the church is to glorify God. In particular they are for the exaltation of Christ who is the head of the body, the church. When a person misses this important point, then he is open to all kinds of mythological bypaths.

It was William Carey, that great missionary statesman to India, who said, "Speak not of Dr. Carey, but of Dr. Carey's Savior!" Such will be the heart-cry of all endued with the gifts of the Holy Spirit of God.

Well says Gerald L. Stover on the purpose of the gifts:

> Gifts are never to be employed to magnify the one who possesses them. The Holy Spirit is not in the business of building great reputations for men; His ministry is to reveal and glorify Jesus Christ (59:46).

When your gifts and mine are used to glorify the Lord Jesus, we have begun to fulfill the primary function for which they were bestowed.

There is a second purpose attached to the Spirit's distribution of the gifts.

B. THE GIFTS ARE GIVEN TO EDIFY OTHERS

Paul's greatest argument with the tongues-speakers of 1 Corinthians 14 was that they were not edifying others.

Prophecy was greater than tongues, for prophecy edified others. Thus Paul pleads, "forasmuch as ye are zealous of spiritual gifts, seek that ye may excel to the edifying of the church" (1 Cor. 14:12). One writer puts it, "all the gifts and operations of the Holy Ghost are eventually for the benefit of the Church of Christ" (46:39). Ironside says, "Gifts are given, not for some individual's happiness, but to be used for the edification of others" (24:55). This is the manward purpose of the gifts. It is the second test for right use of a gift. Does the exercise of this gift edify those around us?

While commenting on the name applied to the gifts in 1 Cor. 12:5, John Owen speaks of "ministrations" as, "powers and abilities whereby some are enabled to administer spiritual things unto the benefit, advantage, and edification of others" (42:836). Then later on he adds:

> They are not in the first place bestowed on any for their own sakes or their own good, but for the good and benefit of others. So the apostle expressly declares, 1 Cor. 12:7, "The manifestation of the Spirit is given to every man to profit withal." These gifts, whereby the Spirit evidenceth and manifesteth his power, are bestowed on men for this very end, that they may profit and benefit others in their edification (42:848).

"Others" is the watchword for our use of spiritual gifts and never the exaltation of self.

Some will probably take exception to this fact, referring us to 1 Cor. 14:4, "He that speaketh in an unknown tongue edifieth himself; but he that prophesieth edifieth the church." They will tell us that one of the gifts at least is to be used to edify self. But is this really what Paul is saying? It seems to me that John Stott is closer to the truth in the following interpretation, in which he is arguing that the consistent emphasis of the New Testament is upon edification as being a ministry to others, and to the church. Then he questions:

> . . . what are we to make of the one and only exception which says that the tonguespeaker "edifies himself"? Surely there must be at least some degree of irony in what Paul writes, for the phrase is almost a contradiction in terms. Self-edification is simply not what edification is all about in the New Testament (58:115).

The gifts—even this one—were given for the edification of others to whom we minister and not for selfish purposes.

Let us yield the closing of this point to the following statement by the late Harry Ironside:

> The gifts abiding in the Church . . . are all given for profit and edification; none are for show, nor to attest the fact of the Spirit's indwelling, nor yet for the happiness of the recipient. All are not evangelists; all cannot preach. All do not possess the ability to shepherd the flock of God; but all have some measure of gift to be exercised for the blessing of the rest (24:57).

He that hath ears to hear, let him hear!

The third main purpose for the gifts builds upon what has already been said.

C. THE GIFTS ARE GIVEN TO EQUIP THE CHURCH

Perhaps the reason for so much mythology growing up around the gifts is that many believers miss this simple fact. The gifts were given to the church as a body, and not just to individuals. The purpose of the gifts is, therefore, tied to the church as a corporate grouping of individuals endowed with spiritual gifts, that the total body may be equipped to function. Thus, Bryant reminds us that:

> Spiritual gifts are not to be considered from an egocentric point of view, i.e., in terms of what they do for the individual. Rather they are to be considered from an ecclesialogical point of view, i.e., in terms of what they do for the Church, the body of Christ (5:66).

Notice again the statements by Paul in 1 Cor. 12:27-28. Keep in mind that the letter is written to a local church.[1]

> Now ye are the body of Christ, and members in particular. And God hath set some in the church, first apostles, secondarily prophets, thirdly teachers, after that miracles, then gifts of healings, helps, governments, diversities of tongues (1 Cor. 12:27-28).

---

[1] See Paul's opening statements in 1 Cor. 1:1-2. Especially note those to whom he addresses the epistle—"unto the church of God which is at Corinth." Putting this together with the direct statement of 1 Cor. 12:27 there can be little doubt that Paul is writing to a local assembly, and that they corporately are Christ's body.

These gifts were given to that local church, that it might be equipped to function properly. This causes Spurgeon to comment, "Every member has its own special office in the body; it is not there merely for its own comfort, but to be a help to the whole system of which it forms a part" (57:457).

This indeed is the background to Paul's analogy of the bodily parts equipping the total structure to move with precision. It is also the reason he goes further to ask in verses 29-30, "Are all apostles? are all prophets? are all teachers? are all workers of miracles? have all the gifts of healing? do all speak with tongues? do all interpret?" Everyone has not the same gift, for the same reason the total physical body is not an "eye," or an "ear." There is a need for the "diversities" of verse 4 if the local church is to be equipped to serve properly as the body of Christ. As Criswell states:

> Each gift is needed and is not to be neglected. Every member is essential to the body. No great church became that way on a one-man ministry. All, each, every one, great, small, rich, poor, old, young, have essential parts (7:151).

"But," says someone, "if the gifts are not primarily for the individual, why does Paul say what he does in 1 Cor. 12:31?" This is an important question; indeed a crucial one. In this verse Paul exhorts us, "but covet earnestly the best gifts." Many have immediately seized upon this verse as an excuse for going on a "personal gift" spree. To them this is proof that the gifts are primarily for the individual.

Is this necessarily so? Could the statement of 1 Cor. 14:1; 12:31 not refer to the church rather than the individual? Could it not be that they are to covet people in their midst who possess these gifts? Surely all of us have longed for "teachers" etc. for our churches. Can it not be that Paul is telling the Church at Corinth to play down the lesser gifts and exalt the primary ones—to emphasize less speaking in tongues and more teaching and preaching?

Remember that the entire text of the passage is to the corporate body of Christ, the local church, and not merely to individuals. For this reason J. Dwight Pentecost also interprets the text in a total-body context, when he writes:

This was a word addressed to the whole assembly of believers. Paul did not say to individual believers that they should covet to be apostles, or prophets, or evangelists, or pastors or teachers. But he says to the assembly of believers as a whole, "You covet, in your midst, the ministry of these gifted men: apostles, prophets, evangelists, pastors and teachers; that through the exercise of all these gifts the whole assembly of believers shall be edified in the faith and shall be built up to the work of the ministry" (44:192).

The gifts are given to equip the church—even these best gifts which we are to "covet earnestly."

This I think leads us to one more thought on the purpose of spiritual gifts.

D. THE GIFTS ARE GIVEN TO ARM SOLDIERS

In 2 Cor. 3:5 the Apostle Paul tells us both his weakness and his strength in serving God: "Not that we are sufficient of ourselves to think any thing as of ourselves; but our sufficiency is of God." Later in verse 8, he tells us how that sufficiency comes. It is "the ministration of the Spirit." Only by means of those "ministrations" could he fulfill his calling.

This word "ministrations" is the same word used in 1 Cor. 12:5 ("administrations"), where the gifts of the Spirit are clearly the context. It is also used in Eph. 4:12 ("ministry") where the work of the gifted men is in view. For this reason, it seems to me that the gifts had the ultimate purpose of equipping the church to punch through Satan's defense line.

The gifts, then, are the weapons by which the church presses the battle to the very gates of hell. As Paul says, "For the weapons of our warfare are not carnal, but mighty through God to the pulling down of strong holds" (2 Cor. 10:4). It was this obvious fact that caused John Owen to comment on this purpose of the gifts using military language.

> There were the weapons of warfare which he furnished his disciples withal when he gave them commission to go forth and subdue the world unto the obedience of the gospel, Acts 1:4, 8; and mighty were they through God unto that purpose, 2 Cor. 10:3-6. In the use and exercise of them did the gospel "run, and was glorified," to the ruin of the kingdom of Satan and darkness in the world (42:838).

The gifts armed the church for spiritual warfare and allowed for great victories in the spread of the gospel.

Once again in closing, what is the purpose of the gifts? To glorify Christ, to edify others, to equip the church and to arm God's soldiers. Wherever biblical gifts are in evidence, each of these aspects of purpose must be fulfilled. The measure of the myth, on the other hand, is how little these aspects of purpose are evidenced today.

PART 3
MYTHS BASED IN TIME
SECTION I. THE FULFILLED GIFTS

9

THE FULFILLED GIFTS

INTRODUCTION

AS SURELY AS there were gifts which were permanently needed in the church, there were also gifts which were temporary in nature. These gifts were as necessary to the founding of Christianity as the others are to its continuance. Yet, as we shall discover from an understanding of what these gifts really were, they have fulfilled their purpose and have been withdrawn.

A. GIFT LISTS AND FULFILLED GIFTS

It is interesting to notice in this respect, that the lists themselves indicate the temporary nature of some gifts. If we take Paul's order of recording the gifts to be 1 Corinthians, Romans and Ephesians, then we begin to uncover evidence that certain gifts were temporary. For example, in Romans there is no mention of healings, miracles, tongues or interpretation. Indeed in Ephesians, there are but four gifts mentioned,[1] indicating that by 63 A.D. a number of authenticating gifts stated earlier (A.D. 54) in 1 Corinthians had passed away, and a number of the gifts in Romans (A.D. 58) were being consolidated as a part of the ministry of the office gifts.

Indeed some have pressed this thought one step further. They refer to 1 Peter 4:10-11 as a fourth list of the gifts of the Spirit. It is pointed out that this Epistle was written some years after the other three, perhaps around A.D. 66. As J. H. Pickford remarks:

---

[1] I am regarding pastor-teacher as a hyphenated gift referring to the same office. The reason for this will become clear when we deal with the grammatical structure of the term.

This list is striking in its brevity, its omissions and its emphasis. The offices and gifts recorded in the Corinthians account are not included: nothing is said about apostles, prophets, healing or speaking in tongues. But the same basic fact remains: every member of the body of Christ has received the charisma to minister in his particular way according to the ability God has given (90:7).

By the same reasoning he claims "that the gifts of the Holy Spirit to the churches converged into two permanent offices: the pastoral and the diaconal" (90:6). Thus, by the time First Peter was written the clear implication was being made that the apostles and prophets mentioned in Ephesians, were passing off the scene.

In discussing the fulfilled gifts, we shall refer three designations to them—*servant* gifts, *service* gifts and *sign* gifts. Some introduction and explanation of these terms is important to an understanding of their use.

B. THE FULFILLED SERVANT-GIFTS

These servants of the church were in themselves the gifts personified. They were Christ's servant-gifts through whose instrumentality God was to lay the foundation for His church and through whom He would also largely write the New Testament Scriptures. However, once the foundation was laid and the Scriptures completed, there was no more need for their specialized function.

Who were these servant-gifts? They were the apostles and prophets listed in the gift list of Eph. 4:11. Their ministry was that of Eph. 2:20 where we read that "the household of God" is "built upon the foundation of the apostles and prophets, Jesus Christ himself being the chief corner stone." The statement concerns completion of purpose and this is in keeping with what we learn about the fulfilled ministry of these servants in the Bible. We shall discover the reason for their impermanence as gifts as we study in more detail what these servant gifts were, as set forth in the New Testament.

C. THE FULFILLED SERVICE-GIFTS

Once it has been determined that there were temporary servants, we should not be surprised to learn that there were also temporary services. Especially is this so when we remember that the service gifts intertwined with the ministry of the gifted men. This is the case with the fulfilled gifts which we are now considering.

Yet again mythological gift theology would tell us that these gifts are for our day. Such theology completely ignores the meaning and purpose of these gifts in connection with the founding days of Christianity. As well might one claim that because God once caused the walls of Jericho to fall He must continue doing so today, as to claim that because God promised these gifts to the early church He must keep on giving them through the church age. When the purpose for which these gifts was given was fulfilled, they were withdrawn. Do not be mistaken about these service gifts!

Now to which gifts do I refer as temporary services? To the gifts of wisdom, knowledge and discernment. I do not deny that these are extant in the world today in a secondary significance (i.e., in the sense in which the words were used, for example, prior to their incorporation as gifts), but in the meaning placed upon them in Scripture as service gifts of the Spirit to the churches they were temporary. We shall look at each of these gifts in turn to discover their nature and function, and how they fulfilled their purpose.

D. THE FULFILLED SIGN-GIFTS

It is hard for us in our smug twentieth century existence to imagine a world without Christianity. Yet that was the very case with the early church. Behind this new religion were no traditions, so it was not readily accepted in the communities where groups of believers gathered. The fact is, Paul could say of the situation, "We are made as the filth of the world, and are the offscouring of all things unto this day" (1 Cor. 4:13).

Now how does one get acceptance for his ministry under such circumstances? The answer is found in the "signs following" of Mark 16:17-18. These were authenticating signs from God, signalling to the world that the fledgling church and its new gospel were real. What God promised to do in these signs He fulfilled; for we read clearly, "And they went forth, and preached every where, the Lord working with them, and confirming the word with signs following. Amen" (Mark 16:20).

These signs that followed the inroads of the gospel in the apostolic age were very important. They were the stamp of God's approval upon this strange new religion. As "Jesus of Nazareth" was "a man approved of God—by miracles and wonders and signs" done in the midst of the people, so the early church (including the apostles, prophets and others) was approved. Moreover, the new message of redemption through the resurrected Christ was "approved" also.

Now which gifts were sign gifts? Which were given to approve the church, the gospel and the leaders? Because of the need to deal with these questions in some length, I shall divide this area into four separate parts. The first will deal with healing, the second will consider miracles and the third and fourth will analyze the complimentary gifts of tongues and interpretation. Combined these form the temporary sign gifts of the Spirit which were fulfilled in the first century and then ceased.

E. AN UNBEATABLE COMBINATION

The servants, the services and the signs were God's unbeatable combination for the mammoth task of *launching* Christianity. The servants were authenticated by the signs (2 Cor. 12:12) as Christ had been also (Acts 2:22). The fledgling church caught the attention of the world, by means of the signs (Acts 2:8), and used the services to deliver the message of God as New Testament revealed truth to the world, which they were commissioned to reach (Acts 2:14-41).

These three components formed God's human instrumentality to found the church, preach the gospel and teach the saints. By this means churches were established, the known world was evangelized and the Scriptures were codified and completed. By their very purpose they were fulfilled before the end of the first century and passed off the scene.

Do not be mistaken, therefore, about their necessity for today. Rather than being a spiritual advance for these to be restored, it would be a disastrous retrogression. It would herald the news that after nineteen centuries, we no longer have a "more sure word of prophecy" (2 Peter 1:19) and need extra-biblical revelation to make up the Scripture's deficiency.

However, in saying so we come into direct controversy with charismatic theology. Because certain gifts are claimed for today, J. Rodman Williams, president of Melodyland School of Theology in Anaheim, California, for example, seems to opt for an open-ended Bible. He seems to claim that by the present-day exercise of these gifts, further inspiration of God akin to Scriptural utterance must not be ruled out. As he puts it:

> The Bible truly has become a fellow witness to God's present activity . . . If someone today perhaps has a vision of God, of Christ, it is good to know that it has happened before; if one has a revelation from God, to know that for the early Christians revelation also occurred in the community; if one speaks a "Thus says the Lord" and dares to address the fellowship in the first person—even going beyond the words of Scripture—that this was happening long ago. How strange and remarkable it is! If one speaks in the fellowship of the Spirit the word of truth, it is neither his own thoughts and reflections (e.g., on some topic of the day) nor simply some exposition of Scripture, for the Spirit transcends personal observations, however interesting or profound they may be. The Spirit as the living God moves through and beyond the records of past witness, however valuable such records are as a model for what happens today (77:16).

Do not be misled by such claims.

As we are discovering throughout this treatment of the gifts, the Bible is God's perfect revelation of Himself to mankind, never to be added to or subtracted from, regardless of what gifts are claimed for today. In this section we shall seek an understanding of the fulfilled sign-gifts, while dispelling myths which have grown up in our day concerning them and their continued use.

10

THE FULFILLED SERVANT-GIFTS

A. CHRIST GAVE SOME APOSTLES

WE HAVE ALREADY made the distinction between "the gifts," and "the gifted." A further difference is now being made, this time concerning the four offices of gifted men. Two of these were permanent gifts for the fulfilling of the ministry until the second coming of Christ. Two of these were temporary gifts for the laying of such a foundation as to ensure that the "building" of the church might endure until Jesus comes.

The myth we face now is that which would have us laying again the foundation, or worse still, never progressing beyond the substructure in the building of the "temple" of the church. Such apocryphal teaching also detracts from the authority of God's Word, which was written by these gifted men of whom we now speak. Do not, then, be mistaken about the temporary nature of, or about the importance of the offices filled by these gifted men.

According to Vincent:

> The distinguishing features of an apostle were: a commission directly from Christ, being a witness of the resurrection, special inspiration, supreme authority, accrediting by miracles, unlimited commission to preach and found churches (67:389).

There is an interesting summary regarding apostles in the *Scofield Reference Bible.*

> (1) They were chosen directly by the Lord Himself, or, as in the case of Barnabas, by the Holy Spirit (Matt. 10:1, 2; Mark 3:13, 14; Luke 6:13; Acts 9:6, 15; 13:2; 22:10, 14, 15; Rom. 1:1). (2) They were endued with sign gifts, miraculous powers which were the divine credentials of their office (Matt. 10:1; Acts 5:15, 16; 16:16-18; 28:8, 9). (3) Their relation to the kingdom was that of heralds, announcing to Israel only (Matt. 10:5, 6) the

kingdom is at hand (Matt. 4:17, *note*), and manifesting kingdom powers (Matt. 10:7, 8). (4) To one of them, Peter, the keys of the kingdom of heaven, viewed as the sphere of Christian profession, as in Matthew 13, were given (Matt. 16:19). (5) Their future relation to the kingdom will be that of judges over the twelve tribes (Matt. 19:28). (6) Consequent upon the rejection of the kingdom, and the revelation of the mystery hid in God (Matt. 16:18; Eph. 3:1-12), the Church, the apostolic office, was invested with a new enduement, the baptism with the Holy Spirit (Acts 2:1-4); a new power, that of imparting the Spirit to Jewish-Christian believers; a new relation, that of foundation stones of the new temple (Eph. 2:20-22); and a new function, that of preaching the glad tidings of salvation through a crucified and risen Lord to Jew and Gentile alike. (7) The indispensable qualification of an apostle was that he should have been an eyewitness of the resurrection (Acts 1:22; 1 Cor. 9:1) (97:1008).

Such a summary gives a good overview of the complex nature of the gift of apostleship, though we would wish to include a greater apostolic role regarding their ministry to the Gentiles as well as to the Jews.

In looking more closely at the gift, let us first of all consider:

1. The Meaning of the Word "Apostle"

Thayer tells us that the Greek word, *apostolos,* means literally "a delegate, messenger, or one sent forth with orders." (62:68). Criswell calls the apostolic gift:

> The first and foremost of all the endowments of the Spirit. . . . The word "apostle" (*apostolos*) was an ordinary, household Greek word meaning "messenger," "one sent forth." In Hebrews 3:1 our Savior is called "the Apostle and High Priest of our profession" because He was "sent forth" from heaven to make atonement for our sins. From the equivalent Latin word of *missio* we gain our English word "missionary" (7:162).

It is clear that the word apostle is used in two senses in the New Testament. Technically, it refers to the twelve who were chosen by Christ (Luke 6:13). In that sense it is used of the "office" of an apostle, and in this sense it is used also of Paul. There are many such as W. A. Criswell who believe that, "in the first chapter of Acts the disciples chose Matthias to be the apostle to take the place of the fallen Judas, but in the ninth chapter of Acts, God chose Saul of Tarsus" (7:163). Others believe that Matthias was indeed God's choice to fill Judas' vacant office, and that Paul was a "special apostle." Still others believe that the disciples had no right to do any business before Pentecost, but were rather simply to "wait for the promise" of the Holy Spirit, and so they acted apart from God's leading in choosing Matthias.

Whatever position is taken, as Criswell points out, it is clear that, in the Bible, there are only twelve apostles. Someday they will sit on twelve thrones, judging the twelve tribes of Israel (Matt. 19:28; Luke 22:29-30). The New Jerusalem is built upon twelve foundations and in these are the "names of the twelve apostles of the Lamb" (compare Eph. 2:20 and Rev. 21:14). These factors indicate strongly that in God's eyes there are eternally only twelve apostles.

There is also a generalized, or non-technical way in which the word is used. Vine writes concerning this usage, calling it "a wider reference" and stating:

> The word has also a wider reference. In Acts 14:4, 14, it is used of Barnabas as well as of Paul; in Rom. 16:7 of Andronicus and Junias. In 2 Cor. 8:23 (R.V., margin) two unnamed brethren are called "apostles of the churches;" in Phil. 2:25 (R.V., margin) Epaphroditus is referred to as "your apostle." It is used in 1 Thess. 2:6 of Paul, Silas and Timothy, to define their relation to Christ (68:63).

It may be that in this secondary non-gift sense the word can be applied to some today. However, to do so causes more problems in the churches than it solves, while at the same time failing to add any more clarity to the biblical references to apostleship.

The second item to be understood concerns:

2. The Making of an Apostle

George Purves, Professor of New Testament in Princeton Theological Seminary at the turn of the century, wrote concerning the apostolic age, saying:

> An apostle must have been a disciple of Jesus throughout His ministry from the close of that of the Baptist. This evidently

assumes that he was to teach Christ's whole message, life, and work, which alone made the resurrection of unique importance . . . to the world they were the official witnesses of the resurrection; to the church, its official instructors and overseers (80:3).

In this he followed Peter's criteria in Acts 1:21-22:

Wherefore of these men which have companied with us all the time that the Lord Jesus went in and out among us. Beginning from the baptism of John, unto that same day that he was taken up from us, must one be ordained to be a witness with us of his resurrection.

Some, however, have gone so far as to apply the term to anyone who is called of God to missionary work. For example, J. C. Lambert, when discussing the word in the *International Standard Bible Encyclopedia,* states:

The apostolate was not a limited circle of officials holding a well-defined position of authority in the church, but a large class of men who discharged one—and that the highest—of the functions of the prophetic ministry (1 Cor. 12:28; Eph. 4:11) (30:203).

In rightly dissenting from this non-restrictive use of this word, Walvoord points out:

In any case it is clear that every minister of the gospel in the apostolic age was not designated by the term apostle, nor can it be proved that all the apostles were missionaries, as Lambert contends (73:175).

Regardless of which position is taken, it is certain that the actual "gift" of apostleship in Scripture was always clearly used in the restrictive sense. It is evidently the most important of the gifts mentioned in 1 Cor. 12:28, and is distinguished clearly from prophets, teachers, and all of the rest. In its strict sense, the gift of apostleship was not merely for "sent ones," but for twelve, particularly-chosen men.

Owen calls apostles "extraordinary officers" of the church. In telling us why, he enumerates the points which set them totally apart from others. These things, he claims, constitute an extraordinary office and make apostleship impossible for today.

1. An extraordinary call unto an office, such as none other has or can have, by virtue of any law, order, or constitution whatever. 2. An extraordinary power communicated unto persons so called, enabling them to act what they are so called unto, wherein the essence of any office doth consist. 3. Extraordinary gifts for the exercise and discharge of that power. 4. Extraordinary employment as to its extent and measure, requiring extraordinary labor, travail, zeal, and self-denial. All these do and must concur in that office and unto those offices which we call extraordinary (42:851).

Using Owen's criteria, the gift of being an apostle referred to twelve men divinely and uniquely chosen for that extraordinary office.

With this in mind, we must now seek to discover:

3. The Ministry of an Apostle

Laying the foundation of the church was the prime ministry of the apostles. In Eph. 2:20 we are told that the church is, "built upon the foundation of the apostles and prophets, Jesus Christ himself being the chief cornerstone." Charles Ryrie calls these "foundation gifts." "There were foundation gifts of apostles and prophets (Eph. 2:20), which gifts do not appear in the periods of building the super-structure of the church" (48:84). This founding ministry was clearly begun at Pentecost, when the first witness, sermon, conversion, baptism and membership is recorded. From there the church multiplied and grew, mainly by the ministry of the apostles who were aided by a witnessing congregation at Jerusalem.

A second part to their ministry was that of *confirming*. I do not refer to the ritual of confirmation carried on today in some churches. Rather the reference is to Heb. 2:3-4 where we are told of that

> great salvation; which at the first began to be spoken by the Lord, and was confirmed unto us by them that heard him; God also bearing them witness, both with signs and wonders, and with divers miracles, and gifts of the Holy Ghost, according to his own will?

The ministry of the apostles was one of authenticating the Word preached, before the Scriptures were written, by these signs of apostleship (2 Cor. 12:12).

A third part of the work of an apostle was *oversight*. An example of this is the delegation sent from Jerusalem to Samaria to see that Philip's new ministry was biblical, or according to correct doctrine (Acts 8:14). Later the Jerusalem Council met to consider the ministry of Paul and to determine what guidance should be given to his converts among the Gentiles (Acts 15:1-29). Of this last recorded conference in which the twelve participated, W. A. Criswell writes:

> They were assembled there with the elders of the local church. Not Peter but James, the Lord's brother, presided. The whole membership of the church participated in the decision (Act 15:22). After the Conference, the Twelve were widely scattered and with a few exceptions are never heard of again (7:164).

Such was the work of the apostles as we find it in the Word of God.

Another mark of this gifted office concerns:

4. The Miracles of Apostleship

When Paul wrote to the Corinthians, he authenticated his claim to apostleship in these words, "I ought to have been commended of you: for in nothing am I behind the very chiefest apostles, though I be nothing. Truly the signs of an apostle were wrought among you in all patience, in signs, and wonders, and mighty deeds" (2 Cor. 12:11-12).

In the early church, such miraculous powers were part of the prerogative of apostleship. On this Samuel E. Pierce comments:

> The Holy Ghost was pleased to crown his descent with external demonstrations of his power, presence, and majesty. He conferred on the apostles and others miraculous gifts . . . These were external extraordinary works, performed by the power of the Holy Ghost, and wrought by the apostles to confirm gospel-truth, and to strike terror into the minds of the opposers and persecuters of it. And these great and miraculous gifts were continued throughout the apostolic day, and then they ceased (46:38).

The earliest list of gifts included at least four that were miraculous among the nine mentioned. In 1 Cor. 12:8-10

these were gifts of healing, miracles, tongues and interpretation of tongues. The Church at Corinth was richly endowed with such gifts so that Paul could write, "Ye come behind in no gift" (1 Cor. 1:7).
Yet, as Unger declares:

> Such miraculous sign-gifts were the special endowment of the apostles, as the God-ordained founders of Christianity . . . These supernatural gifts, which Paul exercised and was able to transmit to others, served not only to establish Christianity but to vindicate his apostleship (65:138).

This is seen clearly in Romans 15:18-19, where he refers to his successful ministry among the Gentiles and states, "I will not dare to speak of any of those things which Christ hath not wrought by me, to make the Gentiles obedient, by word and deed, through mighty signs and wonders, by the power of the Spirit of God."
The miracles performed authenticated both him and the ministry he performed as an apostle.
We have the same thing in Heb. 2:3-4, where the confirming signs clearly refer to the ministry of Christ and of the apostles. Howard Sugden says it well:

> Whenever God begins a new work in the world He does different things. For instance, when He gave the Law there were thunders and lightnings, the voice of God and the sound of the trumpet, and that's the only time it ever happened. The Law has been read ten thousand times ten thousand, but there has never been a trumpet, thunders or lightning. And apostles and prophets have to do with foundations (80:3).

This thought brings us to a fifth and final consideration:

5. The Mirage of Today's Apostleship

I am using the word "mirage" in the sense of "an illusionary appearance." Such is the claim to apostleship today. There are no apostles in spite of the pretentious claims of a variety of groups. Having fulfilled their function, they passed off the scene.
The church was built on the foundation laid by the apostles (Eph. 2:20), and after the foundation was done, their work was done. Says Walvoord, therefore:

The apostolic office died with the first generation of Christians, there being no provision for successors, nor have there been in the history of the church any who could stand with the apostles. The fact that apostles were chosen from those who were eywitnesses of the resurrected Christ eliminates any possibility of later generations participating in the call to apostleship (73:176).

Each age, as Scripture unfolds, was a preparation for that which was to come. The apostolic age was a transition period between the old and the new. The work of the apostles was evidential to the authenticity of the new gospel being preached. However, as W. Graham Scroggie writes:

Now, the New Testament, which was then in process of formation, is completed, and to that we make appeal; that is our power and our authority, rendering the working of miracles unnecessary. If it be claimed that we may now do all that the apostles did, how is it that no one is writing Holy Scripture? We know perfectly well that that was an apostolic prerogative, and we should know also that it was not the only one (79:21).

Because of the standard for the apostolic office, there can no longer be apostles. Peter tells us in Acts 1:22 that to be an apostle one had to, "beginning from the baptism of John, unto that same day that he was taken up from us, . . . be a witness with us of his resurrection." This causes great men of the past such as C. H. Spurgeon to write:

As the result of the ascension of Christ into heaven, the church received apostles, men who were selected as witnesses because they had personally seen the Savior—an office which necessarily dies out, and properly so, because the miraculous power also is withdrawn. They were needed temporarily, and they were given, by the ascended Lord, as a choice legacy (56:178).

It also makes leaders of the present such as W. A. Criswell to state:

The twelve apostles have no successors. For one to be an apostle he had to be baptized by John the Baptist, had to be trained by Christ Himself, and had to be a personal eyewitness of the resurrected and glorified Lord (Acts 1:22). The group did not form a Sanhedrin or a great council. Like the delegates to a constitutional convention, when their work was done the office ceased (7:164).

Do not be misled by pretenders to the office of apostle. This gift was necessary, but it was temporary. Thus, when God's intention for their ministry was complete, He called them home—never to be replaced.

B. CHRIST GAVE SOME PROPHETS

Several times reference has been made to the order of 1 Cor. 12:28. Let me do so again, for here we have the New Testament, gifted officer who was second only to the apostles in the founding days of the church. The fact is that prophets are the only officers of the church mentioned in all four lists of spiritual gifts. This should give some gauge to their importance. This measure is seen in:

1. The Meaning of the Terms "Prophet" and "Prophecy"

The noun *prophetes* in the New Testament refers to one who has insight into divine things and who speaks them forth, or openly. Among the Greeks it denoted an interpreter of the oracles of the gods. *Propheteia* (prophecy) deals with the proclamation of the mind and counsel of God. W. E. Vine tells us that:

> In the Septuagint it is the translation of the word *rôeh,* a seer; 1 Sam. 9:9, indicating that the prophet was one who had immediate intercourse with God. It also translated the word *nābhî,* meaning either one in whom the message from God springs forth or one to whom anything is secretly communicated. Hence, in general, the prophet was one upon whom the Spirit of God rested, Num. 11:17-29, one, to whom and through whom God speaks, Num. 12:2; Amos 3:7, 8[1] (70:222).

Sometimes prophecy was predictive. Examples of this are seen in the prediction by Agabus concerning a coming famine (Acts 11:27-28). In Acts 21:10-14 Paul was warned prophetically that sufferings, and perhaps death, lay ahead for him in Rome. However, the predictive element was secondary to the proclamation of the mind and counsel of God by direct revelation.

This leads us to consider:

---

[1] Vine has an excellent study on both *prophetes* and *propheteia* (Vol. III, pp. 221-223).

2. The Purpose of Prophets and Prophecy

Commenting on 1 Cor. 12:10, Marvin R. Vincent says of prophecy that it had to do with, "utterance under immediate divine inspiration; delivering inspired exhortations, instructions, or warnings . . . The fact of direct inspiration distinguished 'prophecy' from 'teaching' " (67:256). This last statement is important for an understanding of the supernatural element in prophecy—especially in non-predictive prophecy.

Before the completion of revealed truth in the Scriptures, the prophets were the inspired revealers of God's teaching to the churches. They told the infant churches what they should do, believe and teach. James Thomson says of their ministry that:

> These prophets in the N.T. church seem often to have been itinerant preachers. Moving from church to church they built up believers in the faith by teaching the word. Their ministry would probably be characterized by spontaneity and power, since it seems to have included speaking by revelation (1 Cor. 14:6, 26, 30f.) (63:499).

This edifying aspect to the gift is that which Paul has in mind in passages such as 1 Cor. 14:3, "But he that prophesieth speaketh unto men to edification, and exhortation, and comfort." Because of this he goes on to state that he would rather that there was an abundance of "prophecy" in the church, than a lot of tongues-speaking. Prophecy had as its basic purpose the building up of believers by verbalized inspired messages from God concerning faith and practice.

Because of this revelatory aspect to their ministry, John L. Benson is absolutely correct when he writes:

> Prophecy involved secret information which came directly to the prophet's mind from God's mind—information, for instance which spelled out the nature of the church as a mystery organism. God shared with these New Testament prophets mysteries which were hidden in the secret counsels from all eternity and not revealed to any of the Old Testament prophets (2:35).

Because of this, Paul states concerning his prophetic ministry, "But we speak the wisdom of God in a mystery, even the hidden wisdom, which God ordained before the world unto our glory" (1 Cor. 2:7). Then he continues by stating that this is done in chosen words, "not in the words which man's wisdom teacheth, but which the Holy Ghost teacheth" (1 Cor. 2:13). This was the ministry of a prophet, a ministry now incorporated in the Word of God.

The messages of the prophets, therefore, revealed the will of God which otherwise may never have been known. In this way they fulfilled the need, which same need was later to be filled by the completed Scriptures. Accordingly there were certain factors necessary to the gift of prophecy. Walvoord enumerates them as follows:

> (1) the prophet must have received his message from God in the form of some special revelation, (2) the prophet must have divine guidance in the declaration of this revelation, corresponding to the inspiration of the written Word, (3) the message delivered by the prophet must bear with it the authority of God (73:177).

The prophet was then God's spokesman for the inspired message to be delivered.

This brings us to a crucial point:

3. The Passing of Prophets and Prophecy

As with apostles, the purpose for which God gave prophets was to establish the church upon a firm foundation of biblical truth. Their ministry was to span the gap between the Old and the New Testaments. As Spurgeon puts it, "They were needed as a link between the glories of the old and new covenant" (56:178).

This ministry is stated together with that of the apostles in Eph. 2:20 where we are told that "the household of God" is "built upon the foundation of the apostles and prophets, Jesus Christ himself being the chief corner stone." Their ministry was the base upon which the structure of the Christian Church would be built.

Joseph Dillow illustrates the passage with the following diagram:

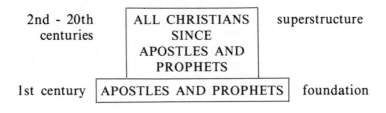

| 2nd - 20th centuries | ALL CHRISTIANS SINCE APOSTLES AND PROPHETS | superstructure |
| 1st century | APOSTLES AND PROPHETS | foundation |

Then he explains:

> The church in Eph. 2:20 is compared to a building which has a foundation and a superstructure. Paul says the foundation represents the first period of church history, Christ and the apostles and prophets. The superstructure represents the succeeding centuries since the first century . . . We are now in the period of the superstructure and not of the foundation. Once the superstructure of a building is laid down upon the foundation, you don't relay the foundation. Prophecy was the foundation, so we can't go back to that. We are above the foundation now. This text is saying, then, that the gifts of apostleship and of prophecy passed during the foundation period of the church (9:115).

Thus the fulfilled purpose denotes the fulfilled office and gift.

By the year A.D. 150 the churches faced their first controversy on this issue, in the claims of Montanus and his two prophetesses. His claim was that the supernatural gifts of apostle and prophet were renewed in him. Accordingly new revelations were given through him, superseding the Holy Scriptures.

Because of this dispute, the churches were forced to declare their position on the issue of extra-biblical prophecy. Out of this discussion, says W. A. Criswell, came their affirmation and conclusion concerning:

> the finality of Scripture. The churches avowed that the Scriptures were closed. There are to be no more Scriptures. They affirmed in no uncertain terms that the ecstatic utterances of Montanus were not Scripture and certainly did not supersede the words of the apostles. Is the Church to expect any further revelation by prophetic visions? No, said the apostolic churches as against a Joseph Smith, or as against a Mary Baker Glover Patterson Eddy (7:19).

Of course, in this they were simply agreeing with the Scriptures themselves, which warn all of us:

> If any man shall add unto these things, God shall add unto him the plagues that are written in this book: And if any man shall take away from the words of the book of this prophecy, God shall take away his part out of the book of life, and out of the holy city, and from the things which are written in this book (Rev. 22:18-19).

The canon of Holy Scripture, of Divine revelation, of inspired utterance and writing is complete. It is closed to all additions or deletions.

For this reason, Peter could write concerning the inspiration of Scripture saying, "We have also a more sure word of prophecy; whereunto ye do well that ye take heed, as unto a light that shineth in a dark place, until the day dawn, and the day star arise in your hearts" (2 Pet. 1:19).

All prophecy in the sense of revelation is ended. The Word of God is all the prophecy we need. It can never be superseded.

We can say, "Amen," to the statement by René Pache concerning those who claim the gift of prophecy today as Montanus did long ago, starting to speak:

> as if they were God Himself: "I, the Lord, declare . . . I announce . . . Do this . . . , etc." . . . However, when these prophets are mistaken, contradict one another, and deliver messages which are decidely inferior to biblical revelation, or even to an ordinary sermon (which, alas, is heard only too frequently), we are forced to conclude that herein, too, counterfeit insinuates itself, and we are led to hold ourselves in prudent reserve, while waiting for God to grant us more reliable proofs of His intervention (43:190).

There will never again be "reliable proof," for the Bible declares "prophecies" to have ended (1 Cor. 13:8).

Let me conclude by saying that the word "prophet" can have a secondary meaning—pale in the full light of the primary. There is a general sense in which the preacher and teacher of the Bible is a prophet. In the past the prophecy of the prophet was new truth revealed. In the present the prophecy of the pastors-teachers is the revealed truth proclaimed.

In this sense, W. A. Criswell says it best:

> It is a gift to be desired by the church (1 Cor. 14:1, 39). In 1 Cor. 12—14 some form of the word occurs twenty-two times. The purpose of the gift is seen in 1 Cor. 14:3: "But he that prophesieth speaketh unto men to edification, and exhortation, and comfort;" in 1 Cor. 14:24, 25: "But if all prophesy, and there come in one that believeth not, or one unlearned, he is convicted of all, he is judged of all;" and in 1 Cor. 14:31: "For ye may all prophesy one by one, that all may learn, and all may be comforted." The Spirit gift of prophecy is bestowed upon the churches for edification, exhortation, comfort, conversion of the lost, and teaching of the unlearned. It should be the gift most commonly exercised in the assemblies of Christ (1 Cor. 14:3, 24, 31). A preacher who gives forth the message of God in the wisdom and power of the Holy Spirit has the gift of prophecy (1 Peter 4:10, 11; 1 Cor. 2:1-16). Prophecy is Spirit-inspired utterance. An inspired preacher was the first gift of the Spirit manifested in the church at Pentecost. He is God's man for the delivering of God's message to a lost world. We must never forget Rev. 19:10, "For the testimony of Jesus is the spirit of prophecy" (7:166).

And we add simply, "Thank you Lord, for such prophets and prophecy today."

11

THE FULFILLED SERVICE-GIFTS

A. THE WORD OF WISDOM

THE GIFT OF WISDOM is mentioned but *once* in the four lists. In 1 Cor. 12:8 we are told that in the "manifestation of the Spirit," "to one is given by the Spirit the word of wisdom." However, in spite of its singularity in the lists, this gift was of utmost importance. Without it the early church could not have continued its ministry. It was a part of the means whereby they understood the very revelation of God for the New Testament age.

Think first of all about:

1. What Wisdom Was

James Thomson explains the meaning in these words:

> This gift would communicate ability to receive and explain "the deep things of God" (Rom. 11:33). In God's dealings with men, much is mysterious, and the ordinary Christian is often in need of a word that will throw light upon his situation; and the person fitted by the Spirit to fulfil this ministry is "through the Spirit" given "the word of wisdom." Because of the strong sense of revelation or insight implied in the phrase, perhaps this gift was akin to a revelational utterance by the Christian prophet (63:499).

It is interesting that both "wisdom" and "knowledge" are tied to the word *logos* in 1 Cor. 12:8. *Logos* is reason, then speech. Jesus is said to be the *Logos* of God (John 1:1-2). The wisdom which is God's gift in this verse, is the *logos* through the Spirit as the channel. Findlay calls it "the truth of God wrought into the man" (13:888).

The character of that wisdom is stated by Paul in 1 Cor. 2:7-8, "We speak the wisdom of God in a mystery, even the hidden wisdom, which God ordained before the world unto our glory: which none of the princes of this world knew." It is a direct intuition into otherwise unknowable mysteries of God. As Benson states: "We are dealing here with an immediate grasp of the secret plans and purposes of God in their totality. This information also became Scripture" (2:35).

This wisdom was illustrated in a very meaningful way when Peter confessed to our Lord, "Thou art the Christ, the Son of the living God" (Matt. 16:16). You will remember that Jesus answered, "Blessed art thou, Simon Barjona: for flesh and blood hath not revealed it unto thee, but my Father which is in heaven" (Matt. 16:17). No one told Peter who Jesus truly was but God gave him the wisdom to perceive the depths of His character. This is exactly what the gift of wisdom was all about.

And such wisdom was needed in the early church. How else could puny man ever cope with the subject matter of Rom. 11:33-36?

> O the depth of the riches both of the wisdom and knowledge of God! how unsearchable are his judgments, and his ways past finding out! For who hath known the mind of the Lord or who hath been his counsellor? Or who hath first given to him, and it shall be recompensed unto him again? For of him, and through him, and to him, are all things: to whom be glory for ever. Amen.

Such vastness, such infinitude as God is, cannot be understood or taught, in man's wisdom or ability. There must be the gift of wisdom to unveil His character and purpose in New Testament truth.

This, of course, is the argument of 1 Corinthians 2. Listen to Paul reason this out so logically in verses 9 to 13:

> But as it is written, Eye hath not seen, nor ear heard, neither have entered into the heart of man, the things which God hath prepared for them that love him. But God hath revealed them unto us by his Spirit: for the spirit searcheth all things, yea, the deep things of God. For what man knoweth the things of a man, save the spirit of man which is in him? even so the things of God knoweth no man, but the Spirit of God. Now we have received, not the spirit of the world, but the spirit which is of God; that we might know the things that are freely given to us of God. Which things also we speak, not in the words which

man's wisdom teacheth, but which the Holy Ghost teacheth; comparing spiritual things with spiritual.

The wisdom Paul used was the gift of the Holy Spirit. Only that wisdom could enable him to reveal and record truths which we today believe are the very Word of God!

Peter speaks of this gift of wisdom in relation to Paul. In 2 Peter 3:15-16 he states that:

> the longsuffering of our Lord is salvation; even as our beloved brother Paul also according to the wisdom given unto him hath written unto you; as also in all his epistles, speaking in them of these things; in which are some things hard to be understood, which they that are unlearned and unstable wrest, as they do also the other scriptures, unto their own destruction.

Paul obviously had the gift of wisdom, which enabled him to intuitively know and understand the great elective purposes of God.

Speaking on the character of this gift, Donald G. Merrett calls it:

> a flash of divine omniscience. All the facts of all time are before God whether they be in the past, present, or future. When God gives to His servants revelatory knowledge of what He is going to do, He has shown something of His infinite purpose. His plan to bring to pass that which He has chosen to do is, of course, His will and His wisdom. If perchance He shows to man what this purpose is, whether it be related to persons or things, that revelation is a word of wisdom (36:173).

In this same way, Clement of Alexandria defined wisdom as, "the knowledge of things human and divine, and of their causes" (49:119).

Let us consider in a practical sense:

2. How Wisdom Was Used

Wisdom was promised to the disciples of our Lord as they looked forward to being brought before courts—religious and secular—for the cause of Christ. Luke 21:14-15 gives that promise:

> Settle it therefore in your hearts, not to meditate before what ye shall answer: For I will give you a mouth and wisdom, which all your adversaries shall not be able to gainsay nor resist.

It is obvious that the wisdom was to be from outside of themselves. This wisdom was to be a spiritual gift.

Coming to the Book of Acts, we see instances of this in operation. When Peter and John were called before the council to explain their behavior in preaching "through Jesus the resurrection of the dead," these educated men were amazed at the spiritual depth and perception which was so obvious. Thus we read:

> Now when they saw the boldness of Peter and John, and perceived that they were unlearned and ignorant men, they marvelled; and they took knowledge of them, that they had been with Jesus (Acts 4:13).

Their wisdom was the spiritual gift promised by Christ.

Later Stephen found himself facing opposition, because he too was ministering in the name of Jesus. But we read that as they disputed with him, "they were not able to resist the wisdom and the spirit by which he spake" (Acts 6:10). Note well that the wisdom is tied to Spirit in this verse, and not merely the human spirit.[1] Stephen was speaking on the things of God by a revelatory wisdom that amazed his detractors.

Wisdom was also a gift used in deciding issues and determining policy. In this sense, we see James using wisdom as he chaired the Jerusalem Council in Acts 15. Read carefully his pronouncement in Acts 15:13-18. It is filled with intuitive insight into Old Testament Scripture. Out of these passages, James brings God's hitherto unknown purpose for the Gentiles (Acts 15:19-21).

So clearly had the wisdom of the Holy Spirit's gift been exerised by James, that we read, "Then pleased it the apostles and elders with the whole church" (Acts 15:22). Because of that wisdom, there was "one accord" (v. 25) in a recognition that they did what they did because, "it seemed good to the Holy Ghost and to us" (Acts 15:28).

You see, in church business the infant assemblies had to depend on the gift of wisdom to interpret God's purposes.

---

[1] The Western text has ". . . the wisdom which was in him and the Holy Spirit by whom he spoke," says F. F. Bruce (3:132). Morgan points out that the expression is "in almost identical phrases" to that which Luke used of Christ in his Gospel (38:182). There can be little doubt, therefore, that Luke here refers to the Holy Spirit by which the wisdom was known and spoken.

They could not seek the New Testament order for things as we can, for the New Testament was as yet unwritten. Thus, the gift of wisdom—as a revelatory gift not unlike that of a prophet—was relied upon for guidance as to God's will in each situation.

Now at this point we need to consider:

3. When Wisdom Passed Away

As with apostleship and prophecy, so with wisdom; the Bible speaks of the gift of wisdom which is a technical term used in a special sense, and it also speaks of the quality of wisdom. While the quality of wisdom lasts throughout the Old and the New Testaments, the technical "gift of wisdom" was temporary and has ceased.

Now the reason for saying this is exactly the same as that applied to apostles and prophets. Wisdom was a service gift—most probably enjoyed by the apostles and prophets—which dealt with "revelation." It was foundational to the coming of the Word of God, but was no longer needed when the Scriptures were complete. Merrill F. Unger puts it this way concerning revelatory gifts:

> It must be remembered that 1 Corinthians is one of the earlier epistles, written in all probability before A.D. 57. When it was penned there was practically no New Testament in existence, except the epistle of James addressed to Hebrew Christians and 1 and 2 Thessalonians. But there were no New Testament manuscripts to preach from. The Old Testament, of course, was available for study, but it did not cover the great distinctive teachings of the new age. The question may be asked, would the Corinthian assembly meet and have a teaching ministry? The answer is yes. God graciously endowed the early church with special revelatory gifts of prophecy, tongues (when interpreted), and knowledge. These special temporary gifts met an urgent need. They were designed to tide the church through the period of partial, piecemeal revelation until the complete and final thing would arrive (1 Cor. 13:10) (65:141).

When the revelation of Scripture was complete and entire—not to be added to, or taken away from—there remained no more need for wisdom. Thus, as a technical gift of the Holy Spirit, wisdom passed away. The Bible forever after was to be our wisdom; from it we receive the fruits of the gift exercised by the men who wrote it.

"But," objects someone, "the Bible tells us to pray for wisdom." Yes, that is true and we will receive wisdom in the general sense of a quality of life, as we ask for it. However, when James 1:5 says, "If any of you lack wisdom, let him ask of God, that giveth to all men liberally, and upbraideth not; and it shall be given him," the very wording used differentiates between the gift and the wisdom spoken of here. The gift of wisdom was not given to "all men." It was sovereignly bestowed by the Holy Spirit "as he will" (1 Cor. 12:8, 11). As everyone was not an apostle, or a teacher, or a prophet and so on (1 Cor. 12:29-30), so also everyone had not the gift of wisdom. Indeed, as they had no control over what they were (for they were what they were by the grace of God [1 Cor. 15:10]), in the same manner they had no control over whether or not they had this gift.

Thus, when James gave an unqualified promise that wisdom would be received by "all men" who asked for it, it is obvious that he was not speaking of the gift of wisdom. If he was, he would have been correcting Paul's statement concerning the sovereign bestowal of the gifts. We must understand, therefore, that he was rather speaking of that wisdom needed by all of us, which we can have indiscriminately for the asking! Do not be mistaken; the gift of wisdom is gone from this age of biblical authority, though the quality of wisdom is available to all who ask in faith.

B. THE WORD OF KNOWLEDGE

Closely aligned to wisdom was another service gift, the gift of knowledge. Paul puts both gifts together in 1 Cor. 12:8 in the words, "For to one is given by the Spirit, the word of wisdom; to another, the word of knowledge by the same Spirit." In relation to wisdom, the Greek states that the gift is bestowed "by," or "through" the Holy Spirit; but in the case of knowledge, it is said to be "according to" the Holy Spirit. Thus, both the means of bestowal and the method of selection are in view in the text.

We must ask immediately:

1. What Is the Word of Knowledge?

As with wisdom, it is tied to *logos*—a reasoned utterance. Paul does not have in mind a knowledge of the written Word of God, or knowledge in a general sense. As Unger stresses:

> He refers strictly to the gift of knowledge. By this special gift the Holy Spirit enabled a first-century believer to know and to instruct the assembly in truth now recorded in the New Testament (65:140).

Knowledge was, therefore, "truth intellectually apprehended and objectified" (13:888). This apprehension was accomplished by the gift installed in the life by the Holy Spirit. It was a supernatural "endowment of the Holy Spirit enabling a first-century believer, through extrabiblical revelation of the future, to declare truth now enshrined in the prophecies of the New Testament" (65:140).

There is absolutely no thought of a knowledge acquired through diligent Bible study such as that of 2 Tim. 2:15. This causes Criswell to state:

> This is the gift of appraisal and of judgment concerning things as they are. It is the ability to grasp the truth about a present situation: seeing, knowing, understanding, as the Holy Spirit sees, knows and understands (7:172).

It was a gift given by God the Holy Spirit which was far beyond the normal and natural capabilities of the individual.

At this point one might ask:

2. Are There Illustrations of Knowledge in the Bible?

The answer is yes; they are in both the Old and the New Testaments. It may seem strange to say that one can see this gift in the Old Testament. However, when we understand that the gift is closely aligned to prophecy, we are not surprised that Old Testament prophets exhibited the gift.

Elisha, for example, exhibited "knowledge" on more than one occasion. Without seeing it or hearing about it, he knew the whereabouts of the Syrian Camp and all that went on there. The distraught King of Syria thought he had a traitorous informer among his men:

and he called his servants, and said unto them, Will ye not shew me which of us is for the king of Israel? And one of his servants said, None, my lord, O king: but Elisha, the prophet that is in Israel, telleth the king of Israel the words that thou speakest in thy bedchamber (2 Kings 6:11-12).

This knowledge Elisha enjoyed was beyond any natural sense. It was something given to him by God's omniscience. Such was the gift of knowledge in the Old Testament; it was probably a service gift of the prophets.

In the New Testament is the account of Peter using the gift of knowledge when interviewing Ananias. No one told Peter of the business transaction completed, or of the lie that Ananias and his wife were living. But God knew and supernaturally gave that knowledge to Peter, who said abruptly:

Ananias, why hath Satan filled thine heart to lie to the Holy Ghost, and to keep back part of the price of the land? While it remained, was it not thine own? and after it was sold, was it not in thine own power? why hast thou conceived this thing in thine heart? thou has not lied unto men, but unto God (Acts 5:3-4).

This was a supernatural revelation from God, a "word of knowledge."

Another instance concerns Paul's journey to Rome on board the doomed ship. God revealed to Paul what no one else on board knew. Thus, he said to all on board:

Sirs, ye should have hearkened unto me, and not have loosed from Crete, and to have gained this harm and loss. And now I exhort you to be of good cheer: for there shall be no loss of any man's life among you, but of the ship. For there stood by me this night the angel of God, whose I am, and whom I serve, Saying, Fear not, Paul; thou must be brought before Caesar: and, lo, God hath given thee all them that sail with thee (Acts 27:21-24).

This knowledge was revealed supernaturally to Paul and his speech was, therefore, "the word of knowledge."

The very mechanics of the gift are laid bare in the seven letters of Revelation 2 and 3. John is the writer, and he reveals things right and wrong at the hidden heart of each church. How did he do it? He wrote what the risen Christ told him to write. The knowledge was nothing more than the message of God through his servant. Such was the "word of knowledge." It was a flash of omniscience from God Himself, revealing what the person normally would not have known, nor could have known.

Because of this we need to be clear that:

3. The Word of Knowledge Is Not Natural Knowledge

We today have what one might call "natural" knowledge. It is acquired by diligent perseverance and hard work. There is a tendency on the part of some to decry such knowledge, but sorry indeed would be our world without Godly scholars.

Paul was knowledgeable, having sat at the feet of such rabbinical masters as Gamaliel. Luke was a trained physician. The great apologists of the second century, Justin Martyr and Origen, used their educated knowledge well in the great theological debates of their day. During the Reformation, scholars such as Melanchthon, Erasmus, Calvin and Luther were saviors of the world from the grip of Rome. Men such as John Fletcher, John Wesley, George Whitfield and Jonathan Edwards have left their scholarly, spiritual impact upon our world.

But what if such men had succumbed to laziness? What if they had relied on some "word of knowledge" to see them through? Would our theological libraries be as rich as they are today through the impact of their educational contributions? I do not think so.

You see, the word of knowledge and "natural" knowledge are two different things. The gift was never meant to replace knowledge acquired, but to augment it with knowledge unacquirable. It was a revelational gift needed, during the infancy of the church, to enable the apostles and prophets to fulfill their unique tasks.

Again we ask ourselves:

4. Is the Word of Knowledge for Today?

We are introduced to this statement in 1 Cor. 13:8, "Whether there be knowledge, it shall vanish away." The word used means literally, they shall be done away. A. T. Robertson says that it is, "rare in old Greek, to make idle, inoperative" (47:179). The idea is that, "they were to be rendered of no effect after their temporary use was fulfilled (68:14)." Thus, Paul continues, "but when that which is perfect is come, then that which is in part shall be done away" (1 Cor. 13:10).

In concluding our study on the word of knowledge, let us just slip into a service at Corinth about the time 1 Cor. 13:9 was written. A believer with the endowment of prophecy stands up, as Merrill F. Unger imagines:

> and, by direct revelation from the Spirit, taught on the rapture or the judgment seat of Christ or the marriage of the Lamb of the New Jerusalem. But all this teaching was bit by bit and fragmentary. Another would rise and discourse in a language he had never studied. He would speak mysteries, and another would interpret to the congregation. So the end result would be equivalent to the gift of prophecy or knowledge.
>
> Another with the gift of knowledge would stand to his feet and discourse on the church, the body of Christ, or the gifts of the Spirit, or the believer's position in Christ, etc. But again this ministry was partial and piecemeal. Here a little, there a little, in contrast to "the perfect [complete] thing" (1 Cor. 13:10). This passage, by strict adherence to the context, necessitates interpreting the complete thing as the New Testament Scriptures, added to the Old Testament and constituting the completed, written revelation of God, forming the canonical Scripture.
>
> Those who study God's Word do not know partially or prophesy partially. The completeness and finality of the Word gives completeness and finality to the teaching of those who faithfully expound it (65:141).

C. DISCERNING OF SPIRITS

Gift number seven in Paul's earliest list, 1 Cor. 12:8-10, is "discerning of spirits." The word literally means, "to separate, discriminate; then to learn by discriminating, to determine, decide" (68:315). In the text it refers to judgment by evidence whether the spirits are evil, or of God.

The nature of the gift of prophecy, as James Thomson points out:

> was such that the danger of false prophets must always have been present. The Spirit, therefore, communicated a gift which enabled some among those who listened to the prophets to

recognize the truth or falsity of their utterances. This was not natural insight or shrewd judgment but a supernatural gift. Paul describes this spiritual gift as a "discerning of the spirits." The fact that the prophet spoke by revelation made the appearance of false prophets almost inevitable; while, therefore, Paul urged his converts not to despise prophesyings they were, nevertheless, to prove all things (1 Thess. 5:20 ff.). The gift of discernment of spirits was an essential. Only then could believers discriminate between the false and the true, when an itinerant prophet claimed to be inspired to speak by revelation (1 Cor. 14:29) (63:499).

Several illustrations of this gift in action are given to us in the New Testament. It was used by Peter when in Samaria. Simon the sorcerer had made profession of faith in Christ and was baptized. However, later when, through the laying on of the hands of the apostles, the people were receiving the gift of the Holy Spirit, Simon's real character came to the fore. Let the Scriptural account tell the story:

> And when Simon saw that through laying on of the apostle's hands the Holy Ghost was given, he offered them money. Saying, Give me also this power, that on whomsoever I lay hands, he may receive the Holy Ghost. But Peter said unto him, Thy money perish with thee, because thou hast thought that the gift of God may be purchased with money. Thou has neither part nor lot in this matter: for thy heart is not right in the sight of God. Repent therefore of this thy wickedness, and pray God, if perhaps the thought of thine heart may be forgiven thee. For I perceive that thou art in the gall of bitterness, and in the bond of iniquity (Acts 8:18-23).

Peter clearly was able to discern about Simon what Philip apparently could not. It is thus that the gift of discernment equipped some to see and understand what others could not.

Another incident of this gift being used is seen in Acts 13:6-11. The false prophet Bar-jesus, or Elymas, is in view here seeking to stop the conversion of Sergius Paulus.

> Then Saul, (who also is called Paul,) filled with the Holy Ghost, set his eyes on him, and said, O full of all subtlety and all mischief, thou child of the devil, thou enemy of all righteousness, wilt thou not cease to pervert the right ways of the Lord? And now, behold, the hand of the Lord is upon thee, and thou

shalt be blind, not seeing the sun for a season. And immediately there fell on him a mist and a darkness; and he went about seeking some to lead him by the hand (Acts 13:9-11).

The gift of discernment saw clearly into the very soul of Elymas. Then, by the apostolic authority of Paul, God's judgment was called upon him.

But even when the prophets were of a high caliber, there were to be checks and balances on their ministry. As W. A. Criswell remarks:

> This necessitated also the gift of discerning of spirits (1 Cor. 12:10), for it was most needed to distinguish between the true revelations from God and false revelations concerning His churches. "The spirits of the prophets are subject to the prophets" (1 Cor. 14:32). "Let the prophets speak two or three, and let the other judge" (1 Cor. 14:29). Prophesyings were not to be despised (1 Thess. 5:20) but their utterances were to be carefully judged (1 John 4:1; Rev. 2:2) (7:166).

For this very reason, we read of those in the Berean Church that they were, "more noble than those in Thessalonica, in that they received the word with all readiness of mind, and searched the Scriptures daily, whether those things were so" (Acts 17:11). Checks and balances were necessary on the prophetic gift and on the service gifts of wisdom and knowledge.

However, as the Scriptures were completed and the gifts of the apostle, prophet, wisdom and knowledge died out (and other gifts too, as we shall see), the gift of discernment also passed away. John F. Walvoord explains:

> As the New Testament had not been completed, there was no written Word to appeal to except the Old Testament. With the coming of the completed New Testament, the written Word made this work of the Spirit no longer necessary . . . Christians are dependent upon the written Word of God as illuminated by the Holy Spirit, and no one is given authority to discern spirits apart from that belonging to all Christians alike (73:188).

Let us beware, then, lest our Lord must charge us also, saying, "Ye do err, not knowing the Scriptures" (Matt. 22:29).

Even today there is need for discernment. This discernment is based upon the Word of God. It is still true, "To the law and to the testimony: if they speak not according to this word, it is because there is no light in them" (Isa. 8:20). Let us, therefore, in this way "try the spirits whether they are of God" (1 John 4:1).

12

THE FULFILLED SIGN-GIFTS

A. THE GIFTS OF HEALING

As DAVID SAID in Psalm 139:14, so can we all say, "I am fearfully and wonderfully made." In relating some of the wonders of the human body, W. B. Riley wrote:

> The brain is enormously more sophisticated in potential pathways and microcircuitry. (There are upwards of 10,000 to 50,000 independent nerve cells in every cubic millimeter of cerebral cortex—10 to 15 billion altogether; each nerve cell is able to receive simultaneous information from thousands of cells, integrating and then funneling this new information to many other cells; consequently, the number of permutations and combinations of circuitry and sequences becomes astronomical.) . . . There are in the human body 600 muscles, 1,000 miles of blood vessels, and 350 arteries important enough to name. The skin, spread out, would cover 16 square feet. It has 1,500,000 sweat glands which, spread out on one surface, would occupy 10,000 square feet and cover five city lots, 20 x 100 feet. The lungs are composed of 700 million cells, all of which we use in breathing, equal to a flat surface of 2,000 feet, which would cover a city lot. In 70 years the heart beats 2,500,000,000 times and lifts 500,000 tons of blood. The nervous system, controlled by the brain, has 3,000,000,000,000 nerve cells, 9,200,000,000 of which are in the cortex of the brain alone. In the blood are 30,000,000 white corpuscles and 180 trillion red ones. It is easy to believe that the very hairs of our heads are numbered— about 250,000. Can anything be more pathetic than for some young freshman, created of God in such intricacy and with such infinite wisdom, to spew his infidelity into the face of the very God Who created him: Who saw his substance before it was in existence and Who wrote down in His book all his members and fashioned them when as yet there was none of them? (82:167).

To any doctor the human body is, therefore, a "fearful" organism to treat medically.

Today, the science of medicine has advanced far beyond the wildest dreams of the physicians of Paul's day. But even yet they must stand in awe of God's creative power. The doctor, with all his modern techniques, merely "treats" the patient and then stands back while God heals.

However, there is a compound gift mentioned in 1 Cor. 12:9, 28 and 30, which exceeded the wonder of the doctor's skillful art. This is called, "the gifts of healing." It referred to the supernatural endowment by God the Holy Spirit, which enabled some individuals to practice a healing art completely removed from their own abilities—either learned, or inherited.

The term in these three verses is in the plural. It is *charismata iamaton,* gifts of healings. Criswell comments that, "as there are different kinds of sicknesses (we can be sick in our bodies, we can be sick in our minds, we can be sick in our souls), so there are different kinds of healings" (7:188). The gift of healing was the complete answer of God to the medical needs of men.

Because of this, in the modern mythology concerning the gifts, there have arisen certain:

1. Mistakes About the Gift of Healing

Through a misinterpretation of this gift, many of these mistakes have been ensconced in the tradition of "faith healing." The greatest of these is that:

a. Healing is in the Atonement

This is usually based on Isa. 53:5. Isaiah, of course, is speaking of the spiritual chastisement Jesus would bear for our sins. He is prophesying concerning the healing of the soul by the atoning death of Christ. With one simple question, J. Dwight Pentecost unveils the fatal flaw in this myth:

> If healing is in the atonement, we would like to ask the question, "Why does any child of God ever die?" Sickness ultimately culminates in death, and death is the outgrowth of sickness. If healing is in the atonement, there could be no such thing as physical death. The fact that believers die negates this

interpretation that Jesus Christ has died to remove all physical sickness (44:185).

The fact of the matter is that we are not promised freedom from sickness or disease until after the resurrection. Rom. 8:22-23 tells us:

> For we know that the whole creation groaneth and travaileth in pain together until now. And not only they, but ourselves also, which have the first fruits of the Spirit, even we ourselves groan within ourselves, waiting for the adoption, to wit, the redemption of our body (Rom. 8:22-23).

This "redemption" is at the second coming of our Lord Jesus Christ, "Who shall change our vile body, that it may be fashioned like unto his glorious body, according to the working whereby he is able even to subdue all things unto himself" (Phil. 3:21). Do not be mistaken about healing in the atonement!

Another part of healing mythology is that:

b. All Sickness is the Result of Sin

This, of course, is related to the previous fallacy. There is no doubt that some sickness does come as the result of sin. Illustrations abound, for example, 1 Cor. 11:30-32 catalogs the judgment of God upon the Corinthians' irreverence at the Lord's Table. Weakness of body, sickness and even death resulted. This instance of judgment could be duplicated, but suffices to make the point.

However, there are a multiplicity of precedents which make it abundantly clear that there are varied known reasons for sickness. It may be satanic in origin (Luke 13:11-16). Sometimes it comes through the burden of service for God (Phil. 2:25-30). At other times it may come from God for a deepening of our spiritual lives (2 Cor. 12:7-10). God's glory may even be the reason for sickness (John 9:1-3).

Whatever the reasons, one thing is clear, all sickness is not the result of sin. If it was, then God would have been wrong about Job (Job 1:8), and Satan and Job's "comforters" would have been right (Job 2:4-5; 4:7-8)! Do not be deceived by thinking that all sickness is the result of sin. "If it were, when the sin is confessed and dealt with, we then could claim relief from the illness itself" (44:186).

A further part of healing mythology states that:

c. God Always Wills to Heal

This myth can be stated negatively or positively: "It is God's will that every sick person be healed," or, "It is not God's will that any of His children should ever be sick." Such mythological teaching, of course, places tremendous pressure on the sick person. If he does not get healed, it is because there is something spiritually wrong with him. It may be sin in his life, or lack of faith, etc., but whatever it is, the sick person is to blame, according to this mythology.

Of course, this doctrine contradicts the Word of God. Consider the case of Timothy (1 Tim. 5:23), of Trophimus, (2 Tim. 4:20), and of Paul himself (2 Cor. 12:7-9). Had it been God's will to heal them, these servants of God would not have had physical infirmities. Says Fife:

> We do not know all His reasons for withholding healing, but often the sufferer and those around him learn through the illness and are drawn closer to Him. Some need an experience of physical suffering to enable them to be more sympathetic to others, some to slow them down and give them a chance to think, and to be alone with Him. And some are taught patience through illness (12:137).

During the earthly ministry of Christ, we see clear discrimination in the healings performed. Take, for example, John 5:1-9. We read that there was a "great multitude" of sick people. Did Jesus heal them all? He certainly could have, if it had been His will; but instead He healed only one man.

Spiros Zodhiates is right in saying:

> All healings of whatever category and degree are the result of His grace. And since they are of grace, they cannot be demanded as rights. We cannot demand to be healthy, but we can receive healing and health, if and when God grants them to us as a free gift. Otherwise Paul would never have called them *charismata*, "free gifts," of healings (82:163).

Do not be deceived that it is always God's will to heal.

Other myths about healing abound in the legendary tradition of the "faith healer." These are merely examples of some of the more prominent. They are given to emphasize that all dependable spiritual truth is objective. It is verifiable by the Bible. What we claim about the gifts of healing, therefore, must come from the Scriptures themselves.

In seeking to find the truth of the Word of God on the gifts of healing, we must clearly differentiate between:

2. The Gifts of Healing and Healing Generally

By this I mean that there is a difference in Scripture between God's general healing of individuals and the gifts of healing mentioned in 1 Corinthians 12. If this were not so, then there would be no healings before the Spirit's sovereign bestowal of the gifts. Further, there could be no healings apart from those people endowed to mediate them. This difference should be patently obvious to any student of the Bible.

One of the early names for God is given in Exod. 15:26. There His name is "Jehovah Ropheca," or, "I am the Lord that healeth thee." God always has healed independently of any gifts of healing bestowed upon an intermediary. Instances of God's healing in answer to prayer can be multiplied. Abimelech was healed in answer to Abraham's prayer (Gen. 20:7). Miriam was healed by God when Moses prayed for her (Num. 12:14). God healed Hezekiah in answer to his prayers (Isa. 38:4-5). All through the Old Testament, God has graciously intervened in the sicknesses of men and healed them.

The life of the Lord Jesus, of course, shows Jehovah Ropheca in action. When Peter preached to Cornelius and his company, in Acts 10:38 he spoke of, "how God anointed Jesus of Nazareth with the Holy Ghost and with power: who went about doing good, and healing all that were oppressed of the devil; for God was with him." When the imprisoned John the Baptist sent two of his disciples to Jesus, asking, "Art Thou He that should come? or look we for another," we read:

> And in that same hour, he cured many of their infirmities and plagues, and of evil spirits; and unto many that were blind he gave sight. Then Jesus answering said unto them, Go your way, and tell John what things ye have seen and heard: how that the

blind see, the lame walk, the lepers are cleansed, the deaf hear, the dead are raised, to the poor the gospel is preached (Luke 7:21-22).

Throughout the gospels we see that God, independently from the bestowal of any gifts, exercised His healing prerogative.

But all of this is different from those "gifts of healing" of which we read in 1 Cor. 12:9, 28 and 30. God was now doing a new thing. He was endowing individuals with the ability to heal as Jehovah Ropheca heals.

This gift was exercised by Peter in Acts 3:1-11, to heal the lame man at the gate of the temple. In Acts 5:12-16 we read:

> And by the hands of the apostles were many signs and wonders wrought among the people; insomuch that they brought forth the sick into the streets, and laid them on beds and couches, that at the least the shadow of Peter passing by might overshadow some of them. There came also a multitude out of the cities round about unto Jerusalem, bringing sick folks, and them which were vexed with unclean spirits: and they were healed every one.

Philip exercised gifts of healing in Samaria (Acts 8:5-7). During Paul's ministry in Ephesus we read:

> And God wrought special miracles by the hands of Paul: So that from his body were brought unto the sick handkerchiefs or aprons, and the diseases departed from them, and the evil spirits went out of them (Acts 19:11-12).

Always the healings are traced to an individual who was supernaturally endowed by God to heal a wide variety of illnesses. There can be no doubt, therefore, that the gifts of healing were parenthetical to the general healing exhibited by Jehovah Ropheca. They were an endowment of specific individuals who could exercise the gifts of healing at will, independent of faith or expectancy in the person being healed.

A case in point is Peter's healing of the lame man at the gate of the Temple in Acts 3:1-11. There was absolutely no expectation on his part, that he would be healed. In fact, he did not even ask to be healed. Neither is there any question of whether he "had faith to be healed," for faith is not mentioned. The miracle was performed solely on the basis of

that which Peter, with absolute assurance, could say, "such as
I have give I thee: In the name of Jesus Christ of Nazareth rise
up and walk" (v. 6). The gift was his to exercise at his
choosing, and he chose to impart the product of that gift to
the lame man, regardless of expectation or faith on the man's
part, and he was healed. This class of gifted individuals was
peculiar to the introductory years of Christianity.

By this understanding, we are led to another conclusion:

3. The Gifts of Healing Were A Sign

At the end of Mark, Christ is recorded as presenting the
great commission for worldwide preaching of the gospel "to
every creature." Then he states among other things, "And
these signs shall follow them that believe; . . . they shall lay
hands on the sick, and they shall recover"[1] (Mark 16:17-18).
It is clearly recorded in this passage, therefore, that gifts of
healing were "sign" gifts.

The word *sēmeion,* "sign," means "a mark, indication,
token" and is used "of miraculous acts as tokens of divine
authority and power" (71:29). Thus we read of Jesus being, "a
man, approved of God among you by miracles and wonders
and signs, which God did by him in the midst of you, as ye
yourselves also know" (Acts 2:22). These were the authenticating signs that Jesus truly was the Son of God.

It was in this sense also that John wrote his purpose
statement, as to why he authored his Gospel.

> And many other signs truly did Jesus in the presence of his
> disciples, which are not written in this book: But these are
> written, that ye might believe that Jesus is the Christ, the Son of
> God; and that believing ye might have life through his name
> (John 20:30-31).

The signs selected proved Jesus to be "the Christ, the Son of
God." They authenticated His claims about Himself.

When the writer to the Hebrews referred to the "so great
salvation" entrusted to mankind he authenticated it as being
the same, "which at the first began to be spoken by the Lord,

---

[1] There is some debate among scholars as to whether the last part of Mark 16,
namely verses 9 to 16, are a part of the original autographs. Some feel that they are a
case of interpolation by some overly zealous scribe to add a more suitable ending to
the gospel than would otherwise be the case.

and was confirmed unto us by them that heard him; God also bearing them witness, both with signs and wonders, and with divers miracles, and gifts of the Holy Ghost, according to his own will?" (Heb. 2:3-4). Unger comments:

> This passage clearly refers to the ministry of the Lord and the apostles who heard Him. "The gifts [distributions] of the Holy Spirit" embrace such *charismata* as are enumerated in 1 Cor. 12:8-10 (65:139).

And among these *charismata* were "the gifts of healing." They were given as God's signature on the Christian gospel that it was truly from Him.

That authenticating work also applied to the servants of God responsible for the dissemination of that gospel. Apart from Heb. 2:4, which states this fact, Paul clearly applies the word "signs" to his own ministry. "Truly the signs of an apostle were wrought among you in all patience, in signs, and wonders, and mighty deeds" (2 Cor. 12:12). Thus, he authenticates his claim to the office of apostle by the "signs" done by him. This causes Benjamin Warfield to state that these miraculous gifts "were part of the credentials of the apostles as the authoritative agents of God in founding the church" (75:6).

What does all of this tell us about the "gifts of healing"? Simply this, they were a sign to authenticate the message and the messenger in the founding days of Christianity. That was their primary function; and when that is realized, it guards from common myths about healing today.

This leads us to another obvious fact:

4. The Gifts of Healing Were Temporary

When the purpose was fulfilled the gift was no longer needed. The Word of God was completed and the message was forever codified. Now the basis for belief would forever be that which was God's revelation of Himself and His work. In this age of grace we are to "walk by faith, not by sight" (2 Cor. 5:7).

W. A. Criswell uses the analogy of the withdrawal of the Old Testament gift of manna to illustrate this point.

> When the Word with its authority was written, the appeal no longer is to the "signs of an apostle" as Paul presented in 2 Cor.

12:12, but to the holy verses of the Holy Book. The sign is no longer needed nor is it necessary. In Josh. 5:11, 12, we are told: "And they did eat of the old corn of the land on the morrow after the passover, unleavened cakes, and parched corn in the selfsame day. And the manna ceased on the morrow after they had eaten of the old corn of the land; neither had the children of Israel manna any more; but they did eat of the fruit of the land of Canaan that year."

The miracle of the manna in the wilderness was no longer needed. They ate of the fruit of the land. So with us. The miraculous sign-gift is no longer needed. We have the living Word (7:191).

So, as the purpose for which the gift of healing was given ended, the gift itself was withdrawn.

We see this withdrawal develop progressively in Paul's life. Remember, there was a time when the gift was so strongly evident upon his life that special miracles were wrought by his hands, "so that from his body were brought unto the sick handkerchiefs or aprons, and the diseases departed from them, and the evil spirits went out from them" (Acts 19:12). What had happened, then, by the time he wrote 1 Tim. 5:23? Why could he not heal Trophimus at Miletum (2 Tim. 4:2)? Harry A. Ironside reminds us that:

Epaphroditus was sick nigh unto death for a long period, and the aged apostle's heart was greatly concerned about him. But God had mercy on him, raising him up at last, not miraculously, but when the disease had run its course. Paul could at one time shake off a viper into the fire, but could not remove his "thorn in the flesh;" instead, he was given grace to endure it (24:56).

Why? Because, as the progressive work of writing the Scriptures was completed, just so progressively was withdrawn the parenthetical gifts of healing.

Some time ago, a professed healer was invited by a local charismatic assembly to hold a week's meeetings in Brantford, Ontario. In the newspaper advertising which preceded his coming was the statement in bold type, "Prominent in his ministry the lame walk, the blind see, and the dead are raised to life." Strangely enough, though to my knowledge we have four Funeral Homes in Brantford, all busily serving bereaved relatives grieving over dead loved ones, none recorded a visit from the evangelist and none reported someone raised to life. Also in Brantford is the W. Ross Macdonald School (formerly the Ontario School for the Blind), serving young blind men and women from across Canada, who would give anything to be able to see, yet not one received his sight. Our city has two hospitals and a sanatorium in which sick people constantly languish, some of them judged incurable, but, during the time of this evangelist's visit to our fair city, not one of those patients was healed!

Why? What is the difference between this healer's claims and that which is recorded of Peter in Acts 3:1-9; Acts 5:12-16; or Acts 9:36-42? The difference is that Peter had the gift of healing and this modern evangelist—for all his miraculous claims—does not! The gifts of healing were temporary, being for a stated purpose; they have long since been withdrawn— that purpose forever fulfilled.

Several years ago, Dr. William A. Nolen, a physician and surgeon from Litchfield, Minnesota, wrote a book entitled, *Healing: A Doctor in Search for a Miracle*. With a background which includes graduation from the Holy Cross and Tufts Medical School, surgical internship at Bellevue Hospital, and being Chief of Surgery at the Meeker County Hospital, Dr. Nolen is well qualified to write his book. However, to add to his understanding of the whole matter of divine healing, he took extended trips to the Philippine Islands to see the "psychic surgeons" visited annually by thousands from around the world who are searching for a miraculous cure; he further spent time with Norbu Chen of Houston, who is a widely recommended Tibetan healer; and finally, he carefully investigated Kathryn Kuhlman's healing meetings, following up on those supposedly healed.

In his analysis of the subject of healing, Nolen is at a loss to find any real cures apart from those dealing with psychosomatic illness. He documents case after case of those supposedly healed, who either returned to their crutches and wheelchairs, or died from the very illness from which they were supposedly cured. In analyzing the late Kathryn Kuhlman's ministry, he states:

> There was lack of medical sophistication—a point that is, in her case, critical. I don't believe Miss Kuhlman is a liar; I don't

believe she is a charlatan; I don't believe she is, consciously, dishonest. I think (and this is, of course, only my opinion, based on a rather brief acquaintance with her) that she honestly believes the Holy Spirit works through her to perform miraculous cures. I think that she sincerely believes that the thousands of patients who come to her services every year and claim cures are, through her ministrations, being cured of organic diseases. I also think—and my investigations confirm this—that she is wrong.

The problem is, and I'm sorry this has to be so blunt, one of ignorance. Miss Kuhlman doesn't know the difference between psychogenic and organic diseases; she doesn't know anything about hypnotism and the power of suggestion; she doesn't know anything about the autonomic nervous system. If she does know something about any or all of these things, she has certainly learned to hide her knowledge.

There is one other possibility. It may be that Miss Kuhlman doesn't want to learn that her ministry is not as miraculous as it seems. If so, she had trained herself to deny, emotionally and intellectually, anything that might threaten the validity of her ministry (40:101).

Such might also be said of many of the, so-called, faith-healers with whom personal sickness and death have not yet caught up.

As a conclusion to his search for a miracle of healing Dr. Nolen wistfully writes:

Two years ago I began looking for a healing miracle. When I started my search I hoped to find some evidence that someone, somewhere, had supernatural powers that he or she could employ to cure those patients we doctors, with all our knowledge and training, must still label "incurable." As I have said before, I have been unable to find any such miracle worker (40:308).

Claims to healing are cheap. Proof is scarce. Do not be deceived by the unsubstantiated charismatic claims.

But let us be clear about what is being said. It is not that God no longer heals today. Were we to say that, we would be guilty of saying that God is no longer God—no longer Jehovah Ropheca. As God always has healed in a generalized way, so He will continue to do, for that is His name. What is being said is that "the gifts of healing" were especially given for a specific purpose and covered a particular period of history. However, as Unger says:

> This does not mean that God upon occasion may not, for His highest glory and to meet a human need, grant special faith to some or the power to perform miracles, including miracles of healing,—if circumstances so necessitate. These divine manifestations, however, are not to be regarded as gifts, but simply as individual acts of God (65:139).

Don't be "myth-taken," therefore, about "the gifts of healing;" they have gone, but the record remains.

5. What About Claimed Healings Today?

How then do we account for contemporary "healings"? There are any number of answers. Let me list some possibilities.

a. They May Be Psychosomatic Healings

Thus the miracle observed is produced by the mind of the individual. Such healing can be produced by the "positive thinking" of the "healer" and the surrendered mind of the seeker. Let no one blasphemously say that these are the answer to John 14:12!

b. In Many Cases No Real Healing Took Place at All, in a Miraculous Sense

As W. A. Criswell puts it:

> But how do these professional miracle workers succeed and continue? For the simple reason that eighty-five percent of all the sick will get well anyway, and to the other fifteen percent the divine healers can blandly and piously say, "You do not have the faith." It is a sure-fire racket, far more certain than betting on horses at the race tracks or playing the game tables at Las Vegas. If the odds are eighty-five percent in your favor, how can you lose? (7:192).

From time to time the newspapers carry the disastrous results which have followed such pronounced cures, as people stop taking medicine vital to their health.

c. No Doubt Some Cures are Satanic in Origin

If Satan could do what Jesus said he did in Luke 13:16, do you not think he would be capable also of undoing it? It is not beyond Satan's machinations as the deceiver of men's souls to produce some physical cure to bring men under his authority or to divert their attention from the real gospel to a pseudo-gospel.

On this point George Shaw delivers a timely warning:

"Divine healing" was never a doctrine preached by the apostles, and, as far as the records of their preaching go, it never had a large place in their thought. We are in danger these days of reducing the great gospel to a mere question of healing the body, and the great doctrines of the gospel are being lost or at least neglected in the strong emphasis laid on healing (52:335).

This must cause Satan much hellish joy!

d. Undoubtedly There are Some Real Healings; the Work of Jehovah Ropheca

These, when they occur, are independent from any "healer" or "healing meeting." They depend not on person, place or practice. Such healings are the work of the God who is "the same yesterday, and today, and forever" (Heb. 13:8).

Charles C. Ryrie puts it well in distinguishing between the miraculous gifts and miraculous happenings.

Distinction should be made between miracles and healings and the gifts of miracles and healings. The spiritual gift is the God-given ability to perform miracles and healings for the purpose of serving Him. However a miracle or a healing may be done apart from the exercise of the gifts. . .

Consequently, then, it does not follow that if one considers the gifts of miracles and healings temporary, he is also saying that God does not perform miracles or heal today. He is simply stating that the gifts are no longer given because the particular purpose for which they were originally given (i.e., to authenticate the oral message) has ceased to exist (48:86, 87).

With this we heartily agree.

To sum up: there is a difference between "the gifts of healing," and God's generalized healing. Does God heal today? Yes. Are "the gifts of healing" for today? No. God always healed and always will, but the gifts of healing were temporary. They passed away as the need for authentication of both the message and the messengers of New Testament truth was swallowed up in the unspeakable power and grandeur of the perfect Word of God.

B. THE WORKING OF MIRACLES

There is a madness for miracles today! On every hand claims are being made concerning miraculous works. Many are running after those who make the most astounding (or should the word be "preposterous") declarations. One miracle worker seeks to outdo the next in the sensationalism of the boast. Is this of God?

Do not be misled by miraculous claims. There is a real danger in today's religious world, that of teasing God to pander to the unbelief of degenerate people. The note of warning which George Shaw sounded over half a century ago, needs to be restated.

> In these days of wonder workers and "divine healers" and pretentious charlatans, I question if miracle working would lead many to the acceptance of the gospel in its work of purifying the heart. There are too many now who run after the spectacular and who are feeding their souls on the phenomena of religion, while their souls are hungering for the Bread of Life (52:340).

Again I say do not be mistaken about "the working of miracles."

Now, having said that, there is much gladness available to us in the Scriptures on this subject. Indeed, we need to remember that what we believe about miracles must be grounded in the teaching of Scripture and not in the miracles themselves. Miracles can be "lying wonders" (2 Thess. 2:9), or they can be mistakenly interpreted (Matt. 12:24), but the Word of God is the unchanging truth from God on the subject.

The gift called "the working of miracles" is recorded but thrice in Scripture. The two lists of gifts in 1 Cor. 12:8-10 and 28-30 present healing and miracles, each in a different order. However, if we regard verse 28 as a descending order of gifts, miracles would come before healing.

Some believe that miracles and healing are one and the same thing. J. Dwight Pentecost, for example, states that:

> The gift of miracles is a general term that includes a number of other spiritual gifts. The gift of healing, the gift of tongues and the gift of interpretation were parts of the gift of miracles.

When the Apostle referred to the gift of miracles, he was referring in a general way to a number of other gifts (44:180).

We could probably agree with this, had not the Scriptures differentiated between these gifts.

No one will argue that healing, tongues and interpretation of tongues are miraculous in nature. But surely so is each of the gifts mentioned in the two lists. They are not natural, human talents; they are supernatural gifts. It was as miraculous for a man to be an apostle or a prophet, as to be a miracle worker or a healer.

It is wise for us, then, to seek:

1. The Definition of Miracles in Scripture

Many definitions have been given to explain what a miracle is. Among them are the following:

> Shaw: A miracle does not change any law, but merely suspends it at a point where the divine will is at work . . . A miracle is a divine event to attest some messenger sent or some message given (52:337).

> Pentecost: A miracle is a sovereign work of God, a manifestation of divine power, given to substantiate and corroborate a message from God (44:180).

> Criswell: A miracle is an interruption, an intervention, in the system of nature as we know it. It is a temporary suspension of the laws that govern this world as we commonly observe them. A miracle is "supernatural," above the "natural" (7:178).

You can see that each one of the above authors presents a miracle as an unexplainable phenomenon in human terms. Miracles are unmistakably the work of God.

The word translated "miracles" in 1 Cor. 12:10, 28, 30 is from *dunamis,* meaning "power, inherent ability." It is "used of works of a supernatural origin and character, such as could not be produced by natural agents and means" (70:75).

In verse 10 the term is used together with "working," from the Greek word *energeo.* Literally this expression means "to work in, to be active, or operative" (71:232). Verse 6 uses it of "God which worketh all in all," while the eleventh verse tells us of the gifts that, "all these worketh that one and the selfsame Spirit."

When put together, these words describe the gift as the active operation of the power of God in an individual's life, giving inherent ability to perform supernatural works. Being a gift of the Spirit in accordance with verse 11, the individual was sovereignly chosen and endowed. Neither the choosing of the gift, nor the power to use the gift originated in the person gifted.

Two other words are used in Scripture for the term miracle. The word "sign" (*semeion*) is used as

> a token and indication of the near presence and working of God. They are signs and pledges of something more than and beyond themselves (Isa. 7:11; 38:7); valuable, not so much for what they are, as for what they indicate of the grace and power of the doer, or of the connection in which he stands with a higher world (64:3).

As such, these miracles which were called "signs" authenticated the divine mission of the doer. We shall see John's use of this word later.

The word "wonder" (*tera*) is used to indicate that "the astonishment which the work produces upon the beholders, an astonishment often graphically portrayed by the Evangelists when relating our Lord's miracles (Mark 2:12; 4:41; 6:51; 7:37; cf. Acts 3:10, 11), is transferred to the work itself" (64:2). Thus miracles described by the term "wonders," show the effect of astonishment they produce in the beholder. The miracle worker, therefore, was a wonder worker.

Speaking of the combination of "signs, and wonders, and mighty deeds" characterized as "the signs of an apostle," Calvin wrote:

> Paul calls them signs, beçause they are not empty shows, but are appointed for the instruction of mankind; wonders, because they ought, by their novelty, to arouse men and strike them with astonishment; and mighty deeds because they are more signal tokens of divine power than what we behold in the ordinary course of nature (61:180).

In this he clearly relates the shade of meaning found in each individual word.

These terms are used three times in Scripture in connection one with another. Each use has a different connection. For example, Acts 2:22 refers to Christ who was "approved of God—by miracles, and wonders and signs, which God did by Him." The Corinthians passage relates to the apostleship of Paul which was authenticated "in signs, and wonders and mighty deeds" (2 Cor. 12:12). In the third passage a warning note is being sounded that "the Wicked" one, "whose coming is after the working of Satan," will deceive the nations by seeking to authenticate his godhead claims (2 Thess. 2:4), "with all power and signs and lying wonders." The combination, therefore, relates to Christ during His earthly life; to Christ's apostles during the introduction of Christianity to the first century; and to the Antichrist during the end of this age.

Each of these terms denotes a different aspect of the same work, rather than three different classes of miracles. For example, as Trench states:

> The healing of the paralytic (Mark 2:1-12) was a wonder, for they who beheld it "were all amazed";—it was a power, for the man at Christ's word "arose, took up his bed, and went forth before them all";—it was a sign, for it gave token that One greater than men deemed was among them; it stood in connection with a higher fact of which it was the seal and sign (cf. I Kings 13:3; 2 Kings 1:10), being wrought that they might "know that the Son of man hath power on earth to forgive sins" (64:7).

A miracle can be described by each or all three of these words, therefore.

In the strict sense, however, miracles can be differentiated from such healings as the one mentioned above. This is why, of course, "the working of miracles" is listed as a gift separate from "the gifts of healing" in 1 Cor. 12:9-10. Each of the first nine plagues was a miracle, as was the dividing of the Red Sea, the provision of manna, quail and water for food, the entrance to Jericho, the sun standing still in the sky, the fire falling from heaven to consume the sacrifice, and so on throughout the Old Testament.

Examples of miracles, which did not include healings in the life of Christ, include the turning of water to wine, walking on the water, stilling the storm, feeding the five thousand and the supply of tax money in the fish's mouth. When examining the

Acts of the Apostles and the Epistles, we discover that such miracles are not so frequently recorded and, apart from the miraculous movement of Philip to Azotus, the release of Peter from prison and the earthquake which accomplished a similar result in Philippi for Paul and Silas, miracles as distinct from healings are few and far between. This is not to say that they were not performed, but simply to call attention to the fact that the early church was not a three-ring-circus wherein the membership gathered to marvel at the latest miracle and where those with the gift sought to outdo one another for the acclaim of the people.

The "evangelist" whom my wife and I recently heard announcing his "revival meetings under the big tent," could learn from this fact. We were travelling through the southern States, listening to "born again radio" as we went along. Suddenly, this rasping voice came on the program to announce that "the miracle of the glass eye" would be performed in the big tent that very night. Apparently, whoever the "evangelist's" guest would be had a glass eye which he would remove in the midst of the "miracle service" and then demonstrate that, through the empty socket, he could "miraculously see everything that is going on" in the service. This circus act was supposed to bring glory to God.

How far removed is this from the meaning of this New Testament gift of the Spirit to the early church. One is never sure whether the aim in such meetings is to feed the sheep or entertain the goats. In the Bible, the gift was poles apart from such pathetic showmanship which is more compatible with "Barnum and Bailey" than with the work of God in the world.

With this background as to what we mean (and do not mean) by a "miracle," we are ready to explore:

2. The History of Miracles in Scripture

There are many today who claim that the Bible is a "Book of miracles." Strictly speaking this is not true. Miracles are not indiscriminately strewn over every page of Scripture. Rather do we find an order to their appearance that is most important.

As Richard Trench wrote:

> We do not find the miracles sown broadcast over the whole Old-Testament history, but they all cluster round a very few eminent persons, and have reference to certain great epochs and crises of the kingdom of God (64:49).

This being the case, we can soon discover that large periods of history (larger by far than otherwise) were without record of miracles. There are no miracles clustered around Abraham, "the friend of God" and the "father of the faithful." Search in vain for miracles in the life of David, Israel's great theocratic king. Even Daniel, during whose lifetime God independently performed notable preserving miracles, performed no miracles himself. Startling is it, as well, to discover that during the ministry of John the Baptist no miracle was done (John 10:41), though there was "not a greater prophet" than he (Luke 7:28).

Where, then, do we find the miracles in the Bible? We find them grouped in three great periods of history. During the periods covered by Moses and Joshua, Elijah and Elisha, and Christ and the apostles. Joseph Dillow presents the following time line to illustrate these periods (9:97).

Moses and Joshua	Elijah and Elisha	Christ and Apostles

$$\text{—o———o———o——o———o———o—}$$

1441 B.C. 1370 B.C.	870 785	A.D. 28 A.D. 90

500 years	814 years

70 years	70 years	70 years

You will notice that each period lasts approximately 70 years, and that the gaps between them form centuries of silence from heaven, as far as miracle workers are concerned. In the Bible there are greater periods without miracles than there are with miracles!

Beginning with the first of these, we find miracles in evidence during:

a. The Period of Moses and Joshua

In Exodus we find God giving to Moses the power of miracle working for the benefit of Pharoah. Exod. 4:1-5 tells us that these were to authenticate Moses as God's deliverer. Thus God says in Exod. 7:3, "And I will harden Pharoah's heart, and multiply my signs and my wonders in the land of Egypt." These and other miracles were done by the hand of Moses before and after the actual deliverance from Egypt.

Later, upon the death of Moses, God called Joshua saying, ". . . as I was with Moses, so I will be with thee: I will not fail thee, nor forsake thee" (Josh. 1:5). Miracles under Joshua authenticated the new leadership at a crucial time in Israel's history, when they were about to enter the promised land. This corroboration of the authority of Joshua, as that of Moses, was done miraculously at Jordan and Jericho, as well as by the other miraculous events of the Book bearing his name.

The second burst of miracles in Scripture comes during:

b. The Period of Elijah and Elisha

They were God's special prophets for a day of decadence in Israel's history. The worship of Baal had reached a peak. Jezebel was eliminating the Levitical priesthood. Israel, as a theocratic nation, was in danger of passing out of existence.

An illustration of the miracles of this period was that performed by Elijah on Carmel. It was the miracle of Elijah calling down fire from God out of heaven, to consume the water-soaked sacrifice which lay upon the altar. Note carefully the "thats" of Elijah's prayer, as he intreats God for the miracle.

> Lord God of Abraham, Isaac, and of Israel, let it be known this day that thou art God in Israel, and that I am thy servant, and that I have done all these things at thy word. Hear me, O Lord, hear me, that this people may know that thou art the Lord God, and that thou hast turned their heart back again (1 Kings 18:36-37).

The miracle was to substantiate God's authority in Israel and to authenticate Elijah as God's appointed representative.

Such also was the nature of the miracles during the life of Elisha. With a double portion of God's blessing upon him, twice the miracles were performed by Elisha. But always they were for corroboration and authentication for the specific period in Israel's history.

The third grouping of miracles clusters around:

c. The Period of Christ and the Apostles

In Christ, God became man. Obviously, proof was needed to substantiate that claim. This was the very purpose for which John wrote his gospel.

> And many other signs truly did Jesus in the presence of his disciples, which are not written in this book: But these are written, that ye might believe that Jesus is the Christ, the Son of God; and that believing ye might have life through his name (John 20:30-31).

Later Peter was to preach on Pentecost concerning:

> Jesus of Nazareth, a man approved of God among you by miracles and wonders and signs, which God did by him in the midst of you, as ye yourselves also know (Acts 2:22).

These miracles were a source of proof to validate the Person of Christ.

The apostolic miracles were the corresponding part of this New Testament cluster. Paul validates his ministry by writing to the Corinthians, "Truly the signs of an apostle were wrought among you in all patience, in signs, and wonders, and mighty deeds" (2 Cor. 12:12). Philip Hughes quotes Hodge as saying, "The signs of an apostle were the insignia of the apostleship. These signs were confirmatory of the apostolic work and word, and therefore of the authenticity of the apostles' mission" (22:456).

On the other hand, Heb. 2:3-4 validates the gospel of salvation by telling us that it,

> at the first began to be spoken by the Lord, and was confirmed unto us by them that heard him; God also bearing them witness, both with signs and wonders, and with divers miracles, and gifts of the Holy Ghost, according to his own will.

The total period of Christ and the apostles is covered in this latter passage.

Joseph Dillow observes that, in each of the three periods of miracle clusters, two things were involved:

> new revelation, and a man (or men) of God whose credentials as the bearer(s) of that revelation needed to be verified. Furthermore, the miracles never broke out before the messenger and his revelation had arrived but only afterward (9:97).

On the basis of this, he goes on to make the point that we should not expect miracles before the next great epoch of history (i.e., the second coming of Christ), but only afterwards. This is something which needs to be emphasized in our generation.

Beyond these three periods there were scattered instances of miracles. However, it cannot be argued from these that miracles were God's normal method of operation. Likewise, it is quite possible that God is performing miracles today. The question is whether this is normative for our age. The Bible says not, as we shall see.

This brings us to a closer look at:

3. The Purpose of Miracles in Scripture

Why did God perform miracles in Bible times? The answer to this question can help us to clear away some mistakes made by those following the charismatic movement's claims. Let us consider four reasons why the clusters of miracles already mentioned appear in Scripture. First in these is:

a. The Introduction of a New Revelation

C. S. Lewis once wrote:

> God does not shake miracles into Nature at random as if from a pepper-caster. They come on great occasions: they are found at the great ganglions of history—not of political or social history, but of that spiritual history which cannot be fully known by men (88:28).

This, of course, is exceedingly evident in each of the three periods mentioned. Moses introduced the law, with its emphasis on the Tabernacles, sacrifices and priesthood. The Pentateuch is largely written (apart from Genesis) to codify these new revelations to Israel. Miracles were given to introduce this era.

Judaism was not only built upon the law, but also "the prophets" (Matt. 22:40). Elijah and Elisha stood for the revival of the prophetic era in an age of critical spiritual decline. Miracles were given by God to draw Israel back to the institution of prophecy.

The total New Testament hangs upon Christ and the apostles. Christ was the one of whom the Old Testament

Scriptures spoke (Luke 24:27). The apostles were those who personified His message during a period when the gospel was not yet codified. Thus, in the life of Christ and the apostles, miracles heralded the new revelation.

The second reason for the miracles was:

b. The Authentication of God's Messengers

Each new revelation demanded new messengers. These were authenticated by the miracles God performed by them. Moses (Exod. 4:1-8) and Joshua (Josh. 3:7) were thus seen to be genuinely God's chosen communicants of His new revelation. Elijah (1 Kings 7:24) and Elisha (2 Kings 2:15) also were verified as God's spokesmen by the miracles they performed. Finally Christ (John 10:25)[2] and the apostles (2 Cor. 12:12) were attested authentic in the same way.

Miracles were, therefore, the testimony of God that those bringing in the new revelations were indeed His official representatives. In this sense, our Lord speaks in John 14:11, "Believe me that I am in the Father, and the Father in me: or else believe me for the very works' sake." The works were God's means of verifying His messenger.

The third reason for miracles seen in the Scriptures is:

c. The Verification of the Message

In the Word of God there are three periods of extensive new revelation. These are presented in the writings of Moses, the prophets and the apostles. Moses wrote the foundational message of Old Testament revelation. The prophets expounded the practical application of the law to the lives of the people. The apostles recorded the fulfillment (Matt. 5:17) and doctrinal explanation (2 Peter 3:15-16) of the Old Testament revelations in the Person of Christ.

Because of the crucial nature of the message of these revelations, it was necessary to authenticate them miraculously; thus it was with Moses (Exod. 7:17-18; 8:22-23), with Elijah (1 Kings 17:24), with Christ (John 10:37-38) and with

---

[2] John never uses the word "miracle" in Greek in connection with Christ but always the word "sign." He does so, because the purpose of a sign is authentication and confirmation. Thus, his purpose for writing is stated in John 20:30-31.

the apostles (Rom. 14:18-19). All of the miracles verified the message as being from God.

The fourth reason for miracles concerns:

d. The Instruction of the Observers

In each period the miracles had an impact on those who saw them. Pharoah was taught the futility of Egypt's gods and the reality and omnipotence of the God of Israel (Exod. 5:2 and compare Exod. 9:27-28; 10:16-17), when each miracle plague was aimed at a specific Egyptian god. Ahab, Jezebel and Israel were instructed concerning the emptiness of Baal worship and the necessity of turning wholeheartedly to Jehovah (1 Kings 18:36-39), when the credentials of 400 prophets of Baal were destroyed by Jehovah's singular prophet. By His miracles, Christ informed the disciples Who He was and what power He possessed (Matt. 8:26). Miracles through the apostles proclaimed that Almighty God was at work in the church (Acts 5:11-13) and caused them to fear greatly.

This use of miracles and the reason for them is set forth clearly in the following chart by John Louis Booth (94). If the purpose of miracles is indeed as expressed in word and chart, what message does this hold for the modern seekers after signs?

To answer this we need to consider:

4. The Passing of Miracles in Scripture

In beginning this discussion, we noted that there is a madness for miracles today. This is predicated upon the assumption that the gift of miracles is for today. Is it? Or, the purpose for miracles having been fulfilled, have they now passed away? In considering these questions we must:

a. Differentiate Between the Gift of Miracles and Generalized Miracles

Perhaps we should divide between miracles and the gift of miracles. Simply stated, the gift of miracles ("the working of miracles") was the ability given by God the Holy Spirit to perform supernatural acts. The performance of these was at the control of the individual himself, since "the spirits of the

GOD'S FOURFOLD PURPOSE IN MIRACLES

Miraculous Era	To introduce the new era	To authenticate the messengers of the new era	To authenticate the message	To instruct observers
Moses and Joshua 1441-1390 B.C.	God was forming a nation (Exod. 19:8; 33:13; Deut. 4:6-8; Exod. 6:6, 7)	Moses (Exod. 4:1-9, 29-31; 14:31) Joshua (Josh. 3:7)	To Pharoah (Exod. 7:17; 8:19) "Let my people go!" To Israel (Exod. 6:6, 7; 14:31)	Israel (Exod. 10:12; 16:2; 14:13, 14) Pharoah (8:10, 22; 9:14) Egypt (14:4; 11:7; 9:26) Nations (9:16; Josh. 2:9-11)
Elijah and Elisha 870-785 B.C.	God establishes the prophets (1 Kings 17:1)	Elijah (1 Kings 17:1; 18:36; 2 Kings 1:10) Elisha (2 Kings 5:8)	Forsake your idols and return to the Lord (1 Kings 17:24; 18:36)	Prophets of Baal People of Israel (1 Kings 18:39; 2 Kings 5:15)
Christ and apostles A.D. 28-95	The offer of the kingdom (Matt. 15:24; Luke 4:18, 19; Matt. 4:23; 10:7, 8) The establishment of the church (Acts 15:12)	Christ (Mark 2:7; Matt. 11:4, 5; John 14:11; 20:30, 31; Acts 2:22) Apostles (Heb. 2:4; 2 Cor. 12:12)	The offer of the kingdom (Matt. 12:28; John 10:37, 38) The re-offer of the kingdom and establishment of the church (Acts 3:1-8; 4:16; 8:5-7; Rom. 15:18, 19; Acts 14:3)	The leaders and people of Israel (Matt. 8:26; Mark 6:50; John 6:3-6; Acts 5:1-11)

prophets are subject unto the prophets" (1 Cor. 14:32). Is this gift still existent in our world today, or has it been withdrawn, the purpose for it having been fulfilled?

Dividing clearly between the gift of miracles and miracles, J. Dwight Pentecost states:

> Let it be very clear that God is still working miracles today, but there is a difference between working miracles and the gift of miracles. The one who had the gift of miracles, referred to in 1 Cor. 12:28, could work a miracle at will. He could use that miraculous power whenever the need presented itself. But God is working miracles today in response to faith (44:184).

The gift has fulfilled its purpose and is gone.

W. A. Criswell reasons very logically when he writes:

> As no one person has all the gifts of the Spirit, so it is possible that no one age has all the gifts. If every Christian does not possess every charismatic endowment, then it could be that every generation does not possess all the gifts. This is certainly true with regard to the sign gift of miracles (7:185).

Certainly we have seen this to be true in the clustered periods of Bible history where the gift of miracles was clearly evidenced.

Surely we are on safe exegetical ground to say that:

b. When the Purpose was Fulfilled the Gift Ended

Dr. Gerry Benn, President of London Baptist Seminary, Ontario, Canada, puts it this way:

> Until the completed Word, God often used the miraculous to substantiate a man's ministry and message. Once the Word or canon was completed the same need is not present. Paul in 1 Cor. 1:22 tells us that the Jews require a sign. Once the scriptures became complete at the end of the first century there was no longer a need for miraculous signs and gifts (83:2).

And with this a host of Bible expositors agree. Let me name two Bible scholars on this point:

> W. Graham Scroggie: The present is not an age of sensuous signs, but of spiritual power, and if, for lack of experience of that power, we resort to what is sensuous, we need not be surprised that the devil makes the most of the opportunity (79:22).

> Merrill F. Unger: A gift implies a settled and continued ability to do something again and again. While God, of course, can do miracles and certainly performs them today, He does not dispense the gift of miracles as in the early church. To establish and authenticate the new faith, apostles and miracle workers were needed and abounded. Now that the faith has been established, no such need exists and no such gifts abound. Faith is to rest in a completed, written revelation, authenticated by miracles and fulfilled prophecy. Now we are to "walk by faith, not by sight" (2 Cor. 5:7) (65:139).

And so we could go on naming and quoting highly regarded men of the Word who believe the ages of miracles to have passed.

In spite of this, books making claims of miraculous happenings appear with regular frequency. One which gained wide readership a few years back was entitled, *Like A Mighty Wind.* The subject matter was a collection of stories from the Indonesian revival which were compiled from talks given in the United States by a 24-year-old former evangelistic team member from the island of Timor.[3] His stories were enthralling, including walking on water, resurrections from the dead, water turned to wine, playback of children's voices without benefit of a tape recorder, clothes that never got dirty and so on. These were not necessarily "eye witness" accounts, but often second- or third-hand stories.

At first many accepted these accounts at face value and they added greatly to the lore of the miraculous within charismatic mythology. However, when others began to trace down and investigate the happenings, they did not find the happenings so miraculous after all. Without exception, those miraculous happenings investigated turned out either to be natural phenomena or not to have happened at all. The findings of the investigations were not, of course, as widely

---

[3] It is interesting to note that when this young man was asked if the Indonesian revival could be duplicated in America he is reported to have said that it could if we will "take out that small computer which is your brain and put it in a little box and shoot it to the moon. Then let God use your heart" (88:29). Allowing for dangerous hyperbole, such a statement well illustrates the subjective attitude we are definitely not to have. God never asks a man to bypass his intellect in order to see miracles, receive gifts or experience revival.

and eagerly accepted and read as was the book which claimed the miracles.

Now this points out a complicating factor in this whole matter. Such tales of miracles make books of the kind in question to be those which earnest and honest people, who long to see the supernatural power of God exhibited in our world, would pass from person to person. But it further illustrates that our reaction must always be on the basis of the Bible's teaching concerning the gift of miracles and not upon our own subjective longing for the miraculous to occur. We need to settle this matter well ahead, so that we might know the perimeters within which our acceptance of such tales will lie. What I am emphasizing is that our appeal must be to the Word of God.

In Mark 16:15-16 our Lord gives the great evangelism call to His disciples to "preach the gospel to every creature." Then Mark 16:17-18 ties that call to "signs" which would evidence the work done to be of God. These were:

> In my name shall they cast out devils; they shall speak with new tongues; they shall take up serpents; and if they drink any deadly thing, it shall not hurt them, they shall lay hands on the sick, and they shall recover.

Each and every one of these, except the drinking of poison, is mentioned as having taken place in the Book of Acts. In fact the fulfillment of these words is recorded by Mark in verse 20, "And they went forth, and preached everywhere, the Lord working with them, and confirming the word with signs following. Amen." It is stated in Mark and illustrated in Acts that God kept His word and fulfilled His promise.

Can we then make the assumption that many seem to make today, that God must "do it again"? Surely it would be as reasonable to say that God must divide the waters of the Red Sea as in Moses' day, or that He must make fire fall from heaven as in Elijah's day, as it is to demand that God must continue to do in our day what the Bible clearly tells us He has fulfilled. These were authenticating signs and God has proven the reliability of both the messengers and the message. There is no longer a need for "signs."

When the writer to the Hebrews was describing how the "great salvation" of which he spoke came to the people of his day, he began to look back. Read Heb. 2:3-4 for yourself. It is all in the past tense. The proofs of the gospel are all regarded as having taken place already. The miraculous had fulfilled its purpose and forever after it was to be the Word of God.

> The test of any man's authority no longer was his ability to work miracles. His authority came from his adherence to the revealed truth of the Word of God. We do not originate a message, and by miracles authenticate a new revelation. We declare to you the message which has been completed. The Holy Spirit bears witness with our spirits that that which is preached is the truth of the Word of God. Thus miracles and signs no longer accompany the messenger (44:184),

says J. Dwight Pentecost.

In his *Notes on the Miracles of Our Lord,* Richard C. Trench comments:

> "Miracles," says Fuller, "are the swaddling clothes of the infant churches;" and, we may add, not the garments of the full grown. They were as the proclamation that the king was mounting his throne; who, however, is not proclaimed every day, but only at his accession; when he sits acknowledged on his throne, the proclamation ceases (64:52).

We have clearly seen in their history and purpose that miracles always were temporary phenomena. At no time in Old Testament history did the clustering miracles last for more than seventy years. So it is with the New Testament. They covered the lifetime of Christ and the apostles, and then they ceased. "They were done once, that they might be believed always" (64:52).

Consider another factor:

c. *The Seeking of Miracles is Not a Sign of Spirituality*

It is the charge of God's Word, "an evil and an adulterous generation seeketh a sign" (Matt. 12:39). Rather than glorifying God, such sign seeking and emphasizing detracts from the splendor of faith in the Bible alone. A. W. Tozer puts it well in analyzing our modern craze for "external evidence." He states:

> Our trouble is that we are trying to confirm the truth of Christianity by an appeal to external evidence. We are saying, "Well, look at this fellow. He can throw a baseball farther than

anybody else and he is a Christian, therefore Christianity must be true." "Here is a great statesman who believes the Bible. Therefore, the Bible must be true." We quote Daniel Webster, or Roger Bacon. We write books to show that some scientist believed in Christianity: therefore, Christianity must be true. We are all the way out on the wrong track, brother! That is not New Testament Christianity at all. That is a pitiful, whimpering, drooling appeal to the flesh (81:13).

One final word on miracles:

d. Miracles are Not the Ultimate Proof of Truth!

Clearly the Bible sets forth this fact in Matt. 7:21-23:

> Not every one that saith unto me, Lord, Lord, shall enter into the kingdom of heaven; but he that doeth the will of my Father which is in heaven. Many will say to me in that day, Lord, Lord, have we not prophesied in thy name? and in thy name have cast out devils? and in thy name done many wonderful works? And then will I confess unto them, I never knew you: depart from me, ye that work iniquity.

Notice that our Lord does not argue over the validity of their claims. The emphasis of their lives had been upon the miraculous "in Thy name"; the profession of their lips had been, "Lord, Lord"; but the mistake of their souls was failing to realize that this was not doing God's will, as found in God's Word; not upon experience, as found in subjective living.

Coupled with this warning must be the warnings given in Scripture concerning a rise in the miraculous in the last days. Consider these Scriptures:

> For there shall arise false Christs, and false prophets, and shall shew great signs and wonders; insomuch that, if it were possible, they shall deceive the very elect (Matt. 24:24).

> And then shall that Wicked be revealed, whom the Lord shall consume with the spirit of his mouth, and shall destroy with the brightness of his coming: Even him, whose coming is after the working of Satan with all power and signs and lying wonders, and with all deceivableness of unrighteousness in them that perish; because they received not the love of the truth, that they might be saved. And for this cause, God shall send them strong delusion, that they should believe a lie: That they all might be damned who believed not the truth, but had pleasure in unrighteousness (2 Thess. 2:8-12).

And he doeth great wonders, so that he maketh fire come down from heaven on the earth in the sight of men, and deceiveth them that dwell on the earth by the means of those miracles which he had power to do in the sight of the beast; . . . And he had power to give life unto the image of the beast, that the image of the beast should both speak, . . . (Rev. 13:13-15).

All miraculous power spoken of in the Scriptures does not originate with God! We are clearly warned that one method used by Satan in "the last days" to remove the minds of men from the Bible as their sole standard of faith and practice, and thereby to deceive, is the use of the miraculous.

Do not be mistaken about the gift of miracles. It is past. The only signs to be given are those written in the Word of God. *Sola Scriptura* keeps us from the Serpent's bite and the deceiver's snare. Let us, therefore, base our faith on the Bible and the Bible alone.

C. DIVERS KINDS OF TONGUES

In Isaiah 8:20 we are warned, "To the law and to the testimony: if they speak not according to this word, it is because there is no light in them." Always and in all places our appeal must be to the Word of God. If the Word of God is contrary to our beliefs and practices, then it is not to be the Bible which is set aside, but our waywardness.

To put it another way, the appeal of a true Christian is not to experience, but his appeal is to the Word of God. Jesus said, "Search the Scriptures" (John 5:39). Luke records of the Berean believers, "These were more honorable than those of Thessalonica, in that they received the Word with all readiness of mind, and searched the Scriptures daily, whether those things were so" (Acts 17:11). Paul exhorts us, "Study to show thyself approved unto God, a workman that needeth not to be ashamed, rightly dividing the Word of truth" (2 Tim. 2:15). At all times and in all circumstances our appeal must be to the Bible.

In no study is this more important than that of tongues. Here our appeal must be solely to the Scriptures. No experience, however wonderful or uplifting, can ever be allowed to supersede the teaching of God's revelation. If what is taught in the Bible is contrary to some experience in life, then a moratorium needs to be called upon any resulting practice; until the biblical foundation is searched out—even if that study destroys one's system of experimental theology.

Our question for this chapter, therefore, must be, "What does the Bible teach about the gift of tongues?" The answer to this inquiry will save us from much that is mythological in modern gift theology. It will also make us unashamed to reject that which is unbiblical and hold fast to that which is good.

To begin, let us search out:

1. The Meaning of the Word "Tongue"

In order to avoid confusion of terms, it is wise for us to determine what is meant by "tongues" as the word is used in the Bible. Immediately we are confronted with:

a. Three Bible Words for "Tongues"

The first of these terms is *glossa*. In its initial sense it can refer to the organ of the body called the tongue and indeed it is so used of the "cloven tongues" of Acts 2:3. Then it refers to the use of that organ and comes to mean simply "language." In this sense it refers to that which is used in common conversation. It is, therefore, known or knowable language and very human.

When Mark 16:17 refers to "new tongues" it literally refers to "new languages." These were "new" in the sense of being different from one's native language, but none the less they were to be actual languages. The same idea holds for 1 Cor. 12:10 which speaks of "divers kinds of tongues." *Genē*, translated "kinds," refers to species or to race and implies great variety of languages. This speech, though of a different variety from one's national language "was not mere gibberish or jargon like the modern 'tongues,' but a real language that could be understood by one familiar with that tongue—" says A. T. Robertson (47:170).

A second term used is *dialektos*, meaning dialect. It denotes, "the language or dialect of a country or district" (69:309). As such it can be more specific than the general language and refer to inflection and tone peculiar to that particular area. Thus the "dwellers at Jerusalem" heard their "proper tongue," or literally "their own dialect" (Acts 1:19). We learn that, on the day of Pentecost, the people heard not only in their own language, but more technically in their "own dialect" (Acts 2:8).

A third term is *heteroglossa* and denotes a tongue of a different sort, or another language. This word is used in 1 Cor. 14:21. There Paul quotes from Isa. 28:11-12 where God warns that He would speak to the Jewish people through men of another language. We shall look a little later at this key prophecy and its interpretation by Paul.

The point to be made here is that whichever of these terms is translated "tongue" in the New Testament, each refers to language. Such language is of a human, understandable, known variety. Because it is unknown to the speaker does not mean it is not known by the hearer. Such a facility, in an unlearned language, is the gift of the Holy Spirit.

b. The Words Used at Jerusalem

In Acts 2, Luke used two of these terms. *Glossa* is used in verses 4 and 11, while *dialektos* is used in verses 6 and 8. This is apart from the usage of *glossa* in verse 3 to denote a tongue as a bodily organ. It is important to note that in Acts 2:1-11 the usages show (1) that the languages spoken were known, (2) that no interpretation was needed, and (3) that they were so properly spoken that the dialect was included.

c. The Word Used in Caesarea and Ephesus

Acts 10:46 and 19:6 each record the gift of tongues being exercised. In both cases the term *glossa* is used, denoting a knowable, translatable, human language as in Acts 2. There is no indication that this was some kind of ecstatic utterance or excited gibberish, but rather a supernatural communication of the Holy Spirit using understandable language. In this it was no different from Pentecost (Acts 11:17) which was described by Peter as "the like [i.e., equal, the same in size, quality, etc.] gift."

d. The Words Used at Corinth

Twenty-one times Paul uses *glossa* to speak of the tongues in Corinth. Only one other word is used and that is the compound *heteroglossa* which is used as a translation of the foreign languages predicted in Isa. 28:11-12. It is clear from the one compound word, which without doubt refers to the actual language of foreign invaders, that Paul is using *glossa* of language and not of some ecstatic utterance or unintelligible gibberish. Therefore, whatever aberrations of the gift may have been seen in the Church at Corinth, we can be assured that Paul was calling them back to the fact that true, biblical tongues involved speaking in a definite, translatable language of earth.

The second important realization one must have for an understanding of this phenomenon concerns:

2. The Receiving of Tongues

According to Kenneth Hagin of Tulsa, Oklahoma, "Speaking in tongues is always manifested when people are baptized in the Holy Ghost" (21:89). With this agrees pentecostalist, Donald Gee, saying:

> The distinctive doctrine of the Pentecostal churches is that speaking with tongues is the 'initial evidence' of the baptism in the Holy Spirit. This article of belief is now incorporated in the official doctrinal schedules of practically all Pentecostal denominations" (17:17).

Hence we discover multitudes in these circles crowding the front of some auditorium, or packing into some prayer room that they might receive "the baptism in the Holy Ghost."

What is "the baptism in the Holy Ghost" according to the Scriptures? It is an historic event predicted by Christ as recorded in Matt. 3:13, Mark 1:8, Luke 3:16, John 1:33 and Acts 1:4-5. Further it is an historic event looked back to in Acts 11:15-17 and 1 Cor. 12:13. What possible event could it be? The obvious answer is the event which occurred on the Day of Pentecost.

Pentecost, like Calvary, was an event universally beneficial to believers. As believers must point to that historic day, when Christ paid the penalty for their sins, making their salvation possible; so they must look back to Pentecost, when the fulfillment of Christ's prophecies in the upper room became their identity in the baptism in the Holy Spirit. For this reason, Paul points back to Pentecost and gathers all other occurrences in one statement saying:

> For by one Spirit are we all baptized into one body, whether we be Jews or Gentiles, whether we be bond or free; and have been all made to drink into one Spirit (1 Cor. 12:13).

A more proper translation is found in the *American Standard Version* as:

> For in one Spirit were we all baptized into one body, whether Jews or Greeks, whether bond or free; and were all made to drink of one Spirit (95).

The reference is to a definite act in the past in which every believer has participated. Says Merrill F. Unger:

> The inescapable truth taught by the apostle is that the one Spirit baptizes all—every believer—into one body and that there is only one body. That which is wrought by the Spirit is an inseparable part of the believer's salvation, "else it could not include each one." Indeed it could not be otherwise, for all the genuinely saved in this age are "in Christ," and no one can attain this position apart from the baptizing ministry of the Spirit (65:100).

As salvation identifies one with Christ on the cross of Calvary, so this identifies one with the baptism in the Holy Spirit in the upper room. The baptism in the Holy Spirit is, therefore, the immediate possession of all who believe in our Lord Jesus Christ and not a subsequent experience to be sought. F. D. Bruner argues the point in these words:

> If this verse is interpreted as speaking of a second, subsequent, and separate baptism in the Holy Spirit, beyond baptism in Christ, for only some Christians, then violence is done not only to the words of the text—"all . . . all"—but to the purpose of the text in its Corinthian context. The burden of Paul's Corinthian message is the oneness of all the baptized in Christ Jesus. Twice, in this single verse, Paul employs the adjective "all," and by it he means all, the entire Corinthian church, and beyond the Corinthians (n.b.: "we were all baptized into one body") "all those who in every place call on the name of our Lord Jesus Christ" (1:2). In 1 Cor. 12:13 Paul is not teaching an unusual spiritual baptism won by only a few, he is teaching the gracious, Christian baptism through the Spirit given to all (4:292).

The baptism is no more repeated than is salvation. It is done, complete and once-for-all.

Now this has clear implications for both the Charismatic and Pentecostal. The Bible asks a series of questions in 1 Cor. 12:29-30.

> Are all apostles? are all prophets? are all teachers? are all workers of miracles? Have all the gifts of healing? do all speak with tongues? do all interpret?

The answer to these is obviously no. In particular to this discussion, "all" do not "speak with tongues," yet "all" have been baptized in the Holy Spirit (1 Cor. 12:13). It would seem logical, therefore, to believe that the baptism in the Holy Spirit is at the least not initially evidenced by the gift of tongues and is more probably not involved in that baptism at all.

Charismatics, such as Kenneth Hagin, try to get around this by declaring about 1 Cor. 12:29-30 that Paul "is talking here about ministry tongues" (21:91). They seek to divide "ministry tongues" from "devotional tongues." Indeed Hagin goes on to interpret Paul's statement in 1 Cor. 14:18-19 in this very manner by saying, "This seems to indicate that his speaking in tongues wasn't in the church" (21:91). By this he implies that verse 18 is "devotional tongues" and verse 19 is "ministry tongues." Rather does he need to do a careful exegesis of the passage to discover the real reason for tongues, for they are clearly a ministry "not to them that believe [i.e., not to them within the church as believers], but to them that believe not." In this sense, Paul the missionary used tongues more than all others at Corinth, because his ministry was to unbelievers of a variety of language groups, as was the case at Pentecost.

As with other gifts, tongues are the sovereign bestowal of the Holy Spirit. Clearly is this stated in 1 Cor. 12:11, "But all these worketh that one and the selfsame Spirit, dividing to every man severally as he will" and again in verse 28, "And God hath set some in the church . . . diversities of tongues. . . ." William Fitch puts it frankly:

> It is very clear that as the other gifts were distributed in the sovereign providence of God by the Holy Spirit, so it is with the

gift of tongues. It is to a select band that this gift is given. It is to a company of men and women, chosen from the foundation of the world through predestinating grace, that this gift is granted by God the Holy Spirit (14:49).

This being the case, the Word of God never urges people to pray for the gift of tongues, but rather to receive from the sovereign hand of God the gifts with which He chooses to equip them for His service.

This brings us to a third important consideration of this gift:

3. The Regulation of Tongues

It is very clear, even from a preliminary reading of 1 Corinthians 14, that Paul is writing to them to plead for exercise of the primary, edifying gift of prophecy. In doing so, he must deal firmly with the gift which, though the least, was causing the church the most trouble. Thus the chapter gives to us the clearest regulation of the use of tongues in all of the Bible. What rules does the apostle impose?

a. Recognize That Tongues are Inferior

This has already been seen in the position given to them in the lists of 1 Cor. 12:8-10 and 28. In both statements, the gift of tongues comes at the end, being ahead of the only gift dependent upon them. Thus we are not surprised to read Paul's admonition in 1 Cor. 14:5, "I would that ye all spake with tongues, but rather that ye prophesied." His reason for this is based upon the inferior usefulness of tongues, "for greater is he that prophesieth than he that speaketh with tongues, except he interpret, that the church may receive edifying."

b. Use Tongues to Edify

Edification is the theme of the chapter. Whatever is done must edify others. Hence Paul writes:

Now, brethren, if I come unto you speaking with tongues, what shall I profit you, except I shall speak to you either by revelation, or by knowledge, or by prophesying, or by doctrine? (1 Cor. 14:6).

To edify, one must have an objective base. Tongues as being used at Corinth were very subjective. Hence, "he that speaketh in an unknown tongue edifieth himself; but he that prophesieth edifieth the church" (1 Cor. 14:4). Tongues may edify oneself, but only real communication of the Word of God edifies others. Thus Paul teaches that "even so ye, forasmuch as ye are zealous of spiritual gifts, seek that ye may excel to the edifying of the church" (1 Cor. 14:12).

c. Warn Unbelieving Jews

If tongues were a sign of impending judgment to unbelieving Jews as 1 Cor. 14:21-22 declares, then unbelieving Jews should be present for the exercise of this gift not to create chaos (v. 23). Because of this their use was limited, as we shall see later in this chapter. Only when those were present for whom God intended tongues to be a judicial sign of God's judgment upon Israel, were they to be used.

d. Provide Decency and Order

In their old lives, before conversion, these Corinthians were "Gentiles, carried away unto these dumb idols" (1 Cor. 12:2). They had been heathen worshippers out of control in emotional hysteria. Now Paul's admonition is, "Let all things be done decently and in order" (1 Cor. 14:40). Thus they were to wait their turn to exercise the gift of tongues. Only one was to speak at a time, and no more than three persons were to speak in any given meeting (1 Cor. 14:27).

e. Be Sure an Interpreter is Present

Since tongues were a foreign language and, therefore, not necessarily understood by all in the congregation, they needed interpretation. Even Paul's ministry needed such a principle as he states in 1 Cor. 14:6:

> Now, brethren, if I come unto you speaking with tongues, what shall I profit you, except I shall speak to you either by revelation, or by knowledge, or by prophesying, or by doctrine?

Only language that is understood can be profitable, "wherefore let him that speaketh in an unknown tongue pray that he may interpret" (1 Cor. 14:13).

Indeed, no person was to speak in tongues before he was sure that someone was present with the gift of interpretation. So emphatic a rule was this, that Paul says, "If there be no interpreter, let him keep silence in the church" (1 Cor. 14:28). This indicates that tongues-speaking was to be planned and that, as with the gift of prophecy (1 Cor. 14:32), the spirit of the tongues-speaker was "subject to" him. The reason for such decorum is stated as, "for God is not the author of confusion, but of peace, as in all churches of the saints" (1 Cor. 14:33). Tongues were always to add to and never detract from worship.

f. Exclude Their Use by Women

In the context of speaking with tongues, Paul warns:

> Let your women keep silence in the churches: for it is not permitted unto them to speak; but they are commanded to be under obedience, as also saith the law. And if they will learn any thing, let them ask their husbands at home: for it is a shame for women to speak in the church (1 Cor. 14:34-35).

There is no doubt that this forbids the exercise of this gift by women in the assembly. F. D. Bruner observes:

> The apparent contradiction observed between this verse and 1 Cor. 11:5 ("any woman who prays or prophesies with her head unveiled dishonors her head") has been variously explained: that in chapter eleven, Paul is speaking more hypothetically, here more concretely; or there of a somewhat private situation, here of a more public one; more plausibly, perhaps, there of intelligible contributions, here of glossolalia; . . . (4:301).

Whatever the reason, it is clear that this regulation forbids the women of the assembly to exercise this gift.

g. Do Not Forbid Tongues in Worship

The statement is made in 1 Cor. 14:39, "Wherefore, brethren, covet to prophesy, and forbid not to speak with tongues." Today there is confusion caused by this text, since those who practice "tongues" point to it as their badge of freedom, while many who do not necessarily believe in tongues are confused into believing that even today they must—however reluctantly—permit the practice of tongues.

The answer is to place the text in the context of the day for which tongues were given. While the reason for tongues had not been fulfilled the gift of tongues must not be forbidden. However, if we find in the Scriptures a basis for believing that biblical tongues have ceased, then we are at perfect liberty to forbid what is not a biblical gift but an un-biblical aberration and extra-biblical phenomenon.

We come in the fourth place to a discussion of:

4. The Reason for the Gift of Tongues

Unfortunately not many people are willing to study the Scriptures to discover such an important matter as the purpose for which the gift of tongues was given. Perhaps to them it is irrelevant and perhaps this is also the reason for today's confusion. In all of the Bible, there is only one God-given, direct, specific reason for the gift of tongues.

a. Reason Needs Understanding

In 1 Cor. 14:18-20 Paul lays groundwork for this reason by pleading for "understanding." Verse 19 uses *nous* or mind, to describe Paul's desire for understanding for himself as he speaks to others. The word denotes generally "the seat of reflective consciousness, comprising the faculties of perception and understanding, and of those of feeling, judging and determining" (70:69). Paul was concerned to be in control of his thought process at all times.

On the other hand, the word *phren* is used in verse 20 to denote the "understanding" Paul desires for the Corinthian believers. Kittel tells us that in its oldest sense the word means "intellectual and emotional involvement" and deals with the field of reason and reasoning power. Therefore:

> To give preference to speaking with tongues as an immediate utterance of the Spirit is childish, 1 Cor. 14:20. The Corinthians should use their reason, which includes emotion and will, and achieve perfection therein (29:220, 230).

Now these Corinthian believers had lots of emotional involvement, but little intellectual involvement. They had never stopped to use their reasoning powers to ask themselves, "Why speak in tongues?" Paul now seeks to make up for that intellectual deficiency by explaining why. Such an understanding would be explosive in that it would move them from childhood to adulthood, and from immaturity to manhood. "The stage of the child, that is not yet responsible for his acts, is followed in human development by that of full understanding, which is the stage of the mature man" (29:230). This was Paul's hope for the Corinthians when they truly understood what tongues were all about.

b. Spiritual Reason Must Be Bible-Based

And what was the reason? It was a Bible-based reason according to 1 Cor. 14:21:

> In the law it is written, With men of other tongues and other lips will I speak unto this people; and yet for all that will they not hear me, saith the Lord.

Paul is quoting from Isa. 28:11-12 which in proper context is a prophecy concerning the Jews. It deals with God's warning sign to the unbelieving Jews of Isaiah's day. Thus, under inspiration of God, Paul tells us that this gift finds its purpose in relation to God's dealings with unbelieving Israel of the first century.

This purpose is the conclusion of verse 22, since the word "wherefore" links what Paul says in verse 21.

> Wherefore tongues are for a sign, not to them that believe, but to them that believe not: but prophesying serveth not for them that believe not, but for them which believe (1 Cor. 14:22).

This serves notice that what he is about to say is the result of a reasoned and intellectually legitimate deduction from the Scriptures just quoted. Remember the word "wherefore" has the same meaning as "so that" and issues in a logical conclusion on the basis of what has just been said.

And what is the "so that" of verse 22? It is that "tongues are for a sign." This is an idiom in Greek that frequently expresses purpose and indicates that the Apostle discovered the true intent of this miraculous phenomenon in the Old Testament passage just quoted. Such a conclusion is further strengthened when we discover "tongues" to be preceded by a definite article in Greek, making the languages very specific, in fact, those of this very phenomenon of tongues-speaking. Paul's argument is that it is not simply foreign languages in general of which Isaiah speaks, but of "the tongues" of which the apostle has been speaking throughout. Hence the purpose of tongues is a God-given sign to "this people" (i.e., the Jews), and refers to the specific phenomenon of speaking with tongues as a warning to unbelieving Jews of impending judgment.

c. Biblical Reason is Verifiable

Now if this purpose is correct, then we should be able to see it verifiable in the New Testament documents. Consider Acts 2:1-13: according to verse 5 the people to whom the "tongues" were spoken were Jews and their nationalities are stated in verses 9 to 11. The fact that they were unbelieving is well seen later in the chapter in verses 22-23 and in the anguished cry of verse 37. Thus, as Isaiah had predicted, God spake to "this people" through men using other languages and the tongues were heard in their "own dialect wherein they were born" (v. 8).

Consider also Acts 10:44-48. The word used to describe the phenomenon of verse 46 is *glossa* meaning a language as in Acts 2:4 and 11. "But," says someone, "these were Gentiles and not Jews." That is true, but there were unbelieving Jews present—including Peter—and for their sakes the phenomenon was repeated. Thus, by way of explanation to the Jews at Jerusalem who still thought that God's dealings were for them alone and not also for the Gentiles (Acts 11:2-3), Peter says in Acts 11:15-17:

> And as I began to speak, the Holy Ghost fell on them, as on us at the beginning. Then remembered I the word of the Lord, how that he said, John indeed baptized with water; but ye shall be baptized with the Holy Ghost. Forasmuch then as God gave them the like gift as he did unto us, who believed on the Lord Jesus Christ; what was I, that I could withstand God?

What was the point of such an explanation? To help those Jews at Jerusalem to understand that God's dealings were shifting from unbelieving Judaism which was under impending judgment to the Gentiles. So we read the outcome in verse 18:

> When they heard these things, they held their peace, and glorified God, saying, Then hath God also to the Gentiles granted repentance unto life.

Hence we have Jews convinced by the sign-gift of tongues of Gentile acceptance by God.

Consider Acts 19:1-9 as a further verifiable use of tongues as "a sign." This is the account of John's disciples caught in a kind of half-way house between Judaism and Christianity. Upon hearing the Gospel of Christ and believing, they received the gift of the Holy Ghost and "spake with tongues" (v. 6). Again the word used is *glossa,* and again the gift is given in connection with Jews who become witnesses of "that way" together with Paul in the synagogue of the unbelieving Jews (vv. 8-9).

This purpose had relevance in Corinth also, and that is the reason for 1 Corinthians 12 to 14. It was given to call these people back to the basic purpose which God intended for tongues-speaking. After all, Corinth was an international city with a thriving community of Jews as well as Gentiles (see Acts 18:1-17). Languages in the church were for the convincing of these Jews who understood them (i.e., as at Pentecost), and when there were Gentiles present who were unfamiliar with Isa. 28:11 and 12 and who did not understand the languages, then the tongues were to be interpreted lest, not comprehending, they say "that ye are mad" (v. 23). Thus when no interpreter was present, there was to be no speaking in tongues. Hence the primary purpose was upheld, that tongues were God's voice to the Jews that they might be warned and believe.

Having now seen the purpose for the gift of tongues, let us note:

5. The Passing of Biblical Tongues

For this we shall turn to 1 Cor. 13:8-12. There are several important facts revealed here. Look first at:

a. The Word Changes in 1 Corinthians 13:8

Two words are used for what will happen to the gifts mentioned in this verse. Prophecies and knowledge are *katargeo.* The word means "to render inoperative, to supersede." It is used four times in this passage, twice in verse 8 and once in verses 10 and 11. In verse 8, the word is found in the future tense and the passive voice. It indicates that in the future, by the action of the coming of something else, these will be rendered inoperative: that they will be suggested.

However tongues are said to be *pauo.* This word means in the active voice, "to make to cease." However in 1 Cor. 12:8 it is not in the active but in the middle voice, denoting that the action is caused by itself or from within. Thus tongues are said "to cause themselves to cease"—but when?

Inasmuch as it has bearing on this question, let us make the intermediate query:

b. What are Prophecy and Knowledge?

Having already dealt with this question at some length, let me answer from a different perspective. Each of these gifts can refer to an action, the exercise of the respective gifts. The prophet stands up in the assembly and he prophecies (Rom. 12:6), the individual so endowed stands up and gives "a word of knowledge" (1 Cor. 13:8)—this is the act of fulfilling one's gift.

From another viewpoint the gifts can be regarded as content. For example, in Matthew 13:14-15 we read of what Isaiah said, but he is not in "the act" of saying it at that moment. Indeed our Lord is quoting a prophecy which was then part of the content of the Old Testament Book of Isaiah. The same can be said about knowledge, when knowledge becomes codified as Scripture, it stands alone, independent of the person who originally exercised the gift. Thus this is no longer the "act" of prophecy or knowledge as a gift being exercised, but now is the "content" of prophecy or knowledge which has become a part of the subject matter of the Scriptures.

Here both prophecy and knowledge apply to content. Notice that in 1 Cor. 14:6 "knowledge" and "prophecy" issue in "doctrine." This implies that the preceding terms apply to "content," since the body of prophecy and the body of knowledge are the body of doctrine, rather than to the "act" of exercising one's gift. The content is nothing less than what we regard today as the Scriptures.

The Bible is the compilation of those messages from God which were written under inspiration of the Holy Spirit. In Jude 3 we read of it as "the faith once delivered unto the saints." The writer to the Hebrews also speaks of this content in his warning of Heb. 2:3-4. Finally God Himself sets the seal upon the completion of this body of revealed truth in the words of Rev. 22:18-19.

c. When are Prophecy and Knowledge Rendered Inoperative, or Superseded by Something Else?

First Corinthians 13:10 has the answer and the word "perfect" is the clue. This word means "complete." It is used in apposition to what is known "in part" and what is prophesied "in part" in verse 9. When does that partial become complete? When the complete revelation has been given. When does the "in part" knowledge and prophecy become inoperative? When it is superseded by the perfect, the complete content of the revelation of God in the Scriptures. Will the content of the Scriptures ever be superseded? Yes, when we meet Christ, according to 1 Cor. 13:12 and we shall be given perfect understanding of all things as opposed to knowledge "in part" now, even with the Canon of the Holy Scriptures before us.

We are now ready to ask the question:

d. When Do Tongues Cease?

It is obvious that it is before Christ comes, for they are not there then. While prophecy and knowledge will endure as the content of Scripture—needed by us, to be studied from our understanding and edification until Jesus comes—tongues are said to cease in and of themselves. Tongues are not mentioned in verses 9 to 12, implying, not that tongues will be rendered inoperative at Christ's return, but that they will not be in existence; for they will of themselves (middle voice) have ceased.

To discover whether the biblical gift of tongues still exists, we only have to answer one question: "Is God still giving warning signs to the Jewish people concerning the judgment of Isa. 28:11-12, or has His purpose for tongues been fulfilled?" In answering this question we look back to Christ's prophecy in Luke 21:20-24. This was the judgment of which tongues were to be the warning sign. Thus when in A.D. 70, the armies of Titus surrounded and destroyed Jerusalem and all the inhabitants left therein, God's judgment had fallen. Says John F. MacArthur, Jr.:

> The message to Israel was clear. No longer would God confine Himself to one people as a channel; no longer would God operate His work of grace through one nation and speak one language. Their unbelief changed that. Tongues, then, were the sign of the removal of national blessing on Israel (32:168).

Now is the season of opportunity for the Gentiles to believe and to receive the Gospel. Rom. 11:25 tells us "that blindness in part is happened to Israel, until the fulness of the Gentiles be come in." The age-long treading of the Holy City, Jerusalem, constitutes a continuing visual lesson in history; that, so long as it continues, God's purposes with the Jews as a nation are in abeyance, and His purpose with the nations is predominant.

Today we can be assured that biblical tongues have ceased. The purpose for which they were given, they have themselves fulfilled. They have worked themselves out of their stated *raison d'être* and have caused themselves to cease. God's stated purpose and guiding prophecy has been fulfilled. As well might we demand that God once again divide the Red Sea, cause Jericho's walls to fall or the sun to stand still in the heavens, as to demand that tongues be revived for today when their purpose is fulfilled. The failure of the modern tongues movement to display any discernible consciousness of the plain biblical reason for this gift, stands as a powerful argument against the movement's genuineness and validity. Do not be misled by today's purported "tongues-speakers." The gift has ceased.

D. THE INTERPRETATION OF TONGUES

The gift of interpretation is mentioned in only one of the gift lists. In 1 Cor. 12:10 it is listed as a gift immediately after the gift of tongues. However, it is implied in the questions of 1 Cor. 12:30 and it is certainly referred to by Paul in 1 Cor. 14:5, 13, 26, 27 and 28. But what does it mean?

Negatively, there are some things we can be aware that it does not mean. It does not refer to the acquired ability to translate one language into another. This act demands long years of study and is not a gift but a human ability developed by hard work. Biblically "interpretation" was a gift conferred and therefore did not depend upon one's intellectual development.

Neither does it refer to the custom used in the synagogues wherein "the translator" . . . in the course of synagogue worship put the Scripture readings into Aramic and also communicated out loud to the congregation the softly spoken sermons . . ." (26:665). Rather does it have a closer resemblance to the Old Testament "prophetic office of interpretation . . . [which] rests on divine inspiration in the strictest sense" (26:664). This is true because this was a gift of the Spirit and not a human ability.

1. The Meaning of the Word

The word used for this gift in 1 Cor. 12:10 and 1 Cor. 14:26 is *hermeneia*. It is a word meaning "to explain, interpret (Eng. hermeneutics), and is used of explaining the meaning of words in a different language" (69:267). The one who had the gift of interpretation was one who could supernaturally translate the meaning of the tongues-speaker, who was using a language unknown to people in the assembly.

In 1 Cor. 12:30 and 1 Cor. 14:5, 13, 27 and 28, a strengthened form of *hermeneia* is used. Here the addition of *dia* (through) adds intensity. The use of the gift, now is said to interpret fully, or to explain thoroughly. It is used of Christ's expounding of the Old Testament Scriptures to the disciples on the Emmaus Road, "in all the Scriptures the things concerning Himself" (Luke 24:27). The gift, therefore, gave the user an understanding of the tongues-message spoken, as God Himself would expound it.

Interestingly enough, both of these words derive "from *Hermēs,* the god of speech" (47:170). *Hermēs* was the Greek name for the pagan god Mercury. He was regarded as the messenger of the gods. In English, the name gives rise to the word hermeneutics, the art or science of interpretation. The one endowed with the gift of interpretation was one who took the message of God, given through the one gifted with tongues, and made it understandable to those who were unfamiliar with the language being spoken.

This leads us to a consideration of:

2. The Purpose of the Gift

The reason for the gift of interpretation was not merely to translate what was said in order to satisfy the curiosity of those present. Rather the gift had the very important purpose of edification. After all, Paul has argued strongly in the early parts of 1 Corinthians 14 that tongues of themselves do not edify. The only way in which they might be helpful in ministry within the Church is by having them interpreted.

Interpretation gave understanding to tongues. Paul's argument is:

> There are, it may be, so many kinds of voices in the world, and none of them is without signification. Therefore if I know not the meaning of the voice, I shall be unto him that speaketh a barbarian, and he that speaketh shall be a barbarian unto me. Even so ye, forasmuch as ye are zealous of spiritual gifts, seek that ye may excel to the edifying of the church. Wherefore let him that speaketh in an unknown tongue pray that he may interpret (1 Cor. 14:10-13).

Interpretation allows the congregation to be intellectually involved and to respond with reason. "Barbarianism" (v. 11) should have no place in the Church, or else it will be perceived as "madness" (v. 23). Interpretation enabled the tongues-speaker to edify the body of Christ.

So important was the gift of interpretation that the gift of tongues was incomplete without it. The person, therefore, who rightly wanted to use his gift of tongues-speaking to the edification of the Church was encouraged to "pray that he may interpret" (1 Cor. 14:13). Only in this way would tongues be worthy of a hearing within the assembly.

So definite was Paul on this matter that he gives to the Corinthians a definite regulation:

3. No Interpreter, No Tongues-Speaker

We have already seen that except in Corinth there is no record of this gift being used. For example, on Pentecost the people asked, "How hear we every man in our own tongue, wherein we were born?" (Acts 2:8). This has led some to believe that the miracle of Pentecost was double, (1) in the speech of the apostles and (2) in the ears of the hearers. However, a more probable interpretation is that there was no need for the words to be interpreted since these people heard directly in their own language.

In Corinth the situation was different. What was happening did not take place in the market square, or in some other public concourse, but in the Church assembly. The purpose of tongues was restricted by virtue of the narrowed scope of congregation. Thus, though some within the confines of the assembly would be Jews to whom God's message would be directed through the gift of tongues, others would be Gentiles who did not understand the language being spoken The gift of interpretation was very important for these people.

So important indeed was this gift in such a setting that Paul states in 1 Cor. 14:28, "If there be no interpreter, let him keep silence in the church; and let him speak to himself, and to God." Says Gerherd Kittel:

> The principle enunciated by Paul, namely, that there must be no speaking with tongues without disciplined ἐρμηνεία (14:26ff.), means in fact the controlling of the wild torrent of spiritual outbursts in the channel of the clear and disciplined but no less genuine and profound operation of the Spirit through the Word" (26:665).

The interpreter avoided the charge of madness in verse 23 and fulfilled the need for edification of verse 26. Of course, this also gives us the clue that the interpreters were well-known to the congregation in general and to the tongues-speakers in particular. They would, therefore, be able to avoid an occurrence of tongues without an interpreter by simply looking around the assembly to see who was present.

A further regulation stipulated:

4. Only One Interpreter

Apparently in the Corinthian Church the practice was for several interpreters to exercise their gift in a given service (1 Cor. 14:26). Sometimes this led to a conflict, since the interpreters would disagree one with the other. Charismatic, Kenneth E. Hagin, illustrates this from personal experience telling us:

> I have been in some services where I have seen the misuse of these gifts and I have gone home confused. . . . This doesn't

mean that the devil was working. It just means that people can get things mixed up (21:95).

Hence the rule of interpretation was laid down in 1 Cor. 14:27: "If any man speak in an unknown tongue, let it be by two, or at the most by three, and that by course; and let one interpret."

Now we have already seen that, "God is not the author of confusion, but of peace, as in all churches of the saints" (1 Cor. 14:33), and that it is His desire to, "let all things be done decently and in order" (1 Cor. 14:40). This was the reason for the statement of verse 27, "let one interpret." The point is that whether one, two or three speakers in tongues were heard, only one interpreter was to be heard. This interpretation was to be given after the gift of tongues had been exercised "by course." In this way no confusion or indecorous conduct would occur and the trumpet of interpretation would not be blowing "an uncertain sound" to the hearers (1 Cor. 14:8-9).

E. WHEN THE GIFT CEASED

Since the gift of interpretation was inseparably tied to the gift of tongues, we are not surprised that both gifts should cease together. If there are no messages being given in God-given foreign languages, then there is no need for the gift of interpretation. Thus the gift, like that of tongues, has ceased and is no longer in use today.

Such an understanding would save many congregations from the following embarrassing incident recorded by W. A. Criswell:

> A seminary graduate who had majored in Hebrew attended a tongues-meeting in California. In the midst of the meeting he stood up and quoted by memory the first Psalm in the original language. After he had finished, the interpreter arose and solemnly, piously made known in plain English what the brother had spoken in an unknown tongue. The interpreter made it an utterance, Spirit-inspired, about women prophesying in church. When the seminarian made known what he had done and what he had said, pandemonium broke loose (7:219).

The word "pandemonium" is better used than perhaps even Criswell realized, since it is composed of two words *pan* (neuter of *pas*) meaning "all" and *daimōn* meaning "demon."

"All demons" can be let loose when people insist on exercising as a gift of the Holy Spirit that which the Scriptures teach no longer exists. "He that hath ears to hear, let him hear."

PART 3
MYTHS BASED IN TIME
SECTION II. THE FULFILLING GIFTS

13

THE FULFILLING GIFTS

INTRODUCTION

WHILE THERE WERE gifts which were by their very nature and purpose temporary gifts to the church, it is very obvious that there were also a number of permanent gifts. These latter are those gifts which did not have an authenticating ministry but a settled ministry. They are the gifts which are needed within the churches for the continuance of the ministry until Jesus comes again.

A. BODY LIFE IS IMPORTANT

In 1 Corinthians 12 Paul argues for the importance of every member in the body. He states the unity of that body, though there may be "many members" in it (vv. 12-14). The body of which he speaks is identified as the Corinthian Church (v. 27). We are told that the members of this church were not placed there haphazardly (v. 18), but sovereignly by God for "God hath set" them "in the church . . ." (v. 28). Further our attention is drawn to the fact that to each member has been given "the manifestation of the Spirit" (v. 7) and that these gifts are divided "to every man severally" as the sovereign Spirit wills (v. 11).

Thus the gifts of the Holy Spirit make each member important to the functioning of the church. Each one has need of every other one (vv. 15-17) and there is room for neither jealousy, nor scorn (v. 21). Whether the gift be a servant gift for public ministry, or a service gift for enablement in some office, or a serving gift to function humbly in a way we may carnally consider "less honorable" (v. 23), all are necessary to the spiritual welfare of the total church.

The gifts are, therefore, interlocking and interdependent. Paul illustrates this by his use of the human body and its functions. Observes G. G. Findlay:

> "God tempered the body together" in this way, "that . . . the members might have the same solicitude for one another." The physical members are obliged, by the structure of the frame, to care for one another; the hand is as anxious to guard the eye or the stomach, to help the mouth or the foot, as to serve itself; the eye is watchman for every other organ; each feels its own usefulness and cherishes its fellows; all "have the same care," since they have the same interest—that of "the one body." This *societas membrorum* makes the physical order both a parable of and a basis for the spiritual (13:894).

As no part of the body is independent of the utility of the rest, so no gift functions in splendid isolation from the rest but is for the edification of all.

If even one person "suffers" because of the scornful opinions expressed (v. 21) about the importance of his gift,[1] being rendered unable to function properly in the use of that gift, then "all the members suffer" loss with him (v. 26).[2] On the other hand if one person is "honored" (Greek *doxazō* from *doxa* meaning "an opinion") through encouraging opinions expressed about his contribution to the life of the church by the proper functioning of his gift, then its use is strengthened and the total church is blessed and rejoices (v. 26). It is said to be important, therefore, to "bestow more abundant honor" (v. 23-24) upon those endowed with gifts which are not as publically acclaimed, because every person's gift is necessary to the health and ministry of the body.

When we comprehend the importance of the gifts of the Spirit to the body life of the local assembly, we are not surprised to discover that there are fulfilling gifts for the ministry of the church today. Indeed, without these our

---

[1] Kittel notes, "the pass. sense and antithetical δοξάζεται show that the meaning of πασχει is in malam partem: 'to suffer harm,' 'to be unfavorably influenced' " (28:912-913).

[2] Kittel further states, "When applied to the community 12:26a does not mean that when a member suffers harm all the members share the loss emotionally. What it means is that in this case they all suffer the loss too" (28:925). When a member loses the function of his gift, all the members suffer the loss of that gift in the life of the Church.

churches could not function as God intends. They can be divided into three basic categories for the purpose of understanding their place and function within the body of Christ.

B. THE FULFILLING SERVANT-GIFTS

As there were fulfilled servant-gifts which were needed in the founding days of the church, so there are fulfilling servant-gifts needed for today. These are gifts which enable the churches to go on fulfilling the ministry of Christ in this and succeeding generations, should the Lord tarry. Rather than having a founding ministry, they have a continuing ministry.

As with the fulfilled servant-gifts, these are personified as the gifts of Christ to the churches in Eph. 4:11. They are "evangelists," "pastors and teachers." Their position, conduct and ministry within the churches have been codified in the Scriptures for succeeding generations to follow. Their ministry is as much needed today as that of the fulfilled servant-gifts of the first century. For details, see Chapter 14.

C. THE FULFILLING SERVICE-GIFTS

While the servant gifts for today are personified, the service gifts are not. They are the endowments of the Holy Spirit which enable believers to hold some position within the church. Those who are possessors of these gifts are enabled to perform formal service within the churches, in such a way that the whole body is helped to function properly.

There are four such gifts: governments, ruling, ministry and faith. Each one has a specific equipping for those who would perform a public ministry within the church. They function as leadership qualifications and without them those who seek to hold a position find in themselves an inexplicable inadequacy. Those job-oriented gifts are necessary to the smooth running of the entire church body and are, therefore, fulfilling gifts for today. For details, see Chapter 15.

D. THE FULFILLING SERVING-GIFTS

While the servant gifts are personified and the service gifts are mainly position oriented, the serving gifts are the enablement for individualized functions within the church body. The operation of these gifts does not depend upon public service, or even upon organized use. They are gifts which enable individuals to contribute to the life of the church in a personal—indeed often private—manner and in such a way that the needs of others are met.

Because these gifts are by their very nature "background gifts," they are not often publicized. Yet without them it is doubtful if any church could truly survive as a sharing and caring assembly. I am referring to the gifts of exhortation, helps, mercy and giving. While each of these may at times enter the scrutiny of public use, on the whole they are continually being carried on in the seclusion of quiet service rendered to God for His praise alone.

In a very real sense these gifts are to the church what oil is to machinery. They are the lubricant which enables the church to function properly. Without them the operation of the body breaks down and the servant and service gifts are rendered less effective. Though often taken for granted because of their quiet, unassuming place in the assembly, those endowed with these gifts are as necessary for the life of the church today as were the apostles in the first century.

With this background on the meaning of the terms and the identification of the gifts covered by them, we are ready to begin our analysis of these fulfilling gifts of the Spirit. These are gifts which are in operation today to enable us to fulfill the responsibilities God has given to us as we live and work for Him. Each of us is endowed with one or more of these gifts, and they render us without excuse for not fulfilling our particular function within the body of Christ. For details, see Chapter 16.

14

THE FULFILLING SERVANT-GIFTS

A. CHRIST GAVE SOME EVANGELISTS

WHILE BEING AN evangelist may not be an office within the church, there can be no doubt about it being a gift. The word is used only three times in the New Testament, these being Acts 21:8, Eph. 4:11 and 2 Tim. 4:5. It is interesting that this final occurrence is recorded in Paul's last letter, written shortly before his death about A.D. 65. To the last, Paul was concerned that the "work of an evangelist" be carried on.

The word *euangelistēs* means literally "a messenger of good;" being composed of *eu* meaning "well," and *angelos,* meaning "a messenger" (69:44). It denotes a preacher of the gospel, and Eph. 4:11 and 2 Tim. 4:5 make it clear that this is an abiding function of the churches of Jesus Christ.

One very quickly sees the ministry of an evangelist, when he realizes the similarity of the term to that of "the gospel." In the original the gospel is *euangelion,* from which we get our English reference "evangel," or good news. Thus, while the term evangelist is used only three times in the Scriptures, one can readily see that the function is at the core of New Testament preaching.

The evangelist is the one to *euangelizō,* "to bring or announce glad tidings" (69:168). His proclamation concerns the death, burial and resurrection of Christ (1 Cor. 15:1-4). He tells of God's grace to sinners (Acts 20:24), and the full and complete forgiveness available to all who will repent and believe the gospel (Mark 1:15, Acts 3:19). This function was so exact and of such great importance, that we read of Paul's concern for the Galatian believers in these words:

> I marvel that ye are so soon removed from Him that called you into the grace of Christ unto another gospel [*euangelion,* "glad

tidings"]: Which is not another; but there are some that trouble you, and would pervert the gospel [*euangelion,* "glad tidings"] of Christ. But though we, or an angel from heaven, preach any other gospel [*euangelizetai,* "should announce glad tidings"] unto you than that which we have preached [*euengelisametha,* "what we announced"] unto you, let him be accursed. As we said before, so say I now again, If any man preach any other gospel [*euangelizetai,* "announces glad tidings"] unto you than that ye have received, let him be accursed (Gal. 1:6-9).

It is clear, therefore, that the message of the evangelist was to announce the evangel of the gospel and nothing more.

Now having said these things, we are ready to note that:

1. The Evangelist Is a Gift

This is clearly indicated in Eph. 4:11. Among the ascension gifts of Christ mentioned is this statement, "and some, evangelists." The evangelist is, therefore, an ascension gift of Christ for the preaching of the gospel.

Notice the order in which the gifts are presented. "And he gave some, apostles; and some, prophets; and some, evangelists; and some, pastors and teachers" (Eph. 4:11). Unlike the order of 1 Cor. 12:28, it would seem that the order here is sequential. The apostles were primary in that they began their ministry during the earthly ministry of Christ. Prophets, by their function, were needed to deliver God's revelations to the congregations of the churches prior to the closing of Scripture. Then the pastors-teachers carried on a more settled ministry of spiritual upbuilding of the young churches begun. Evangelists, on the other hand, were there to preach the gospel and to establish those congregations of believers.

Not just anybody could be an evangelist, anymore than anyone by personal choice could be an apostle, or a prophet. As with the others, this was a gift and a calling upon the individual's life. "And no man taketh this honor unto himself, but he that is called of God, as was Aaron" (Heb. 5:4). It was incumbent upon the churches, therefore, to recognize their ministry as a fulfilling gift from God for the gospel's sake.

J. Dwight Pentecost, writing of the gifts of evangelist, states:

An evangelist had the particular gift of preaching the gospel to unsaved men so that they would hear and believe. This is a continuing gift to the present day. There are men who have an incisive knowledge of the Word of God, who stand up before an audience of the unsaved, and are doctrinally correct as they preach Christ, but they give the invitation and nothing happens. Is there something wrong with their doctrine? No. Another man preaches Christ and there is great response. What is the difference? One has the gift of evangelist and the other doesn't (44:173).

Let us not mistakenly believe then, that every preacher has the gift of being an evangelist.

Another factor about this gift comes out clearly in the Scriptures:

2. Evangelists Could Be Laymen

I use the word "laymen" advisedly but not in any disparaging sense. It is used simply to distinguish between the ministry now being described and that of an ordained pastor-teacher. So in this sense, a person could be an evangelist without any thought that he should "live of the gospel" (1 Cor. 9:14).

This seems to be the case in the life of at least one New Testament evangelist:

a. Philip Was a Deacon

Apparently he worked out in the world for his living as many others in the local Church at Jerusalem did. But when the dissension arose and the apostolic call for deacons was given, Philip was among those seven men chosen. By the way, it is by this fact that he is identified as the same person as the evangelist of Acts 21:8:

> And the next day we that were of Paul's company departed, and came unto Caesarea: and we entered into the house of Philip the evangelist, which was one of the seven; and abode with him.

Philip was, therefore, a layman who was chosen as a deacon in his home church in Jerusalem.

In Acts chapters 6 and 7 there is nothing mentioned that particularly distinguishes the ministry of this individual. We are told in Acts 6:7 that:

The Word of God increased, and the number of the disciples multiplied in Jerusalem greatly; and a great company of the priests were obedient to the faith.

But whether this was through the ministry of the deacons, or was a result of the burden being shifted from the apostles' shoulders so that verse 4 might be fulfilled, we do not know.

We do know that Stephen's ministry certainly stood out among the rest of his fellow deacons, although Philip is not mentioned again in chapters 6 and 7. All we can do is assume that he went faithfully about his responsibilities to the glory of God. In all of this time, Philip is not referred to as an evangelist, and it may well be that the gift had not yet been discovered.

However, something happened to disturb the peace of the Jerusalem Church, and,

b. Philip Became an Evangelist

In Acts 6:1 the peace of the church was disturbed from within, and deacons were instituted as a ministry within the church. However, in Acts 8:1 the peace was broken from without, and the gift of an evangelist began to be exercised outside the church. We read that because of the "havoc" Saul was making of the Church in Jerusalem, believers were "scattered abroad." "Then Philip went down to the city of Samaria, and preached Christ unto them" (Acts 8:5). Suddenly deacon Philip becomes "Philip the evangelist" (Acts 21:8).

Now there is a biblical principle involved here. In 1 Tim. 3:13 we read, "For they, that have used the office of a deacon well, purchase to themselves a good degree, and great boldness in the faith which is in Christ Jesus." Philip had used his Jerusalem office well, and so God has given him evangelistic boldness to preach the evangel in Samaria. He thereby moves from being a server of tables (Acts 6:2), to becoming a flaming evangelist.

Philip, by the very circumstance of life (and we may add "providential" circumstance, for the Church at Jerusalem had shown little enthusiasm for the fulfillment of the great commission to non-Jews), is shown to have the gift of being an evangelist. However, let us emphasize again that this was a gift and not a natural ability. As John F. Walvoord puts it:

Of primary importance in propagating the gospel is the gift of evangelism (Eph. 4:11). By its title, it is clear that this gift has reference to effective preaching of the gospel message to the unsaved, and as such, it is to be compared to the teaching gift which gives instruction to the unsaved. It is clear, experimentally, that knowledge of the gospel does not bring with it the ability to preach it with success to others. Men may possess the gift of teaching, for instance, without possessing the gift of evangelism, and vice versa . . . While all are called to bring the gospel to the lost by whatever means may be at their disposal, . . . it is the sovereign purpose of God that certain men should have a special gift in evangelism (73:169).

Another important fact we must note about this gift is that:

3. Evangelism May Vary as to Congregation

Today our thinking on evangelism has been colored by the massive crusades "put on" by world famous evangelists. But if I am reading my Bible correctly, evangelism has a three-fold connotation. First of all:

a. It Can Encompass a City

We read in Acts 8:5 that, "Philip went down to the city of Samaria." There, without any advance party or great publicity, we read simply that he, "preached Christ unto them." Here was a single individual driven from his home city and province by the providential circumstances of life, who began to evangelize a city with the Gospel!

Moreover, because he had the gift of being an evangelist, "the people with one accord gave heed unto those things which Philip spake" (Acts 8:60). "And there was great joy in that city" (Acts 8:8). He was successful, though he was alone, without any back-up organization, because he had the ascension gift of Christ for being an evangelist.

So amazing were the results in Samaria (and let us remember as John 4:9 reveals, "the Jews have no dealings with the Samaritans") that, "when the apostles which were at Jerusalem heard that Samaria had received the word of God, they sent unto them Peter and John" (Acts 8:14), to see what was going on. It seemed that the believers at Jerusalem were skeptical to say the least, as to the authenticity of what was going on. Peter and John were the envoys to determine whether it was real!

Such is the amazing power of evangelism exercised by one who has this gift. Results follow the preaching of the Gospel in a way that others only dream of. And one who is an evangelist in the Eph. 4:11 sense can as readily capture a city for Christ, as another might a single person.

Now this is not to downplay individual evangelism, for:

b. This Gift Can Encompass a Person

The fact is that the greatest illustration of this is seen in the life of the very same evangelist who could encompass a city in his evangelism. At the very height of the awakening in Samaria, "the angel of the Lord spake unto Philip, saying, Arise, and go toward the south unto the way that goeth down from Jerusalem unto Gaza, which is desert" (Acts 8:26). The purpose of this was that Philip might come in contact with "a man of Ethiopia," one single individual.

Had not God made a mistake in directing Philip away from the mighty moving of the Spirit of God in Samaria? No, for God is interested in the individual as much as He is in the city. Furthermore, the gift of evangelism is as much needed for the individual as for the multitude. As Eric S. Fife says:

> The point that needs to be grasped is that Philip was as much an evangelist when talking to one person, as when he was talking to the multitudes. There are various definitions of an evangelist. I would define him as a person with the God-given ability to bring people to faith in Jesus Christ (12:156).

Hence, in Acts 8:27-39 we have one of the greatest illustrations of personal soulwinning to be found in all the Bible by one who has the gift of evangelism. Within a short period of time an individual, who had never heard of Jesus, not only was introduced to Him, but believed on Him and was baptized. It is interesting to notice that the same result occurred after the conversion of the Ethiopian, as occurred after the salvation of the Samaritans in verse 8. We read that, "he went on his way rejoicing" (Acts 8:39).

But not only can the gift encompass a city and a person:

c. It Can Encompass a Church

Timothy was the pastor of the Church in Ephesus. He was Paul's "son in the faith." Much that he knew, he had been taught by his spiritual father. Now Paul was about to lay down his life for the Gospel's sake. Hence, he could write, "I am now ready to be offered, and the time of my departure is at hand" (2 Tim. 4:6).

In such a situation and at such a time, what message would be paramount in importance to this local church pastor? Well among other things immediately before Paul spoke of his "departure," he wrote these words, "But watch thou in all things, endure afflictions, do the work of an evangelist, make full proof of thy ministry" (2 Tim. 4:5). You see, evangelism could encompass a church. Indeed, for a "full proof" ministry it must encompass the church where every man of God pastors. This was the aged apostle's last message to Timothy, and to us.

This may be done either personally, or by proxy through someone with the gift of being an evangelist. Whatever the method used, it is a must for the survival of the local church. In every congregation, for a complete ministry to be exercised, evangelism must play a part. Every pastor must foster the spirit of evangelism among his members, making it a part of the very atmosphere of his church.

Indeed it may well be that Philip exercised his gift in this way also. After the Ethiopian had been led to Christ we read, "But Philip was found at Azotus: and passing through he preached in all the cities, till he came to Caesarea" (Acts 8:40). Thereafter we hear no more about him until Acts 21:8, where we read that Paul and his company came to Caesarea and, "entered into the house of Philip the evangelist, which was one of the seven; and abode with him." Apparently for some twenty-five years Caesarea had been Philip's home. Did he function as a deacon, or an evangelist? Was he a deacon attached to the local church there, or was that his base for evangelistic outreach? We do not know. One thing we do know is that he would be as faithful in his relationship to the church there as he was at Jerusalem.

One more aspect of this New Testament gift must be noted. It would seem that:

4. Evangelism Involved Church Planning

While it is important to notice the exercise of the gift of evangelism, it is at least of equal importance to be aware of the product. It seems to me that the product of the biblical gift was always a local church. This was the ultimate aim; not merely the gathering of decisions for Christ.

Thus, in a very real sense, evangelism was church oriented. The authority of the local church was upon the ministry carried out (Acts 8:14-25). Further, the issue of the gift seems also to be a local church. For example, through the ministry of Philip, a local church was planted in Samaria. Traditional history tells us that through Philip's ministry to the Ethiopian eunuch, the Church in Ethiopia was begun.

Though Paul is not called an evangelist, he is most probably one of the clearest examples of this gift in the entire New Testament. Wherever he went, people were converted and baptized. Always when he left, there seems to have been an organized local church. In this sense, he illustrates the church planting aspect of evangelism.

Is it any wonder that W. A. Criswell writes with longing heart concerning the gift of being an evangelist that it:

> is a distinct gift which few men possess in superlative degree, but when it is found, it is the third of all the gifts of the Holy Spirit, preceded only by the gifts of apostleship and prophecy. The famous evangelists through the years have been men so greatly used of God to bless the world. We need them desperately. May God grant that the gift with increased frequency and meaning may fall upon our preachers today (7:168).

So let it be, Lord Jesus!

But lest some feel discouraged because they do not have this great gift, let me close with a wonderful principle stated by Jesus:

> Say not ye, There are yet four months, and then cometh harvest? behold, I say unto you, Lift up your eyes, and look on the fields; for they are white already to harvest. And he that reapeth receiveth wages, and gathereth fruit unto life eternal: that both he that soweth and he that reapeth may rejoice together. And herein is that saying true, One soweth, and another reapeth (John 4:35-37).

There is a necessity for some to sow the seed, who may never see the harvest. Others reap who never did any labor in preparation. Whether we sow or reap matters little, as long as we use to the maximum the gift God has entrusted to us for His glory.

B. CHRIST GAVE SOME PASTORS

The last two ascension gifts mentioned by Paul in Eph. 4:11 are "pastors and teachers." Many believe that both of these gifts refer to the same office. Says John F. Walvoord, "In Eph. 4:11, the use of *kai,* linking pastors and teachers instead of the usual *de,* implies that one cannot be a true pastor without being also a teacher" (73:170). William McRae categorically states, "This gift is the only dual gift in the New Testament. There are not two gifts here. It is one gift which has two distinct dimensions" (35:59).

Having said that, and agreeing in principle with the position of these men, for the purposes of this chapter, I shall deal with each word separately. These are important terms! If we are to fully understand and appreciate the office they represent, we must first realize the significance of their use.

In considering the first title, we must make ourselves aware of:

1. The Different Words for Pastor

There are at least three different denominations given to the office of pastor in Scripture. Let us begin with the one on hand:

a. The Term "Pastor"

Of all designations of the office, this is the most wonderful. It is probably the one most appreciated by every local-church minister. Yet in all of the New Testament, it is used but once. Among the ascension gifts of Christ in Eph. 4:11 we are told, "He gave some, . . . pastors."

The Greek word is *poimēn,* meaning simply "a shepherd." In its initial form it refers to one who tends the flock (70:167). It means more than merely one who feeds them; it means one who cares for them. Hence, metaphorically the word is applied in the Scriptures to the men given, by the ascended Christ, to the church to care for it.

In John 10:11 our Lord takes this term as a name for Himself. "I am the good shepherd," He tells us. What a high and holy privilege it is for any man to be called "pastor." Yet it is the same word.

Peter reminds us in 1 Peter 2:25, "Ye were as sheep going astray; but are now returned unto the Shepherd and Bishop of your souls." As our "good Shepherd," Christ drew us to Himself and tended to our needs. So, the man who is Christ's gift to the church is a pastor. He too tends the sheep of God.

Later 1 Peter 5:4 refers to the second coming of Christ. There the pastors are being reminded of their duties and Peter says, "And when the chief Shepherd shall appear, ye shall receive a crown of glory that fadeth not away." Our Lord is the "chief Shepherd," and His ascension gifts are under-shepherds. Their ministry is carried on as understudies of Christ.

When the writer to the Hebrews was ending off that tremendous epistle that so exalts and magnifies Christ in His mediatorial work, he used a benediction. In it he summed up the ministry and work of Christ in these glorious words:

> Now the God of peace, that brought again from the dead our Lord Jesus, that great shepherd of the sheep, through the blood of the everlasting covenant, make you perfect in every good work to do his will, working in you that which is wellpleasing in his sight, through Jesus Christ; to whom be glory for ever and ever. Amen (Heb. 13:20-21).

Christ is now the "great Shepherd" and wonder of wonders, He shares some of that care for the sheep with poor, fallen humanity through His gifts to the church, His pastors.

Of all the appellations by which a minister of the gospel can be called, none is so elevating and at the same time so humbling, as the term pastor. Yet this is the very term heaven chose to describe the gift Christ gave to the church, when He ascended up on high. What a privileged office for mortal man to fill: a pastor!

Another word used to describe the same office is:

b. The Term "Bishop"

The designation is found in Acts 20:28; Phil. 1:1; 1 Tim. 3:2; Titus 1:7 and 1 Peter 2:25. Five times a pastor is called by the term "bishop." The Greek word is composed of two parts, *epi* meaning "over," and *skopeo* meaning "to look or watch."

Episkopos, therefore, literally refers to one who looks over or watches over a local church (68:128). The pastor is now being called an overseer.

In our day the term bishop has connotations of hierarchy. It is used mainly in churches with a form of government which calls for an office to oversee a number of churches and their pastors. However, the word is not so regarded in Scripture, where it is used interchangeably with the term pastor.

Whereas the word "pastor" refers to the minister's relationship to his flock, the word "bishop" refers to the work of the pastor. He is to seek to safeguard the church from error's pathway, or from the incursion of grievous wolves. His responsibility is to ensure that all things are done decently and in orderly fashion. Great indeed is the responsibility, therefore, of the bishop of a local church.

The third name applied to the office of a pastor is:

c. The Term "Elder"

Presbuteros is the word in the original. It is an adjective which originally referred to age, and hence the translation "elder." However, the term held much more significance than that, and indeed the matter of age became secondary. According to Samuel Bagster, the word held the notion of "dignity," and a "local dignitary" might be called an elder (1:340).

In relation to the office of a pastor the term also "refers to the dignity and rank of his position" (7:168). It had connotations of "spiritual maturity" (69:21). The office was not one for a novice, but for one who had gained experience in the ranks of the local church ministry.

Poimēn, presbuteros and *episkopos* are terms which describe the same office, and may be used interchangeably. An example of this is Luke's account of Paul's last farewell to the Ephesian pastors. In Acts 20:17, these are referred to as, "the elders [*presbuterous*] of the church." But when Paul addresses them in verse 28 he says:

> Take heed therefore unto yourselves and to all the flock over the which the Holy Ghost hath made you overseers [*epis-*

kopeus, "bishops"], to feed [*poimainein,* "to shepherd" or "pastor"[1]] the church of God which He hath purchased with His own blood.

Thus, in this single passage we have illustrated for us the fact that these three terms apply to and describe the same ascension gift of Christ.

The second important understanding we must seek in regard to this gift has to do with:

2. The Qualifications of a Pastor

One method of determining the importance of a gift is to note the qualifications which are given for one who would exercise it. Of all the gifts there are qualifications laid down for only one, and that is this ascension gift of pastor. Not only are there qualifications laid down, but they are of the most stringent nature, being found in three different passages of Scripture (1 Tim. 3:1-7; Titus 1:5-7; and 1 Peter 5:1-4).

For one to exercise the gift of pastoring:

a. There Are Personal Qualifications

By the very nature of the office, a pastor must "be," before he can "do." Thus, qualifying marks for a bishop are extremely high. Indeed the Scriptures sum them up by saying that he "must be blameless" (1 Tim. 2:2).

The words used to describe the character of one of God's gifts to the church are:

vigilant, sober, of good behavior, . . . not given to wine, no striker, not greedy of filthy lucre; but patient, not a brawler, not covetous (1 Tim. 3:2-3).

For a bishop must be blameless, as the steward of God; not self-willed, not soon angry, not given to wine, no striker, not given to filthy lucre . . . sober, just, holy, temperate (Titus 1:7-8).

Without going into a word study, one can quickly see that the standard set by God for the personal life of these men is overwhelming. Is it any wonder that they are to be regarded as Christ's ascension gifts to the church?

But the standards touch other areas, for example:

---

[1] This shepherding or pastoring aspect is emphasized in verse 29, in contrast to the vivid imagery of "grievous wolves" (compare John 10:11-12).

b. There Are Family Qualifications

To be the bishop of a church family, a pastor must be able to demonstrate his spiritual leadership at home. Thus he must be, "one that ruleth well his own house, having his children in subjection with all gravity" (1 Tim. 3:4). Only those are to be "ordained" as elders who are, in this respect, "blameless, the husband of one wife, having faithful children not accused of riot or unruly" (Titus 1:6).

Now the reason for such a qualification is clearly stated. "For if a man know not how to rule his own house, how shall he take care of the church of God?" (1 Tim. 3:5). At home a man's family is his congregation. If a pastor fails the test in the spiritual upbringing of his family, he fails.

How our modern society needs such men of God, whose homes are an example of what family life should be. In a world of marriage breakdown and rebellious families, there is a tremendous need for pastors to illustrate in their own homes that it need not be so by the grace of God. Only by the gift of Christ, is it possible for such pastors to be found.

Beyond these standards, we find that:

c. There Are Community Qualifications

By this I mean that the community in which the man lives must know the life of the pastor pleases God. If a man's testimony before the world outside the church is questionable, he will be a liability and not an asset to the ministry. Thus we read, "Moreover he must have a good report of them which are without; lest he fall into reproach and the snare of the devil" (1 Tim. 3:7).

Tragic as it is to say, the good name of a local church has often been besmirched by pastors who did not qualify here. A man who does not pay his debts, or who is testy in his attitudes before the world, or whose moral character has been tainted, can bring grief and shame upon the church family. How the ascension gift of Christ is needed to safeguard against such tragedy.

For the office of a pastor we find also that:

d. There Are Maturity Qualifications

These qualifications are not often considered in our youth oriented society, but it is still true today that you cannot put an old head on young shoulders! The Scriptures state, "Not a novice, lest being lifted up with pride he fall into the condemnation of the devil" (1 Tim. 3:6). Surely, in light of this Scripture we do not help "a novice" by placing him unadvisedly in the position of overseer to the church.

We do well to remember our word study on the interchangeable term "elder" at this point. If the word does not in its metaphorical sense mean maturity in years, it certainly does mean maturity in all that deals with the spiritual welfare of the church. For a young pastor to behave as an "elder," he must have and be the gift of Christ to the church. He must also be surrounded by those who know, esteem and love him as such for the sake of the total work of the church (1 Thess. 5:12-13).

We come to a closer ministry standard now.

e. There Are Doctrinal Qualifications

In Titus 1:9 we read that the pastor must be one, "holding fast the faithful word as he hath been taught, that he may be able by sound doctrine both to exhort and to convince the gainsayers." Going together with this, 1 Tim. 2:3 tells us that he must be, "apt to teach." Peter likewise emphasizes this by exhorting, "Feed the flock of God which is among you." The pastor must be doctrinally sound, and spiritually aware of the protection needed by the flock (Acts 20:28-30).

We tend to forget how quickly doctrinal problems can arise in a local church. By the time Jude was writing his letter, spiritual wolves were already among the flocks. Thus he says:

> Beloved, when I gave all diligence to write unto you of the common salvation it was needful for me to write unto you, and exhort you that ye should earnestly contend for the faith which was once delivered unto the saints. For there are certain men crept in unawares, who were before of old ordained to this condemnation, ungodly men, turning the grace of our God into lasciviousness, and denying the only Lord God, and our Lord Jesus Christ (Jude 3-4).

Pastors are needed who can doctrinally withstand such an attack from without and from within the church.

It is obviously in this area that the teaching gift is so necessary. Nothing feeds the flock, protects the flock, and strengthens the flock of God's people like good, solid, consistent Bible teaching. Gifted men, the ascension gifts of Christ, are needed for this awesome responsibility.

Once more, the standard for the pastoral office also has congregational aspects to it. Thus we say:

f. There Are Church Qualifications

It is Peter who mainly emphasizes these in 1 Peter 5:2-3.

> Feed the flock of God which is among you, taking the oversight thereof, not by constraint, but willingly; not for filthy lucre, but of a ready mind; Neither as being lords over God's heritage, but being ensamples to the flock.

He is speaking mainly of church relationships in the pastor's work.

If he is to be a shepherd to the flock, the pastor must work willingly. His motivation must be love for the flock, and not for his paycheck. In demeanor he must be firm, loving, kind and tender; not arrogant, proud, lordly and sharp. The example of his life will be as important as his ministry.

Is there such a man abroad in the world today? Only if he is the ascension gift of Christ. This, and each qualification presented as a standard for the pastoral office, merely identifies God's chosen and gifted servants for the ministry of the gospel among the churches.

We come now to a third important understanding needed with regard to pastors as the ascension gifts of Christ. This concerns:

3. The Ministry of a Pastor

In as much as we have already dealt with the pastor's ministry in embryonic form in considering his qualifications, there is not a great need for expanded discussion here. However, it is important to recognize some practical considerations in this regard. Because of the very nature of his office:

a. The Pastor Must Study the Bible

A pastor who does not spend time studying the Bible will never be able to teach the Bible. Commenting on 2 Tim. 2:15, John Calvin wrote:

Since we ought to be satisfied with the Word of God alone, what purpose is served by hearing sermons every day, or even the office of pastors? Has not every person the opportunity of reading the Bible? But Paul assigns to teachers the duty of dividing or cutting, as if a father in giving food to his children, were dividing the bread and cutting it in small pieces (89:28).

Then in a sermon on 2 Tim. 1:13-14 he asks:

How many [ministers] does one see who have only superficially glanced at Holy Scripture and are so pitifully poorly versed in it that with every new idea they change their views (89:29)?

There can be no doubt about it that the first responsibility of a pastor is to study the Word.

Then again, the responsibility of the ministry means:

b. The Pastor Must Seek the Lord

It is impressive to note the number of times Jesus is said to have sought prayer fellowship with the Father. He breathed the very atmosphere of prayer. If the "chief Shepherd" so needed to pray, does not the under-shepherd?

Read Paul's Epistles with special regard to his prayer life. Again and again he makes mention of people for whom he is pouring out his heart to God in prayer. Surely, if such a seasoned and successful servant of God needed so to pray over his ministry, should not each pastor do so as well?

It is interesting that when the first trouble erupted in the Jerusalem Church, the apostles saw it as a diversionary tactic of Satan. Thus we read their statement of the problem and their suggested solution:

It is not reason that we should leave the word of God, and serve tables. Wherefore, brethren, look ye out among you seven men of honest report, full of the Holy Ghost and wisdom, whom we may appoint over this business. But we will give ourselves continually to prayer, and to the ministry of the word (Acts 6:2-4).

They recognized that the greatest ministry they could perform was that of prayer and the ministry of the Word of God. Can we improve upon New Testament methodology today?

Then the ministry means that:

c. The Pastor Must Preach the Word

Preaching and teaching go hand in hand here. Paul wrote to Timothy with this solemn statement:

> I charge thee therefore before God, and the Lord Jesus Christ, who shall judge the quick and the dead at his appearing and his kingdom; Preach the word; be instant in season, out of season; reprove, rebuke, exhort with all longsuffering and doctrine. For the time will come when they will not endure sound doctrine; but after their own lusts shall they heap to themselves teachers, having itching ears; and they shall turn away their ears from the truth, and shall be turned into fables (2 Tim. 4:1-4).

There is no greater need among our churches than for pastors who will preach and teach the unadulterated truths of the Bible.

John F. Walvoord goes to the heart of the question when he writes:

> While it is not necessary for a teacher to have all the qualities of a pastor, it is vital to the work of a true pastor that he teach his flock. It is obvious that a shepherd who did not feed his flock would not be worthy of the name. Likewise in the spiritual realm the first duty of a pastor is to feed his flock on the Word of God (73:170).

It is the "sermonette" which creates the "Christianette." The pastor must expound the Word, and the congregation is to "endure sound doctrine" (2 Tim. 4:3).

The great need of our day is for Bible teachers. Men with the gift of teaching, who can in turn create a love of God's Word in the lives of the hearers. Eric S. Fife is correct when he admonishes:

> The fact that teaching occurs in all three lists of gifts, and that in Ephesians the man who possesses the gift is described as pastor and teacher makes it clear that the primary function of the pastor is to teach.

> * * *

> When your church is looking for a pastor, don't look for an administrator—look for a teacher. Do not look for a crowd-pleaser—look for a teacher. Do not look for a good visitor—look for a teacher. If we get our priorities right much of the

visitation and other work can and should be done by well-taught laymen who may be elders or deacons. The pastor is not called and paid to do all the work that the church members want to avoid; his main function is to teach (12:158).

After Paul wrote Eph. 4:11 he continued to give the purpose of the pastor's ministry as being:

> For the perfecting of the saints, for the work of the ministry, for the edifying of the body of Christ: till we all come in the unity of the faith, and of the knowledge of the Son of God, unto a perfect man, unto the measure of the stature of the fulness of Christ: that we henceforth be no more children, tossed to and fro, and carried about with every wind of doctrine, by the sleight of men, and cunning craftiness, whereby they lie in wait to deceive (Eph. 4:12-14).

This can never happen except as the pastor studies the Bible, spends time alone with God in prayer, and, fresh from the presence of God, brings spiritual food for the hungry through his preaching and teaching ministry.

Beyond this the Scriptures teach that:

d. The Pastor Must Care for the Sheep

Vincent is very shrewd in observing, "No man is fit to be a pastor who cannot also teach, and the teacher needs the knowledge which pastoral experience gives" (67:390). The pastor who does not spend time with his "flock," cannot truly minister to their needs. He may indeed be powerful in his preaching and deep in his teaching, but he will also be miles apart in his ministry.

When Jesus was recommissioning Peter after the resurrection, twice He used the word *boske,* meaning specifically to nourish or provide food. "Feed my lambs" (John 21:15). "Feed my sheep" (John 21:17). This refers most obviously to the preaching and teaching ministry of the pastor.

But between both of these, our Lord used another word, *poimaine,* in relationship to the work He wanted done. "Feed my sheep" (John 21:16). This word means "to act as a shepherd." There is more to shepherding than merely feeding the sheep, and this word refers to that work. Peter is to care for the sheep as well as to teach and preach to the sheep.

Later, when Paul was instructing the elders of Ephesus with regard to their pastoral tasks he used the same word, "feed [*poimainein*] the church of God, which he hath purchased with His own blood" (Acts 20:28). This shepherding would involve protecting the church from "grievous wolves," from "perverse" doctrines, from schism and divisions (Acts 20:29-30). They were to pastor or shepherd the church in the same way that a shepherd would care for his sheep. This cost "the good Shepherd" His life (John 10:11), and "His own blood" was invested in the sheep. The undershepherd must show himself not to be "an hireling" (John 12:12) in being shepherd to God's sheep.

Such care involves tenderly pursuing those who have gone astray and bringing them back to the fold (Luke 15:3-7). It involves the reflection of Christ's Messianic ministry described in Isa. 61:1-3:

> The Spirit of the Lord God is upon me; because the Lord hath anointed me to preach good tidings unto the meek; he hath sent me to bind up the brokenhearted, to proclaim liberty to the captives, and the opening of the prison to them that are bound; to proclaim the acceptable year of the Lord, and the day of vengeance of our God; to comfort all that mourn; to appoint unto them that mourn to Zion, to give unto them beauty for ashes, the oil of joy for mourning, the garment of praise for the spirit of heaviness; that they might be called trees of righteousness, the planting of the Lord, that he might be glorified.

The pastor must in like manner care for God's sheep.

The ministry also means that:

e. The Pastor Must Administer the Church

I am not saying that the total administration of the church should rest upon his shoulders, but rather that he is responsible to see that the work of God throughout the congregation is carried out in a proper manner. There may well be others who possess the gift of administration who can greatly aid the pastor in this matter. However in the final analysis, the shepherd is responsible to God for the order, decency, and decorum with which the business of God's church is carried out.

Hollis Green is correct when he refers to the design that Christ had in mind for the church through the gifts listed in Eph. 4:11.

The purpose of these primary gifts to the church is "to equip the saints for work of service in building up of the body of Christ." This rendering of the verse is supported by the fact that there is a change of preposition in the verse from *pros* to *eis; pros* denoting the ultimate, *eis* the intermediate object. The gifts in verse 11 do not monopolize the church's ministry; their function rather is to help and direct the church so all members may perform their several ministries for the good of the whole (20:67).

In this sense, the pastor is to be the administrator of the local church.

Yet the warning sounded by John L. Benson on this matter is worthy of our attention also.

> A pastor who fancies that his first role is an administrator has not understood the New Testament emphasis upon his teaching ministry. But the preacher who does nothing for his flock except feed them had better beware lest he make them fat and useless. The flock of God need care and comfort, challenge and correction, healing and help too (2:43).

When a minister reduces his pastoral role solely to the level of an administrator, he has robbed his church and destroyed his ministry, no matter how effective he seems to be from the outside.

In bringing this chapter to a conclusion, let me refer to:

4. The Respect of a Pastor

We live in a rebellious age, and unfortunately the spirit of the age sometimes invades our churches. It is important for all of us, therefore, to give thought to the biblical teaching on the respect our Lord enjoins from His people for their pastors. Take for example 1 Thess. 5:12-13:

> And we beseech you, brethren, to know them which labor among you, and are over you in the Lord, and admonish you; and to esteem them very highly in love for their work's sake. And be at peace among yourselves.

It does not take a great exposition of this passage to explain the meaning of, "esteem them very highly." God expects His churches to appreciate His gifts to them.

Because of the sensitive nature of the subject, let me yield the closing statement on it to one who is not a pastor, Peter Wagner.

As I understand God's way of operating, there is one person and one person only who, under God, bears the chief responsibility for a local church—that person is the senior pastor. God will hold all members responsible for their church, of course, but none to the degree of the person who has accepted the top position of leadership. I believe that the attitude church members need to have toward their pastor is described in Hebrews 13:17: "Obey your leaders and follow their orders. They watch over your souls without resting, since they must give to God an account of their service. If you obey them, they will do their work gladly; if not, they will do it with sadness, and that would be of no help to you" (TEV). Not enough sermons are preached on this text. It is extremely difficult for a pastor to preach a sermon on it in his own church because his motives can so easily be misinterpreted . . . Many pastors are suffering untold personal grief and frustration because their people do not understand or practice the biblical principle of obedience to those in authority. The total effect of overlooking or neglecting this principle is that it becomes an obstruction to church growth (72:249-250).

A pastor, a bishop, an elder—call the person what you will—he is an ascension gift from Christ to His church. Stringently qualified for the spiritual office to which he is divinely called, the true pastor studies, prays, preaches, shepherds and administers the church of God. What a high and holy calling for any man. Do not be misled by those who would deprecate the office. It is written into the very Word of God as His continuing gift for this church age.

C. CHRIST GAVE SOME TEACHERS

As stated in Chapter 14, B, the last two terms mentioned in Eph. 4:11 are regarded by many Bible scholars as a single gift. For example, J. Dwight Pentecost claims concerning "pastors and teachers" that:

the words ought to be hyphenated. There is one gift: pastor-teacher. There will be two emphases in the ministry. As a pastor, he cares for the flock. He guides, guards, protects, and provides for those under his oversight. As a teacher, the emphasis is on the method by which the shepherd does his work. He guides, he guards, he protects by teaching. We teach the truths of the Word of God, so our flock will not fall prey to error. In so doing we have discharged the gift of pastor-teacher (44:173).

The reason for this view relates to the structure of the Greek in the text. Marvin Vincent, in his *Word Studies in the New Testament,* states, "The omission of the article from teachers seems to indicate that pastors and teachers are included under one class. The two belong together" (67:390). The last ascension gift, therefore, is "pastors-teachers."

We have already dealt with the first half of this hyphenated gift. What about this second part? There is something important for us to realize just now. Though all pastors by virtue of their embodiment of Christ's ascension gift are teachers, all teachers are not necessarily pastors.

Now this basic fact leads us to our first point with regard to the second half of this hyphenated gift.

1. Teaching Is a Gift of the Spirit

There are only two gifts which appear in the three major lists of *charismata* in the New Testament. One of these is prophecy and the other is teaching. When we look more closely, we discover that in 1 Cor. 12:28 the third gift mentioned is "teachers." In Rom. 12:6-8 the third gift mentioned is "teaching." And in Eph. 4:11 it is the third continuing gift mentioned, being joined to that of pastor.

Because of its rank and the number of times it is mentioned, we are led to believe that this gift is of major importance for the ongoing spiritual well-being of the church. It is foundational to the total ministry of the local church. Most probably the reason why it is joined to the office of pastor, is that this office cannot function without a teaching ministry.

The teacher differed from the prophet in the very nature of his gift. A prophet spoke the revealed will of God without any necessary reference to Scripture. What he said, he said by revelation as the mouthpiece of God. However, the teacher takes the Word of God already given and explains what God has previously made a part of Scripture. He does not give new revelation, though he may give new insights into that already written.

The word translated teacher is *didaskalos* in the Greek. It is applied to Jesus by Nicodemus in John 3:2, "Rabbi, we know that thou art a teacher [*didaskalos*] come from God." Jesus was the greatest teacher our world has ever known.

The product of the *didaskalos* was *didaskō,* "to teach or to give instruction" (71:111). In Matt. 4:23 we read, "Jesus went about all Galilee, teaching [*didaskōn*] in their synagogues." Jesus the teacher ministered to the people by means of teaching. It was an important part of His earthly labor. The teacher, therefore, walks in his ministry where Jesus walked.

We must remember that because we are referring to what the Bible calls a spiritual gift, natural abilities do not substitute for it. As John L. Benson reminds us:

> The fact that the man is spiritually gifted indicates that all of the rhetorical, pedagogical, psychological, and theological training do not make him what he is. These advantages may contribute to his usefulness, but, in addition to all of these cultural benefits, he has a God-given, divinely bestowed ability to understand and impart spiritual truth (2:43).

What we are speaking of is beyond the native talents and abilities of ordinary human powers. It is the supernatural endowment of the Spirit of God in the individual's life.

Yet the gift is so down to earth that as J. Dwight Pentecost describes it:

> This gift can be exercised in a Sunday school class or a home Bible class. When somebody comes to you and says, "I wish I knew something about the Word of God," and you take your Bible and turn to a passage and teach that hungry babe some truth from the Word of God, you are doing the work of a teacher (44:174).

The main thing to keep in mind is that no matter where or how it is exercised, teaching is a spiritual gift from God.

Let us then take a second exploratory step to discover:

2. The Function of the Teaching Gift

John F. Walvoord explains the function of the teaching gift as:

> a supernatural ability to explain and apply the truths which had been already received by the church. As such it is related to, but not identical with, illumination, which is a divinely wrought understanding of the truth (73:168).

W. A. Criswell adds that, "It is the God-given ability to explain the Holy Word, especially to newborn babes in

Christ" (7:168). When we come to the Scriptures, a number of functions are tied to the teaching gift. Among them, and primary to all others is:

a. To Unveil Christ in the Scriptures

After His resurrection, Christ met two sad, dejected, unbelieving disciples on the Emmaus Road. They were leaving Jerusalem, the center of faith and worship, and in disillusionment were discussing the events of Christ's crucifixion and seeming non-resurrection. Their discouraged conclusion was, "But we trusted that it had been He which should have redeemed Israel: and beside all this, today is the third day since these things were done" (Luke 24:21). This in spite of the fact that the women had told them the tomb was empty, and that angels had testified that He was alive.

Meanwhile Jesus had caught up with them and joined them in their journey and conversation. But when it became very obvious that they had become agnostic in their unbelief, we read, "Then he said unto them, O fools, and slow of heart to believe all that the prophets have spoken: Ought not Christ to have suffered these things, and to enter into his glory?" (Luke 24:25-26). However, the conversation did not end with Christ's shock treatment upon their melancholy discussion and skepticism, for, "beginning at Moses and all the prophets, He expounded unto them in all the scriptures the things concerning himself" (Luke 24:27). This is Jesus the teacher in action!

Notice that He gave no new truth. He dealt with the Scriptures already there and gave new insights into them concerning Himself. The word used for this is *diermēneuō*. It is composed of two words; *hermēneuō* meaning "to interpret," and the intensive *dia* meaning "through." Literally the word means "to interpret fully"[2] (69:63).

Now this gives us the teacher's method. From this word we get our English word hermeneutics, "the art or science of interpretation." Jesus took the already existing Scriptures

---

[2] This is the same word used for the gift of interpretation of tongues. When interpreting the message God had given through the tongues-speaker, the interpreter was not able to embellish the message, or add to the message, but merely to state thoroughly all that God had said through the speaker.

and systematically went through them, thoroughly interpreting them as God's revelation of Himself.

This is the first function of the teaching gift. A teacher has the ability to take the Scriptures and unveil Christ to His hearers. Indeed not only is this a God-given ability, but also a solemn responsibility. The most important purpose of teaching is to make men see our Lord in the Word of God.

A second important function of the teaching gift is:

b. To Instruct New Believers

In His final instructions to the disciples before leaving for heaven, Jesus gave what has come to be known as "the great commission." The most complete, and probably the most famous record of it is given in Matt. 28:19-20. There we read:

> Go ye therefore, and teach all nations, baptizing them in the name of the Father, and of the Son, and of the Holy Ghost: Teaching them to observe all things whatsoever I have commanded you: and, lo, I am with you always, even unto the end of the world. Amen.

Christ's last command to His disciples involved "teaching" others.

Now there are two different words used in these verses. The first one is *mathētēs,* literally "a learner." This word comes from the root *math,* indicating thought accompanied by endeavor. There is the concept of discipling in the term, since a disciple was not only a pupil, but also an adherent and hence an imitator of his teacher (68:316). Thus, those disciples won to Christ were to become imitators of Him. So successful were the early disciples in this that we read, "and the disciples were called Christians first in Antioch" (Acts 11:26). They were unmistakably like Christ!

But it is the second use of the word teach that is particularly relevant, inasmuch as it is *didaskontes.* This is the present active participle of *didaskō,* to instruct thoroughly or completely. Hence the job of the church is to go on thoroughly indoctrinating those who become learners, or disciples, "teaching them to observe all things whatsoever I have commanded you" (Matt. 28:20). How was such a work to be accomplished? By those in the church whom God had endowed with the ability to teach, through the gift of teaching from the Holy Spirit.

The first obvious teachers in the early church were the apostles. After the great evangelistic service on Pentecost when 3000 were converted and in turn were made disciples by baptismal initiation into the church, we read, "And they continued steadfastly in the apostles' doctrine and fellowship, and in breaking of bread, and in prayers" (Acts 2:42). The operative word is "doctrine," *didachē*—from *didaskō,* to teach. Literally these young converts were steadfastly continuing "in the teaching of the apostles." Thus from the very first, the function of the teaching gift was to thoroughly instruct young converts "to observe all things" Christ had commanded.

A third function of the teaching gift was:

c. To Teach at the Student's Level

Probably each of us has had the experience of listening to a teacher who was so simple his teaching seemed anemic, or conversely to one so deep that we thought we would drown. Well, from Scripture it would seem that the genius of the spiritual gift of teaching was to have the ability to meet the needs of those being instructed, at the level of their personal development. The function of the teacher, therefore, was to give only what the student could assimilate into his life.

We see this clearly illustrated in the life of Paul in relationship to the Corinthian Church. In 1 Cor. 3:1-2 he writes to them, "And I, brethren, could not speak unto you as unto spiritual, but as unto carnal, even as unto babes in Christ. I have fed you with milk, and not with meat." Milk is the proper food of babies. Indeed spiritual babes in Christ are taught by Peter to "desire the sincere milk of the Word that ye may be able to grow thereby" (1 Peter 2:2). There is nothing wrong with spiritual milk in its place.

However, what Paul is saying is not complimentary. He is referring to an abnormal situation. These people should long ago have been weaned from milk, and have learned to assimilate more substantial food related to growth and maturity. The tragedy was, they had not grown. They were still "even as babes in Christ," unable to eat meat.

Hence, we see Paul functioning with the spiritual perception which was born of the gift of teaching. He says, "I have fed you with milk and not with meat; for hitherto ye were not able to bear it, neither yet now are ye able" (1 Cor. 3:2). The teaching of Paul was adjusted to their stage of spiritual development in life. It was just right for their level of immaturity.

Later the writer to the Hebrews speaks in similar tones when he states:

> For when for the time ye ought to be teachers, ye have need that one teach you again which be the first principles of the oracles of God; and are become such as have need of milk, and not of strong meat. For every one that useth milk is unskillful in the word of righteousness: for he is a babe (Heb. 5:12-13).

The milk of the Word is needed by spiritual babes in Christ and by the spiritually immature. One with the gift of teaching knows this level intuitively, and has the competency to regulate his presentation to the ability of his hearers to digest the truths expounded.

However, with the same gift the teacher can satisfy the spiritual hunger and appetite of the mature believer. In this respect Hebrews 5:14 continues, "But strong meat belongeth to them that are of full age, even those who by reason of use have their senses exercised to discern both good and evil." The gift of teaching enables the person endowed to as readily present more difficult truth (Heb. 5:11)[3] to those able to absorb it. In this way, no matter what the development of the student's spiritual comprehension the gifted teacher can promote further learning. This is part of the function of the gift of teaching.

A fourth function fulfilled by the teachers is:

d. To Cause the Church to Grow

Immediately after the statement of the hyphenated pastor-teacher gift, Paul continues in Eph. 4:12-13:

> For the perfecting of the saints, for the work of the ministry, for the edifying of the body of Christ: Till we all come in the unity

---

[3] A comment with regard to such difficult truth being found in the writing of Paul is made by Peter in his second Epistle. There he speaks of those unable to comprehend such truths, who in their immaturity misinterpret them (2 Peter 3:15-16).

of the faith, and of the knowledge of the Son of God, unto a perfect man, unto the measure of the stature of the fulness of Christ.

Several words are used here to indicate this matter of spiritual growth.

One is the word "perfecting," found in verse 12. The original is *katarartismon,* and it means to render fit or complete. It signifies the path of progress, and implies a process leading to consummation (70:174). Thus it has the idea of moving toward full growth in one's Christian life.

Also in verse 12 there is the word "edifying." This is *oikodomēn,* composed of two parts; *oikos* meaning "a home," and *demō* meaning "to build"[4] (69:17). Literally the word denotes the act of building a physical structure, but figuratively it is used in the New Testament of promoting spiritual growth, hence edification. The function of teaching, therefore, is that of building up.

Another is the word "perfect" (v. 13), which is *teleion* in the original. In Eph. 4:13 it is applied to *andra,* a man. The import is thus, that the man is "fully grown and mature" (70:174). Once more the thought is that of growth in one's spiritual life.

Then, together these words have a standard in, "the measure of the stature of the fulness of Christ" (Eph. 4:13). The objective of growth is to be like Christ. The goal of growth is to reach the stature of Christ's spiritual fulness.

Now how does all this growing come about? It is produced by the ministry of the ascension gifts of Christ. They were given "for" this reason. The preposition "for" is *pros* in the original, which with the accusative (as is "perfecting") is used of the place to which anything tends. So the exercise of the gifts mentioned in Eph. 4:11 is meant to move the Church toward full growth and maturity.

This was the work accomplished by the teaching of the apostles and prophets in their day (Eph. 2:20). It is to be the ultimate teaching function of the evangelist, and pastor-teacher of our day. Thus, the end purpose of the teacher

---

[4] Hence the picture of the church as an *oikodomē,* building in Eph. 2:21-22, in which believers are the building materials. See also 1 Peter 2:5 for the same figure.

becomes the, "edifying [or building] of the body of Christ" (Eph. 4:12). Church growth is the goal of the teaching gift. The third point of understanding concerning this gift is:

3. The Preparation for Teaching

Because an individual possesses the gift of teaching, this does not negate the need for preparation. The fact is that the totality of life preparation affects the use of the teaching gift. It is not that preparation produces the gift, it is that it prepares it for use.

In this sense the pastor-teacher needs to fulfill the admonition of 1 Tim. 4:13-14:

> Till I come, give attendance to reading, to exhortation, to doctrine. Neglect not the gift that is in thee, which was given thee by prophecy, with the laying on of hands of the presbytery.

For a teacher to be used of God in the presentation of biblical truth, he must diligently read.

Paul himself is a great example of the way in which a true teacher seeks to prepare himself for teaching. Remember that long before he was converted, Saul sat at the feet of Gamaliel and was taught the Old Testament truths of Judaism. When God saved him, he had been a scholar in his own right. After God called him to full-time service he seems to have spent some three years in private, personal, preparation for the presentation of New Testament truths (Gal. 1:15-18).

All through his mighty ministry he emphasized the need for study. It was his habit of life. Even when he knew the time of his "departure" was "at hand," he sent word to Timothy saying, "The cloak that I left at Troas with Carpus, when thou comest, bring with thee, and the books, but especially the parchments" (2 Tim. 4:13). Paul, the teacher, was a student to the very end of his life.

Such a fact tells us that the teacher is not to use his gift as an excuse for laziness. As Eric S. Fife puts it:

> Good teaching requires hard work and lots of it. I am constantly appalled when I visit pastors in their offices. Almost always that is what they are, "offices," when they should be studies. Jowett, the great British preacher, once said, "If the study is a lounge the pulpit is an impertinence." A poor library makes for poor preaching (12:130).

The teacher must develop his gift by diligent application to "the books, but especially the parchments."

For this reason also we read the emphasis Paul placed upon Pastor Timothy's need to study. To this minister of the Church in Ephesus, he wrote, "Study to shew thyself approved unto God, a workman that needeth not to be ashamed, rightly dividing the word of truth" (2 Tim. 2:15). The gift of teaching is from God, and the study is to gain approval of God as it is used.

A "teacher" may have been an apostle or a prophet in the early church. Today the pastor must teach to fulfill his spiritual calling and gift. Beyond this are a host of uncommon believers, distinguished from their fellows by the gift of teaching. All are responsible to God for the use they make of this gift.

Don't be misled by those who believe the gift is unimportant. It is needed today as much as it ever was. May God distribute more among the churches that the winds of erroneous doctrine might not toss God's people upon the rocks of deceit.

15

THE FULFILLING SERVICE-GIFTS

INTRODUCTION

SERVICE GIFTS DIFFER from servant gifts in that the latter are personified, but the former are not. Rather, service gifts are those which enable persons who possess them to be of help to the whole church without necessarily holding any office. They are the endowed abilities of the Holy Spirit to enable the church as a whole to perform its total ministry.

What, then, are these gifts? They are the gifts of governments, ruling, ministry and faith. These are the spiritual donations which enable the recipients to function in their office, position, or job in such a way that the total church is blessed. Let us take them one by one as we seek to understand their nature and purpose.

First of all, there is:

A. THE GIFT OF GOVERNMENTS

We find this gift in 1 Cor. 12:28, where Paul records, "God hath set some in the church . . . governments . . ." Whatever the gift is, it is there by the sovereign placement of God for the good of the entire church. But what does the word mean?

In Greek the term is *kubernēseis,* from *kubernaō* meaning "to guide," and is found only here in the New Testament. The word has nautical overtones, in that it refers to the pilot who "steers" the ship (69:168). Even today, an English sailor might refer to the helmsman as "the governor." This leads Leon Morris to comment that the word, "denotes the activity of the steersman of a ship, the man who pilots his vessel through shoals and brings her safe to port" (39:179). The kindred word *kubernētēs,* meaning "shipmaster or steersman," appears in Acts 27:11 (67:260). There Paul was seeking to warn the ship's crew of impending disaster, but the centurion in charge preferred to believe "the master [*kubernētē*] and the owner of the ship."

Some versions have the marginal rendering, "wise counsels." This is based on the Septuagint usage, for example in Prov. 1:5, where the word is used to translate the actual term "wise counsels" (67:260). The one with this gift is able to benefit the church in the midst of difficult decision making. He is able to see the heart of a matter, and generally cut through the morass of foggy thought around him.

Marvin R. Vincent tells us that Ignatius used the word in a letter to Polycarp. It is a plea to Polycarp to give leadership in the midst of desperate days of church history. In part the letter states and Vincent comments:

> The occasion demands thee, as pilots [*kubernētai*] the winds." The reading is disputed, but the sense seems to be that the crisis demands Polycarp as a pilot. Lightfoot says that this is the earliest example of a simile which was afterward used largely by Christian writers—the comparison of the Church to a ship (67:260).

Polycarp was regarded by Ignatius as having the gift of "governments." In this sense W. A. Criswell defines the gift as, "the ability to guide the church through all the fortunes and vicissitudes of daily life, maintaining order and holding the congregation to its heavenly assignment" (7:175).

Discussing the word "governments," Gerherd Kittel writes:

> The reference can only be to the specific gifts which qualify a Christian to be a helmsman to his congregation, i.e., a true director of its order and therewith of its life. What was the scope of this directive activity in the time of Paul we do not know. This was a period of fluid development. The importance of the helmsman increases in a time of storm. The office of directing the congregation may well have developed especially in emergencies both within and without. The proclamation of the Word was not originally one of its tasks. The apostles, prophets and teachers saw to this . . . No society can exist without some order and direction. It is the grace of God to give gifts which equip for government. The striking point is that when in verse 29 Paul asks whether all are apostles, whether all are prophets or whether all have gifts of healing, there are no corresponding questions in respect of *antilenpseis* and *kubernesis*. There is a natural reason for this. If necessary, any

member of the congregation may step in to serve as deacon or ruler. Hence these offices, as distinct from those mentioned in verse 29, may be elective. But this does not alter the fact that for their proper discharge the charisma of God is indispensable (19:1036).

This gift refers us, therefore, to those who are possessed of a God-given ability to be "helmsmen" within the church. For this reason some translate the term by the more modern word "administration." Those who have this gift can thereby make the local church to be alive with activity. They enjoy organizing, overseeing business matters, helping staff relations, dealing with details and generally making sure the work of the local church runs smoothly.

Ted Engstrom describes the gift of administration from the life and work of Solomon. He reminds us that to give Israel a solid economic base, and to build his temple successfully, Solomon formulated well-laid plans which are spelled out in detail in 1 Kings chapters 5 through 7.

> As a part of the whole plan, Solomon devised a method to divide the land into districts for tax revenue to support the government's efforts to strengthen the nation's economy. He did not follow the pattern set forth when the land was split up along tribal lines after the Israelites first entered Canaan. The plan was so efficient that the indescribably beautiful temple was completed in record time, and it remained the spiritual center of the people for centuries. Solomon evidenced a real gift to administer the plan and make it effective to obtain a positive result (11:52).

Then, in contrast, Ted W. Engstrom continues by reminding us that:

> Because his successors could not follow Solomon's plan and maintain the nation's unity, the kingdom became fragmented into party rivalries and eventually split into the southern kingdom (Judah) and the northern (Israel). The kings who ruled after him did not have the gift to administer or organize the people consistently (11:52).

Not only does this illustrate the gift, but also the fact that not everyone has it.

The gift may belong to the pastor, but not necessarily so. Many a local church is blessed with laymen who have the gift of administration and who can relieve the pastor of many cumbersome details, allowing him to spend more time in "prayer and to the ministry of the Word"(Acts 6:4). A pastor should not, therefore, feel threatened by this involvement by members of his congregation, neither should the laymen become pompous. It is a gift and should neither produce fear, nor pride. When properly exercised, the gift glorified God in the smooth running of the local church.

The second of the service gifts under consideration is:

B. THE GIFT OF RULING

Some commentators regard this as the second half of a hyphenated gift which includes "administration." However, in the original language in which the New Testament was written, the word used has a different connotation than that of administration. Hence, I am referring to "ruling" not only as a separate, but also as a distinct gift of the Holy Spirit.

The word is *proistamenos* in Rom. 12:8. It comes from *proistēmi* which is composed of two words, *pro* meaning "before or in front of" and *histermi* meaning "to set or make to stand" (1:344, 203). It means literally, "he that is placed in front." The reference is to any position of superintendence within the local church, and no ecclesiastical office is necessarily referred to (67:158).

In Titus 3:8 the word is used in connection with the maintenance of "good works." There the term "to maintain" is *proistasthai*[1] meaning "to be forward in," or "to take the leadership in." Christians are to be out in front of the world as far as "good works" are concerned!

The reference in Rom. 12:8 is in the middle voice, which in the Greek takes the action to itself. Thus the one with this gift has that capability of "taking over," or taking the lead in a particular matter or situation. In this same sense it is used of "bishops" and "deacons" who, as fathers, are to show excellence in "ruling" or giving leadership within their own homes. The conclusion being that if a person does not show

---

[1] Present, infinitive, middle of *proistēmi,* from which also comes the word "ruling" in Rom. 12:8.

the gift of leadership within his own home, he cannot be expected to show it within the church.[2]

The word is used specifically of "elders" in 1 Tim. 5:17. There we read, "let the elders that rule[3] well be counted worthy of double honor, especially they who labor in the word and doctrine." Not only is the gift here related to the office of "elder" (pastor), but especially to that aspect of leadership having to do with preaching and teaching. Such leadership was to be doubly honored (practical honor in the form of remuneration is at least partially in view in the immediate context of verse 18) by the local church because of his spiritual benefit to all.

Commenting on 1 Tim. 5:17, John L. Benson states:

> Some churches think this calls for a man in addition to the pastor who will exercise jurisdiction and authority in the church. The Presbyterians recognize both a teaching elder and a ruling elder. We Baptists insist that both of those functions adhere to one office. That is, the pastor of the church is the elder and the bishop. The pastor and the deacons are the only officers in a New Testament church (2:44).

With this we would heartily agree.

Within the local church all members are equal, but in God's sovereign plan some have been equipped to lead, and some to follow. This fact causes C. Peter Wagner to define the gift of ruling as:

> the special ability that God gives to certain members of the Body of Christ to set goals in accordance with God's purpose for the future and to communicate these goals to others in such a way that they voluntarily and harmoniously work together to accomplish those goals for the glory of God (72:162).

This is leadership in action.

Romans 12:8 tells us that this leadership is to be done "with diligence." W. A. Criswell explains:

---

[2] See 1 Tim. 3:4-5, 12, regarding the qualifications for bishops and deacons.

[3] *Proestōtes,* the perfect active participle form of *proistēmi,* from which the gift of ruling derives in Rom. 12:8.

The Greek word *spoude* means "speed," "haste," "diligence," and finally "earnestness." The man who presides over the congregation of the Lord is to be deeply sensitive to the needs of the group and is to be diligently earnest in his response to them (7:175).

In this way no rulers will become "lords over God's heritage" (1 Peter 5:3).

The third of the four service gifts under present consideration is:

C. THE GIFT OF MINISTRY

During war years when a soldier joins the army we say of him that he has gone into "the service." By this we mean that he has gone to serve his country on the battlefields of the world. In the same fashion, when a young man is called to the ministry, people commonly say that he has gone into "full-time service." This is meant to indicate that his life vocation has now become the service of God. The same thought is contained in the gift of "ministry," for the prevailing thought is that of service.

Romans 12:7 states that if our gift is, "ministry, let us wait on our ministering." The word translated "ministry" is *diakonian* meaning "service, serving, waiting, attendance, the act of rendering friendly offices" (1:92). Marvin R. Vincent states that:

> as it is distinguished here from prophecy, exhortation, and teaching, it may refer to some more practical, and, possibly, minor form of ministry. Moule says: "Almost any work other than that of inspired utterance or miracle-working may be included in it here." So Godet: "An activity of a practical nature exerted in action, not in word" (67:157).

Thus the gifts of the Spirit reach down into the practicalities of church life.

When commenting on this verse James Denney reminds us that even practical service is spiritual in God's economy. He states that:

> although *diakonia* probably refers to such services as were material rather than spiritual: they were spiritual however (though connected only with helping the poor, or with the place

or forms of worship) because prompted by the Spirit and done in it (8:690).

So, the service of the one who has this gift is "spiritually" practical!

Interestingly enough a kindred word, *diakonos,* is used of the office of a deacon. It may well be that the gift about which we are thinking is essential to the office of deacon, though not confined to it. For example, when the apostles called the church together in Acts 6, they said, "It is not reason that we should leave the word of God, and serve tables" (Acts 6:2). The word they used for "serve" was *diakonein,* which is also related to the word "ministry" in Rom. 12:7. Then they suggested the election of seven men, "whom we may appoint over this matter" (Acts 6:3). The purpose for these men was that of *diakonoi,* "servants" or deacons.

This causes W. A. Criswell to define those with this gift as:

> men who are able to assist the pastor in his work of guiding the welfare and destiny of the congregation. Happy is the pastor who has these God-appointed and God-blessed deacons (7:175).

There is no doubt that to fulfill the office of deacon well, a man needs to be possessed of this gift. However, whether, as Criswell seems to imply, only deacons have this gift is another matter.

Since this gift relates to the totality of the practical needs of the local church, it differs from the serving gifts in that it is not necessarily person centered in the service rendered. It is a task oriented gift, with the service directed more to the institution than the individual. Therefore, it is more general in its purpose than the serving gifts, which tend to particularize their ministry to people.

Because service is such a general need, this gift usually equips its possessor with a wide range of abilities to meet those needs. For this reason, C. Peter Wagner defines the gift as:

> the special ability that God gives to certain members of the Body of Christ to identify the unmet needs involved in a task related to God's work, and to make use of available resources to meet those needs and help accomplish the desired goals (72:226).

Such people can be counted on in the most adverse circumstances and for the widest variety of service.

The fourth of these service gifts in a very real sense adds life to all of the rest. This is:

D. THE GIFT OF FAITH

It is obvious that the gift now spoken of does not refer to "saving faith." Every child of God without distinction has been made partaker of that faith, or he is not a Christian. The Bible says, "For by grace are ye saved through faith; and that not of yourselves: it is the gift of God" (Eph. 2:8). Saving faith is, therefore, common to all believers.

Having said that, there is a gift of faith which, like the other spiritual *charismata,* is the sovereign bestowal of the Holy Spirit. Therefore, not everyone had this gift of faith any more than everyone was a prophet, or a teacher, or possessed of the other gifts. Because of this, Kenneth Kinghorn of Asbury Theological Seminary gives the timely warning that, "the person who has the gift of faith should not chide others for their lack of faith. After all, not every Christian possesses this gift" (25:67). This statement, of course, once again separates the gift from "saving faith."

It would seem too that of all the gifts of the Spirit, this is the only one which is also a part of "the fruit of the Spirit." In Gal. 5:22 we read, "But the fruit of the Spirit is . . . faith." With this matter of faith, therefore, it seems that one may receive it as a gift, or have it grow in one's life as a fruit. Either way the faith is the product of the Spirit's work in the life of the individual.

Again as we read the chapters of Corinthians in which the gifts are revealed, we come to 1 Cor. 13:2. There we read this superlative, "Though I have all faith, so that I could remove mountains." Yet at the same time we are reminded that Christ said, "If ye have faith as a grain of mustard seed, ye shall say unto this mountain, Remove hence to yonder place; and it shall remove; and nothing shall be impossible unto you" (Matt. 17:20). Can it be that this gift has not to do with the amount of faith, but with the vitality of faith? Does mustard seed faith accomplish exactly the same thing as "all faith?"

J. D. Macauley suggests a solution to this problem in these words:

The Holy Spirit will give a man all the faith for which he has capacity, but when he has all that he can contain, he has no more than a grain of mustard! Our capacity is so small! But there is this about it—a mustard seed is a living thing, and it can grow and become a tree. So it is with faith. Our capacity may be small, but the faith imparted by the Holy Spirit is a living thing, and it can grow until its branches are spread abroad, giving shelter and blessing to many who otherwise would find no resting-place. How else can we explain a Francke of Germany, a Mueller of Bristol, a Hudson Taylor of China, a Moody of Chicago? The faith of these men was small, but living, and it grew and spread its branches in the forms of orphanages, world missions, Bible training institutes and other establishments which bless the world to this day (33:75).

So it is that the gift of faith opens the door to trust in a manner others never dream of. This is why G. G. Findlay describes it as "potent faith" (13:888).

We should notice the placement of this gift of faith. It comes immediately after the revelatory gifts of wisdom and knowledge. These were the apostolic and prophetic gifts upon which the church was founded (Eph. 2:20). Further, it is clearly distinguished from the sign gifts by which the message was authenticated, by virtue of its enumeration before them as a gift in its own right. We hear much today about "faith healing" and "miracles of faith" but, clearly, this is not the faith spoken of in 1 Cor. 12:9. The faith of this gift is a faith apart from whatever might have been involved in the sign gifts. It was clearly not a part of them any more than it was a part of the preceding revelatory gifts.

Yet, when we come to Rom. 12:6 we discover that the prophet could only exercise his gift to "the proportion" of the gift of faith he had. Says Marvin R. Vincent:

In classical Greek it is used as a mathematical term. It signifies, according to the proportion defined by faith . . . Those who prophesy are to interpret the divine revelation "according to the strength, clearness, fervor, and other qualities of the faith bestowed upon them; so that the character and mode of their speaking is conformed to the rules and limits which are implied in the proportion of their individual degree of faith" (67:156).

Hence, though the gift was distinct, it seems to have been intricately attached to the founding prophetic messages of the New Testament.

Commenting on Paul's statement, "let us prophesy according to the proportion of faith," James Denney states that it, "implies that the more faith one has—the more completely Christian he is—the greater the prophetic endowment will be" (8:690). Therefore, the gift of faith greatly affected the prophetic gift, though it was separate from it.

Indeed, more basic still is the thought that the gift of faith seems to be tied to our level of psychological adjustment. In Rom. 12:3 Paul states that a person rightly thinks about himself, "according as God hath dealt to every man the measure of faith." A person with the gift of faith ought, therefore, to be "well adjusted," not only in his spiritual life but also in his mental outlook. He ought to have come to spiritual terms with his self-image and his abilities in life.

The gift of faith is seen in the lives of individuals in the Bible. Abraham, for example, seems to have been possessed of something akin to this gift. In Heb. 11:17-19 we read that by faith he believed that God would raise up his son Isaac from the dead, if the lad were slain by his father in obedience to God's command. Such faith was based upon the foundational promise of the Word of God to him. Hence we read:

> By faith Abraham, when he was tried, offered up Isaac; and he that had received the promises offered up his only begotten son, of whom it was said, That in Isaac shall thy seed be called: accounting that God was able to raise him up, even from the dead; from whence also he received him in a figure (Heb. 11:17-19).

His was wondrous obedience by faith.

Obviously Elijah needed analogous faith to believe that God would use the meager supply of the widow of Zarephath to care for both of them and her son, through the three years of drought that God sent upon the land. Yet we read:

> She, and he, and her house, did eat many days. And the barrel of meal wasted not, neither did the cruse of oil fail, according to the word of the Lord, which he spake by Elijah (1 Kings 17:15-16).

His was daily living by faith.

Stephen, you will recall, was a man, "full of faith and of the Holy Ghost" (Acts 6:5)—an unbeatable combination! So great was his faith, that again within verses we read, "and Stephen, full of faith and power" (Acts 6:8). There is little doubt that here was a man possessed of this spiritual gift. His was a life witness by faith, even unto the death of martyrdom.

The gift of faith is a very practical, a very down to earth gift. Says George Shaw:

> Many a poor woman struggling against great odds and keeping a strong faith in God the meanwhile has this gift of faith. Faith does not always operate in the outward things. To maintain a quiet and abiding confidence through dark and stormy days; to rest contented and happy in days of adversity; to hold an unwavering trust in God when Providence is casting gloomy shadows across your path; to be able to say with Christ when on the cross of sacrifice, and when all is dark and mysterious about the soul, "Father, into Thy hands I commend my spirit," this is to have a gift of faith. To say with Abraham when the divine voice has called you to offer the child of your hopes and the son of promise, "The Lord will provide a lamb," this is the gift of faith. To hold steadfast an unwavering confidence in the work of Christ in an age of gross skepticism is to have a gift of faith (52:334).

I like how George Shaw describes the daily exhibition of faith in those words, for it brings faith into the very life situations which each of us meets day after day.

Such faith as is the bestowal of the Spirit's gift gives great confidence in the power of God to intervene in routine life situations. Often this is the need within our churches, as difficulties arise and the enthusiasm petrifies amongst God's people. By the gift of faith exhibited in an assured confidence in God's ability to undertake, one single man can preserve a whole church from the frigid death of unbelief.

It may well be that more is in Rev. 3:20 than any of us has ever comprehended. Think of these words, "if any man hear my voice and will open the door I will come in." Christ had been pushed out of the Laodicean Church by a self-sufficient rejection of dependence upon God (Rev. 3:17). Yet one man—"any man"—but especially one endowed with the gift of faith, could turn the tide, change the whole backslidden picture and start revival amongst the whole church! Such is the service rendered within the church by one with the gift of faith.

John Owen well says on this point that:

> where God stirreth up any one unto some great or singular work in His church, he constantly endows them with this gift of faith. So was it with Luther, whose undaunted courage and resolution in profession, or boldness in the faith, was one of the principal means of succeeding his great undertaking. And there is no more certain sign of churches being forsaken of Christ in a time of trial than if this gift be withheld from them, and pusillanimity, fearfulness, with carnal wisdom, do spring up in the room of it (42:874).

Oh, that God would write this upon the heart of every church member!

Without the gift of faith exhibited in the lives of some among us we die! Is it any wonder C. Peter Wagner honestly states, therefore, "I may not have the gift of faith, but I love to be around and support those who do" (72:159). Who among us who has faced the alternate flinty-granite of unbelieving negativism, cannot add a hearty "Amen" to that sentiment? Faith is that service gift that gives life and glorious expectancy to all the rest.

Yes, there are service gifts extant in the church today. They are the gifts of "governments," "rule," "ministry," and "faith." Do not be mistaken that the work of God can be carried on without them. They are as necessary today as when the New Testament was being written. Thank God, they are among us still!

16

THE FULFILLING SERVING-GIFTS

INTRODUCTION

WE COME NOW to a study of what may be termed "quiet" gifts. There is not a great deal of excitement generated by the mention of their names. Great charismatic conferences are not built upon the fervent seeking or exhibiting of them. George E. Gardiner analyzes the situation correctly when he writes:

> Everyone wants the gifts that will get attention! It has been my observation that no one starts a "helps movement," or a "giving movement," or a "showing mercy movement." Yet these are gifts of the Spirit just as much as were "tongues" and "healing" whose names are commonly linked with movements! (16:27).

Indeed, not only are they gifts of the Spirit, but the church cannot function properly without them.

These are serving gifts, possessed by many of God's "hidden ones" (Ps. 83:3). Their names are not emblazoned in neon lights. They are rarely mentioned when the "front men" are receiving the congratulatory acclaim for the success of the work. However, they are some of God's choicest children who, by their faithful gift-service, enable the church to function and grow.

The first of these enablements is:

A. THE GIFT OF EXHORTATION

In Rom. 12:6-8 Paul writes that whatever the gift we have received, it is to be used to perform that specific task. Thus, "he that exhorteth, on exhortation" (Rom. 12:8). Literally he is saying that the one who has the gift of exhorting is to use that gift to exhort; this is the plan of the Holy Spirit in bestowing the gift.

The Greek verb is *parakaleō*. It is made up of two parts; *para* meaning "to the side," and *kaleō* meaning "to call." Literally, the word means to call to one's side, and it has the idea of comfort or encouragement as its objective (69:60).

The noun which goes along with it is *paraklēsis*. It has a meaning akin to the verb form, to call to one's side and hence to one's aid. Encouragement is also the connotation of this word (69:60).

When Jesus was preparing His disciples for the moment of His return to heaven, He said, "It is expedient for you that I go away: for if I go not away, the Comforter[1] will not come unto you; but if I depart, I will send him unto you" (John 16:7). Here the word "Comforter" is a noun used like a verbal adjective. It is *paraklētos,* with a meaning similar to the previous words mentioned, literally "the One called alongside" with the idea of giving aid (68:208). This, of course, refers to the ministry of the Holy Spirit in our lives. He has been given to come to our aid in living the Christian life amidst every conceivable circumstance.

In 1 John 2:1 the word is used again, this time in relation to Christ. There we are told, "If any man sin, we have an advocate with the Father, Jesus Christ the righteous." The verbal adjective is used here also, illustrating for us the judicial connotation of the term. It could be used in a court of justice to denote a legal assistant, counsel for the defense, an advocate; then generally one who pleads another's cause, an intercessor or advocate (68:208).

Now let us keep in mind that we are dealing with shades of meaning in the word that is used to describe the gift of exhortation. Clearly the essence is that of comfort, encouragement, assistance and consolation. Therefore, we should expect to find those qualities exhibited in the life of one with the gift of exhortation. Do we?

One man stands out head and shoulders above all others in the Bible as exhibiting this gift. He is called Joses. Of this man we read in Acts 4:36 that he, "by the apostles was surnamed Barnabas, (which is, being interpreted, The son of consolation)." Now why did they do that? What quality or

---

[1] See also John 14:16, 26: and 15:26 for the same use of the word *paraklētos*.

gift did they see in him that his name should be changed to Barnabas? The interpretation of his new name should give us a clue. "Son of consolation" (*huios parakleseos*) is from the same root as our word "exhortation" in Rom. 12:8. He was called, "Son of exhortation," for that is what they saw in him. It was his gift.

And what a mighty ministry it enabled him to perform. Using his gift of encouragement, he took Paul under his wing shortly after he was converted. The other disciples were still fearful and skeptical about the reality of his profession (Acts 9:26).

> But Barnabas took him, and brought him to the apostles, and declared unto them how he had seen the Lord in the way, and that he had spoken to him, and how he had preached boldly at Damascus in the name of Jesus (Acts 9:27).

He fostered and encouraged the new-born Christian, Saul of Tarsus, possibly saving him from a discouragement that, humanly speaking, could have caused him to quit before he had really got started in his future ministry. This causes Leslie Flynn to comment, "Do we realize that had not Barnabas used his gift of encouragement we might be missing half of the New Testament books?" (15:88). Such was the effect of Barnabas' gift upon the one who would afterward become the mighty apostle Paul.

Later Barnabas was sent by the Jerusalem Church to the city of Antioch. His mission was to minister to the new converts coming out of a spiritual awakening that had arisen, when those scattered by the Jerusalem persecution after Stephen's martyrdom preached the gospel in Antioch. How the gift and spirit and character of the man are caught in the description of his ministry there.

> When he came, and had seen the grace of God, [he] was glad, and exhorted them all, that with purpose of heart they would cleave unto the Lord. For he was a good man, and full of the Holy Ghost and of faith: and much people was added unto the Lord (Acts 11:23-24).

Did you notice the pertinent word "exhorted?" That is the word in Rom. 12:8 and that is the gift in action. When one with the gift of exhortation uses it as God intended it to be used, others will always be blessed through the service rendered.

Later still, Barnabas and Paul were to part company in a "contention" directly attributable to Barnabas' use of his gift. On an earlier missionary journey John Mark had accompanied them as their attendant. However, due possibly to homesickness or to some other reason judged by Paul to be trifling, Mark had deserted the mission and gone home (Acts 13:13). So it was that when Barnabas determined to again take Mark along on a second missionary journey:

> Paul thought not good to take him with them, who departed from them from Pamphylia, and went not with them to the work. And the contention was so sharp between them, that they departed asunder one from the other (Acts 15:38-39).

Notice that Barnabas was so possessed of the gift of exhortation, that he was willing to part company with a dear friend and fellow missionary, rather than not exercise that gift. To Barnabas, Mark had a greater need of his company and encouragement than Paul. And so Barnabas took Mark, and sailed unto Cyprus (Acts 15:39). What Paul, who may not have had this gift, could not see in Mark at that time, Barnabas could see.

Was he right? In effect Paul later says that he was, when shortly before his execution in Rome he sent a letter to Timothy saying, "Take Mark, and bring him with thee: for he is profitable to me for the ministry" (2 Tim. 4:11). It takes one with the gift of exhortation to have such far-sighted interest in a young deserter like Mark, as to turn him into a Gospel writer and a useful servant to an aged apostle.

W. A. Criswell describes this endowment of the Spirit as, "the gift of 'encouragement,' 'strengthening' so desperately needed by so many of the members of Christ's body (7:174)." And C. Peter Wagner describes it as, "the special ability that God gives to certain members of the Body of Christ to minister words of comfort, consolation, encouragement and counsel to other members of the Body in such a way that they feel helped and healed" (72:154). There is a sense in which all of us are to be involved in the role of exhorter. In Heb. 10:24-25 we read:

And let us consider one another to provoke unto love and to good works: Not forsaking the assembling of ourselves together, as the manner of some is; but exhorting one another: and so much the more, as ye see the day approaching.

But in the final analysis, the greatest blessing comes in this connection from those sovereignly gifted by the Spirit with the charisma of *paraklēsis,* exhortation.

The second of these spiritual enablements for serving is:

B. THE GIFT OF HELPS

There is only one reference to this gift in the New Testament. However, the spirit of it is woven into the very warp and woof of the Scriptures. In 1 Cor. 12:28 we read, "And God hath set some in the church . . . helps." As a gift, the word does not appear again in any of the other lists, yet its importance is obvious.

People in our world tend to strive after the illusion of self-sufficiency. Nations want to be independent one from another. States and provinces seek sovereignty as much as possible. Individuals do not like to be indebted to others. Yet it's all a delusion, for from the global village, to the nation state, to the community person, we are all interdependent.

Nowhere is this more evident than in the church, the body of Christ. This, of course, is the whole point of 1 Cor. 12:14-27. As surely as the total physical body is dependent on the "help" of each part, so also is the church. Now this is where "the gift of helps" comes in. It was not by accident that Paul excluded it from his earlier list in 1 Cor. 12:8-10, for its significance depends upon an understanding of the inter-dependence of the members of the local church.

The word is *antilēpeis,* from *antilēpsis.* This term is composed of two parts, *anti* meaning "in exchange," or in its local sense "in front," and *lambanō* meaning "to take or to lay hold of" so as to support. Together the significance is a laying hold of, a taking instead of, and from that to help or support (69:213).

In the sense of a gift these ideas are intensified and made a part of the recipient's spiritual character and personality. He exists (or is "set") in the church to help the body function properly. This is his way of serving God. Thus C. Peter Wagner defines the gift as:

> the special ability that God gives to some members of the Body of Christ to invest the talents they have in the life and ministry of other members of the Body, thus enabling the person helped to increase the effectiveness of his or her spiritual gifts (72:224).

It is the utilitarian gift of receiving maximum satisfaction and efficiency in one's spiritual life, by helping individual members of the body to function.

Such people are not necessarily officers within the church. Indeed they may hold no formal position whatsoever. However, they are always available whatever the need might be. This caused Charles H. Spurgeon to write:

> It strikes me that they were not persons who had any official standing, but that they were only moved by the natural impulse and the divine life within them to do anything and everything which would assist either teacher, pastor, or deacon, in the work of the Lord. They were the sort of brethren who are useful anywhere, who can always stop a gap, and who are only too glad when they find that they can make themselves serviceable to the church of God in any capacity whatever (55:589).

In the same sermon, he describes these people as having "tender hearts" of sensitive concern; "quick eyes" to comprehend the situation; and the serving qualities of "a strong hand" and "a bending back." Such are those possessed of the gifts of "helps."

So important is this matter, that when Paul gave his final exhortation to the Elders of Ephesus, he said, "I have shewed you all things, how that so laboring ye ought to support the weak, and to remember the words of the Lord Jesus, how he said, It is more blessed to give than to receive" (Acts 20:35). The word "support" is *antilambanesthai,* related to "helps" and holding the idea of aid or assistance. Paul wanted these elders to realize that this matter was at the very heart of Church work.

The shining example of this gift in action in the New Testament is found in 1 Cor. 16:15-16 where Paul speaks of "the house of Stephanas . . . that they have addicted themselves to the ministry of the saints." According to G. G.

Findlay, the word "addicted" (*tassō,* to place, arrange, set, or appoint), "implies a systematic laying out of themselves for service" (13:950). And verse 16 indicates that they were involved in "manifold" labor "to the point of toil and suffering," on behalf of the church (13:950). There is no indication of office or official title in all of this. It was a ministry of helps, without which it is doubtful the church could have survived. Such an exercise of gift involved an all-out, spiritual effort and commitment in serving within the body. Old or young, rich or poor, educated or uneducated, bond or free, it mattered not; so long as this was the gift possessed, this was to be the work performed.

Is it any wonder, then, that the inimitable prince of preachers, Charles H. Spurgeon finished up his sermon on "helps" to his own congregation by saying:

> I would stir you all up to help in this work—old men, young men, and you, my sisters, and all of you, according to your gifts and experience, help. I want to make you feel, "I cannot do much, but I can help; I cannot preach, but I can help; I cannot pray in public, but I can help; I cannot give much money away, but I can help; I cannot officiate as an elder or a deacon, but I can help; I cannot shine as 'a bright particular star,' but I can help; I cannot stand alone to serve my Master, but I can help." There is a text from which an old Puritan once preached a very singular sermon. There were only two words in the text, and they were, "And Bartholomew." The reason he took the text was, that Bartholomew's name is never mentioned alone, but he is always spoken of as doing some good thing with somebody else. He is never the principal actor, but always second. Well, let this be your feeling, that if you cannot do all yourself, you will help to do what you can.
>
> Gather we not, this night, as a meeting of council, to present degrees to such disciples as through many sessions of labor have merited them? I confer upon you who have used your opportunities well, the sacred title of "Helps." Others of you shall have it when you deserve it. Go and win it. God grant that it may be your joy to wear the holy vestment of charity, fringed with humility, and to enter into heaven, praising God that he helped you to be a helper to others (55:599).

Such is the challenge of serving for those with the gift of helps. They are the unsung heroes of the church, but not the unrewarded servants of God. As surely as the exercise of every other gift brings His, "Well done," so does the quiet gift of "helps."

The third spiritual enablement for serving is:

C. THE GIFT OF MERCY

The apostle Paul, in Rom. 12:8, makes mention of this charisma in the words, "He that sheweth mercy, with cheerfulness." What a treasured gift is this, and how like the very character of God Himself! Well wrote the hymnwriter, "Streams of mercy, never ceasing, call for songs of loudest praise" (102:104). Rich indeed is the church which abounds in this gift.

The word God used to describe the gift was *eleeō*. This is the outward manifestation of pity. It not only assumes need on the part of the recipient, but also resources adequate to meet the need on the part of the exhibitor (70:60). The verb signifies a feeling of sympathy with the misery of another, especially when manifested in action (70:61).

We see the thought of such sympathy in the relationship of God to His people in Psalm 103:13, "Like as a father pitieth his children, so the Lord pitieth them that fear him." Isaiah 63:9 shows the same empathy on God's part, "In all their affliction he was afflicted, and the angel of his presence saved them: in his love and in his pity he redeemed them; and he bare them, and carried them all the days of old." When Jesus lived our lives, He exampled mercy in all that He did, so that Peter could preach about, "How God anointed Jesus of Nazareth with the Holy Ghost and with power: who went about doing good, and healing all that were oppressed of the devil; for God was with him" (Acts 10:38). The very atmosphere God breathes is that of mercy.

Because of this, in God's way of reckoning, this gift is highly prized. Matthew records the sentiments of the Master in these words:

> He that receiveth you receiveth me, and he that receiveth me receiveth him that sent me. . . . And whosoever shall give to drink unto one of these little ones a cup of cold water only in the name of a disciple, verily I say unto you, he shall in no wise lose his reward (Matt. 10:40, 42).

Not a deed of mercy shall be done without a heavenly record being kept against the day of rewards.

Near the end of His ministry, our Lord told of the day when, the sheep and goats being separated, each shall receive his eternal reward. To the sheep on His right hand, the King shall say:

> Come, ye blessed of my Father, inherit the kingdom prepared for you from the foundation of the world: For I was an hungered, and ye gave me meat: I was thirsty, and ye gave me drink: I was a stranger, and ye took me in: Naked, and ye clothed me: I was sick, and ye visited me: I was in prison, and ye came unto me. Then shall the righteous answer him, saying, Lord, when saw we thee an hungered, and fed thee? or thirsty, and gave thee drink? When saw we thee a stranger, and took thee in? or naked, and clothed thee? Or when saw we thee sick, or in prison, and came unto thee? And the King shall answer and say unto them, Verily I say unto you, inasmuch as ye have done it unto one of the least of these my brethren, ye have done it unto me (Matt. 25:34-40).

When the gift of showing mercy is rewarded, the Savior will have a personal interest in all those so honored.

Defining this gift one writer states, "The gift of mercy is the gift to sympathize with and to suffer alongside those who fall into grievous affliction" (7:173). Another author adds:

> Every Christian is expected to be merciful. This is a role that reflects the fruit of the Spirit. But those with the gift of mercy make compassion and kindness their life-style. They do not simply react to emergencies, as every Christian is supposed to do. They continually seek opportunities to show pity for the miserable (72:223).

No wonder God so highly prizes this gift among His people.

Interestingly enough, when Rom. 12:8 tells how the gift of mercy is to be exercised, it says simply, "with cheerfulness." The word is *hilaroteti*—a word which almost translates itself by its very pronunciation (hilarity). Only found here in the New Testament, the term refers to an attitude of mind and signifies joyfulness and thus cheerfulness (68:184). The opportunity to minister to one in need exhilarates the person with this gift.

Marvin R. Vincent comments on the word "cheerfulness" that it refers to:

> the joyful eagerness, the amiable grace, the affability going the length of gaiety, which make the visitor a sunbeam penetrating into the sick-chamber, and to the heart of the afflicted (67:158).

James Denney adds to this the further thought that:

> A person of a grudging or despondent mood has not the endowment for showing mercy. He who is to visit the poor, the sick, the sorrowful, will be marked out by God for His special ministry by this endowment of brightness and good cheer (8:691).

Those with the gift of mercy can maintain a mental attitude of cheerfulness when others cannot. They are so equipped by the nature of their gift.

Of course, there is a time when one possessed of this gift will, "weep with them that weep" (Rom. 12:15). W. A. Criswell tells the story of a little girl who came home from school and told her mother about her playmate whose mother had died and who was so sad. The mother asked her child, "And what did you say, dear?" The child replied: "I did not say anything. I just went over to her desk, sat down by her side, and cried with her." (7:174). Such is the gift of mercy exhibited at the right time, in the right place, and in the right manner.

Those who have ever visited First Baptist Church of Hammond, Indiana, where Dr. Jack Hyles is pastor know that his congregation shows this gift in organized action in an unusual proportion. Their outreach of loving sympathy encompasses large ministries to the blind, the deaf, the "educable slows," the "skid row" transient, the ghetto children, the physically handicapped, as well as a cross-section of upper society. No wonder they have been called, "the church with a heart," for the gift of mercy is seen in operation at every level of their ministry.

However, although there are isolated examples of the organized gift of mercy, as the one above, usually this is the personal serving gift of individual believers. Often times the deeds of mercy are done, and no one but the recipient knows anything about it. It is another quiet, unassuming gift without which the church cannot fulfill its calling. But, as with secret prayer, it is true of those using their gift of mercy, "Thy Father which seeth in secret shall reward thee openly" (Matt. 6:6).

There remains only one more enablement for serving, that is:

D. THE GIFT OF GIVING

The Scriptures offer much help on the subject of giving. As far back as Deut. 16:16-17 there is a commandment to the man of Israel to appear before the Lord three times each year. In coming, the passage states, "they shall not appear before the Lord empty: Every man shall give as he is able, according to the blessing of the Lord thy God which he hath given thee." It was important to God that the Israelites not only learn to worship, but to give.

Later in the Book of Proverbs, the principle was enunciated in these words:

> There is that scattereth, and yet increaseth; and there is that withholdeth more than is meet, but it tendeth to poverty. The liberal soul shall be made fat: and he that watereth shall be watered also himself (Proverbs 11:24-25).

Giving now was taught to have God's blessing attached to it.

As we come into the New Testament, the law of the Old becomes the gift of the New. Hence, when enumerating the Romans' lists of *charismata,* Paul writes, "He that giveth, let him do it with simplicity" (Rom. 12:8). Giving is finally introduced as a "grace gift" of the Spirit of God.

The word "giveth" is *metadidous,* from *metadidōmai.* There are two parts to the word; *didōmi* meaning "to give," and the preposition *meta* meaning "with." Together the word signifies to give a share of, or to apportion as distinct from straight giving (69:149).

In turn this sharing is to be done in "simplicity," *haplotēti.* This term denotes sincerity or unaffectedness. It derives from *haplous* meaning "single or simple," as contrasted to *diplous* meaning "double." In other words, the gift of giving is to be exercised in a different fashion from that of the Pharisees. They had a "double" reason, one part of which was to "be seen" of men. Thus Jesus teaches us:

> But when thou doest alms, let not thy left hand know what thy right hand doeth: That thine alms may be in secret: and thy Father which seeth in secret himself shall reward thee openly (Matt. 6:3-4).

In contrast to the double standard of the Pharisees, the gift of giving is to be done with singularity of purpose, or with "simplicity."

Commenting on this word, James Denney says:

> It is not exactly "liberality," though in these passages it approaches that sense: it is the quality of a mind which has no *arrière-pensée*[2] in what it does; when it gives, it does so because it sees and feels the need, and for no other reason; this is the sort of mind which is liberal, and God assigns a man the function of *metadidonai* when He bestows this mind on him by His Spirit (8:691).

Such "simplicity" is a part of this grace-gift of the Holy Spirit. Without it giving is a chore, and may even be spiritual duplicity!

Perhaps an illustration of this may be seen in the mental set of Ananias and Sapphira. They had watched as Barnabas, "having land, sold it, and brought the money, and laid it at the apostles' feet" (Acts 4:37). Apparently he had the gift of giving, and decided to share with the church the wealth realized from his land sale. Obviously such a gesture raised the stature of this good man in the eyes of the people,[3] so Ananias and Sapphira thought they too would try such a gesture.

However, their mental attitude towards giving was not conditioned by the gift of giving. Therefore, when they too sold land and brought the gift they did it with a *diplous* (double) mind-set. They wanted to keep the money for themselves, but they also wanted to give a part making the gesture look more generous than it really was. Hence while they said that they were giving everything, their "duplicity" in giving caused them to keep back part for themselves.

---

[2] Literally "back thoughts," the French term refers to hidden intentions or motives, which would denote hypocrisy in the action.

[3] I am sure Barnabas did not contemplate people's admiration of him ahead of time, and use it as a factor in his decision to give. However, as a natural by-product of the deed, his socio-spiritual standing would rise.

Such giving was not motivated by the gift of the Holy Spirit. Rather it was the direct result of a Satanically filled heart. Thus Peter confronted Ananias saying:

> Ananias, why hath Satan filled thine heart to lie to the Holy Ghost, and to keep back part of the price of the land? Whiles it remained, was it not thine own? and after it was sold, was it not in thine own power? why hast thou conceived this thing in thine heart? thou hast not lied unto men, but unto God (Acts 5:3-4).

A man may fake the gift of giving, but it will be a sin against the Holy Spirit. Hence God's immediate judgment fell upon both husband and wife "within the space of three hours."

Well, are there illustrations in the New Testament of giving "with simplicity?" Oh yes, there are a number. For example, it would seem that such giving was a natural part of the Jerusalem life of the infant New Testament Church. In Acts 2:44-45 we read, "And all that believed were together, and had all things common; and sold their possessions and goods, and parted them to all men, as every man had need." There was no coercion in this. Not one word of instruction seems to have been given advocating it. There were those in need, and these young Christians responded with singleness of heart to meet that need through the grace of giving. Apparently the gift of giving was in operation in the earliest days of the church.

Later the gift was very evident in Macedonia. Lest we think that the gift of giving is the prerogative of the rich, let us put in perspective the setting in 2 Cor. 8:1-2. Paul is using the Macedonian believers as an illustration of the grace of giving. Hence he asks us to consider:

> the grace of God bestowed on the churches of Macedonia; how that in a great trial of affliction the abundance of their joy and their deep poverty abounded unto the riches of their liberality (2 Cor. 8:1-2).

What they did, they did by the grace of God (remember we are talking about a "grace-gift," charisma, in this matter of giving), out of "deep poverty." They were not a "rich man's club;" they were a congregation of poverty stricken believers in Christ.

Now it is in this setting that we read of their exercise of the gift of giving. Verses 3-4 state:

For to their power, I bear record, yea, and beyond their power they were willing of themselves; praying us with much entreaty that we would receive the gift, and take upon us the fellowship of the ministering to the saints (2 Cor. 8:3-4).

To the limits of their human capabilities, and beyond, they gave. This was "the riches of their liberality" (*haplotētos,* simplicity), and their singularity of mind-set for this was created when they, "first give their own selves to the Lord, and unto us by the will of God" (2 Cor. 8:5). When first of all the totality of their beings was given,[4] then their "simplicity" (liberality) burst forth also. This is the methodology set forth in Rom. 12:8. This is the gift of giving at its peak of fulfillment.

Because of such examples of the gift of giving in Scripture, C. Peter Wagner defines the gift as, "the special ability God gives to certain members of the Body of Christ to contribute their material resources to the work of the Lord with liberality and cheerfulness" (72:96). When W. A. Criswell defines it, he does so with reference to the "simplicity" as well as the giving, and states, "This gift refers to a material ministry manifesting the love of Christ, a giving, not by sentiment or by emotions, but by the wisdom of the Spirit of God" (7:174). Combined, these explanations probably come as close to an interpretation as a definition could possibly come, in setting forth the nature of the spiritual gift. In the final analysis, however, the definition that really counts must be the example of the real-life individual biblically serving God by means of his gift.

Such a definition is seen in the life of John Wesley. During his lifetime he lived in voluntary poverty. When he died, he left an estate of two silver spoons and a well-worn frock coat. However, during his lifetime Wesley is reported to have given $150,000.00 to the Lord (37:126). This man set forth the gift of giving in the service of his life.

George Mueller of Bristol, England, sustained the work of several orphanages by prayer and faith alone. He once said, "It pleased the Lord to give me something like a gift of faith,

---

[4] In the Greek, "gave" in 2 Cor. 8:5 is *edōkan,* first aorist, indicative, active of *didō mi,* "to give;" the same word as is used in Rom. 12:8 for the gift of giving.

so that unconditionally I could ask and look for an answer" (7:176). When he died his total personal estate was $850.00, but when his books were audited after his death, it was discovered that he had given a total of $180,000.00 to the Lord's work. The entry of this is most instructive. It is identified simply as from "a servant of the Lord Jesus, who, constrained by the love of Christ, seeks to lay up treasure in heaven" (37:127). Mueller was evidently possessed of the gift of giving.

Another more modern example of the gift in action might be R. G. Le Tourneau. To him the question was "not how much of my money I give to God, but rather how much of God's money I keep" (31:280). In answer to this, Le Tourneau gave 90% of his business to the Lord by way of a Christian foundation, and then tithed 90% of the part he kept for himself. Surely this was the gift of giving.

A contemporary example of giving because of the constraint of this gift is seen in the life of Stanley Tam. He owns, or should I say rather, owned a silver business in Lima, Ohio. He literally made God his senior partner by legally turning 51% of his business over to his Christian foundation. Over the years this has been rasied to 100%, a move that more than amply demonstrates the gift of giving (72:95).

For the ultimate definition of this gift, however, we must reach back into the Gospels. There we read of a day when, "Jesus sat over against the treasury, and beheld how the people cast money into the treasury: and many that were rich cast in much" (Mark 12:41). As He watched, a widow came along holding all her earthly riches in her hand. She only had "two mites, which make a farthing," but she gave it wholeheartedly to God's work. With perfect understanding of her heart, her poverty, and her gift, Jesus commended this giving to His disciples, saying:

> Verily I say unto you, that this poor widow hath cast more in, than all they which have cast into the treasury: For all they did cast in of their abundance; but she of her want did cast in all that she had, even all her living (Mark 12:43-44).

Such a quality of giving is the greatest joy of one who has the gift of giving. As J. Dwight Pentecost remarks, "Spiritual giving is not related to your bank account; it is related to the supervision of the Holy Spirit over you and your bank account. That is why it is called a spiritual gift" (44:174).

Of course, it goes without saying that everyone does not have this gift. Larry Coy tells the story of a man who could not decide what his true gift really was. He couldn't decide between giving and serving. He decided to give himself to giving. His testimony in two months was, "I gave the Lord all my money and He took it!" (78:8). Needless to say his joy was quenched quickly. But the joy of one who had the gift of giving would not be quenched. Rather he would be exhilarated, because God's receiving of his gift would have been the fulfillment of his heart's purpose (2 Cor. 9:7).

Serving gifts: the gifts of exhortation, of helps, of mercy, and of giving. In general, they represent the unassuming *charismata* of the Holy Spirit. While they are found modestly at work behind the scenes, they are of utmost importance to the work of the Lord. Of none of them can the church say, "I have no need of thee" (1 Cor. 12:21). Rather, unless each member possessing them exercises these gifts to their fullest extent, the whole church suffers loss. "Having then gifts differing according to the grace that is given to us" (Rom. 12:6), let us use them to God's glory, the church's good, and our own spiritual fulfillment.

CONCLUSION

17

A MORE EXCELLENT WAY TO DISPEL MYTHS

GOD'S GREATEST exposition on the meaning of love is given incidentally to His greatest concentration of teaching on the gifts of the Spirit. First Corinthians 13:1-3 is set between the two earliest chapters dealing with the gifts in the New Testament and is presented as a better way to develop body life within the church. It was Paul's antidote, written under inspiration of the Holy Spirit, for the charismatic confusion of his day.

These Corinthian believers were mistaken about the gifts. Pride and arrogance had set in as a result of not understanding the nature and biblical reason for their bestowal. The more flamboyant gifts were being elevated to a position exactly the opposite of God's design. Chaos had descended upon their services and devotion was being smothered by self-adulation.

So it is that in closing chapter 12 of 1 Corinthians, Paul states that there is a superior way of conducting church affairs. This "more excellent way" is the subject of chapter 13 and the background against which he is able to present the exhortations of chapter 14. It is the explanation necessary to dispel the myths causing the church, then and now, to plunge into God dishonoring disorientation. Hence, people deceived by current charismatic doctrine, need this better way as a foundation for a more biblical gift theology.

It is the way of love—*agapē*. What a word is this! The Holy Spirit could have moved Paul to use the word *philanthrōpia,* which denotes tender affection, love for mankind and kindness, but He did not. *Agapē* is the highest form of love, used to state the character of God when we read twice over, "God is love" (1 John 4:8, 16). It describes the attitude of the eternal Father to His Son as expressed by Christ in John 17:26, "And I have declared unto them thy name, and will declare it: that the love wherewith thou hast loved me may be in them, and I in them." It is used in John 3:16 to express God's concern for lost humanity, "for God so loved the world, that he gave his only begotten Son, that whosoever believeth in him should not perish, but have everlasting life." Then it is used to convey His will to His children concerning their disposition one to another in the words, "A new commandment I give unto you, That ye love one another; as I have loved you, that ye also love one another" (John 13:34).

In this latter sense, the word *agapē* is used throughout 1 Corinthians chapter 13. Hogg and Vine state that this:

> love can be known only from the actions it prompts. . . . Christian love, whether exercised toward the brethren, or toward men generally, is not an impulse from the feelings, it does not always run with the natural inclinations, or does it spend itself only upon those for whom some affinity is discovered. Love seeks the welfare of all (70:21).

And this is the contrasting point of love in 1 Corinthians chapter 13 as against the Corinthians' use of the gifts of the Holy Spirit, especially tongues, in 1 Corinthians chapters 12 and 14.

Notice that Paul begins by stating that:

A. TERMS NEED LOVE FOR PROFIT

No matter with what gifts a person or a church may have been blessed, the work of God cannot be accomplished without love. Love is indispensable!

1. Love Is Indispensable to Language

Note it well in 1 Cor. 13:1, "Though I speak with the tongues of men and of angels, and have not charity, I am become as sounding brass, or a tinkling cymbal." Whether the language is ordinarily or supernaturally produced, it matters not. Without love it becomes merely a senseless noise without any real communication at its heart. Speech, of whatever sort it is, signifies nothing without love.

Henry Drummond illustrates this well in reference to David Livingstone. He writes:

> In the heart of Africa, among the great lakes, I have come across black men and women who remembered the only white

man they ever saw before—David Livingstone; and as you cross his footsteps in that dark continent, men's faces light up as they speak of the kind doctor who passed there years ago. They could not understand him; but they felt the love that beat in his heart. They knew that it was love, although he spoke no word (10:21).

Love is indispensable to the gift of tongues.

2. Love Is Indispensable to Prophecy

What a marvelous gift this was. It was the greatest of the gifts. But notice, "Though I have the gift of prophecy . . . and have not charity, I am nothing" (1 Cor. 13:2). Remember, Paul would say in 1 Cor. 14:1, "Desire spiritual gifts, but rather that ye may prophesy." But without love, prophecy had no edification. Love was indispensable to prophecy.

3. Love Is Indispensable to Wisdom

"And though I have the gift . . . [to] understand all mysteries . . . and have not charity, I am nothing" (1 Cor. 13:2). Can you possibly imagine what a gift that must have been, to be able to plunge into the depths of the mysteries of God and understand them? This miraculous ability, which was used to explain those mysteries to God's church, was a gift of the Holy Spirit.

O the depth of the riches of the wisdom and knowledge of God! how unsearchable are his judgments, and his ways past finding out! For who hath known the mind of the Lord? or who hath been his counsellor? Or who hath first given to him, and it shall be recompensed unto him again? For of him, and through him, and to him, are all things: to whom be glory for ever (Rom. 11:33-36).

To know and explain this was the gift of wisdom. Yet without love, the person with that gift was worthless. Love is indispensable to wisdom.

4. Love is Indispensable to Knowledge

This was another supernatural endowment of the Holy Spirit. But Paul says, "Though I have the gift of . . . all knowledge . . . and have not charity, I am nothing" (1 Cor. 13:2). Being able to have a mental and spiritual grasp of the totality of revelation would add absolutely nothing to a person's value, if it was devoid of love. Love is indispensable to the gift of knowledge.

5. Love Is Indispensable to Faith

"Though I have all faith, so that I could remove mountains, and have not charity, I am nothing" (1 Cor. 13:2). This is miracle-working faith. The force of the original is that by it the person can remove mountain after mountain. It is the faith that multiplies Matt. 17:20. But while men may applaud and heap acclaim on the miracle worker, God sees the missing ingredient. Without love, the gift of "all" faith adds up to a life which is one big zero. Love is indispensable to the gift of faith.

6. Love Is Indispensable to Giving

"Though I bestow all my goods . . . and have not charity, it profiteth me nothing" (1 Cor. 13:3). Take everything you have, all your earthly possessions and give them away in the exercise of your gift of giving and without love you are without reward. Remember, Jesus had said, "Whosoever shall give to drink unto one of these little ones a cup of cold water only in the name of a disciple, verily I say unto you, he shall in no wise lose his reward" (Matt. 10:42). But without love the greatest philanthropic gestures are profitless.

W. A. Criswell points out that:

> Paul does not say that philanthropy in itself profits nothing, even though it is unaccompanied with love. A bequest of a million dollars will profit an institution whether bequeathed in anger to rob a hated son, or given in vainglory or ostentation. Philanthropy that blesses a good cause can be used as a selfish instrument to minister to one's hope to be known as a generous soul, or to advertise one's affluence, or to buy one's way into heaven, or to uphold one's image in a business community. But without love, the philanthropy profits the giver nothing (7:230).

Be as magnanimous as you possibly can and at the bottom of the judgment ledger will be "No reward." Love is indispensable to the gift of giving.

7. Love Is Indispensable to the Gift of Mercy

Read it again, for this is important, "Though I bestow all my goods to feed the poor . . . and have not charity, it profiteth me nothing" (1 Cor. 13:3). The word "bestow" has the picture of a mother putting morsels of food in the mouth of her young (68:121). It means to feed out in morsels, to dole out adequate to the need of the hour (67:263). Now, in the gift of mercy such a concern for the poor and needy is greatly evident. But if the great motivating force is not love, it is all of no account in God's eyes.

W. Graham Scroggie believed that Paul was being almost satirical in such a supposition as this. He wrote:

> It may seem incredible that sacrifices such as these would or could be made by a loveless person, and yet, that is what the passage supposes, and not without some ground. Dean Stanley has said: "Who that ever witnessed the almsgiving in a Catholic monastery, or in the Court of a Spanish or Sicilian Bishop's or Archbishop's palace, where immense revenues are syringed away in farthings to hordes of beggars, but must feel the force of the apostle's half satirical, 'If I bestow all my goods?' " (51:29).

Love is indispensable to the real exercise of the gift of mercy.

8. Love Is Indispensable to Serving

Jesus once said, "Greater love hath no man than this, that a man lay down his life for his friends" (John 15:13). But such laying down of one's life is motivated by love. What if that love is missing? What if it is mere duty, or demonstration? Then, "though I give my body to be burned, and have not charity, it profiteth me nothing" (1 Cor. 13:3).

W. Graham Scroggie remarks on this matter that:

> It is on record that an Indian, a Buddhist in the time of Augustus, burnt himself. His tomb at Athens may have been seen by the Apostle Paul, with this inscription: "Zarmochegas, the Indian from Bargosa, according to the ancient customs of India, made himself immortal, and lies here" (51:30).

But Paul's point is that a person can serve his fellowman unto the death, to martyrdom, yet there will be no eternal profit in it. He gains nothing. Love is indispensable to the gift of serving.

The fact is that whatever the gift spoken of, without love, it is useless.

What, then, is life without love? The apostle's fivefold "if" and fourfold "all" create such a person as never lived, one who has matchless eloquence, profound insight, wide knowledge, tremendous faith, the will to utmost sacrifice, yet, he says, though all of these qualities were found in a single person, if he were without love, what he did would profit him nothing, and he himself would be nothing. In the sight of God all gifts without love are worthless, but love, even where there are no gifts, is everything (51:30).

Love is the ultimate grace. All of our abilities are saved from hollowness and hypocrisy by love. It is the gift of gifts, without which none of the rest avail anything within the church. Love is indispensable! No wonder it is a "more excellent way."

In the second place Paul explains this better way, saying that:

B. TEMPERAMENT NEEDS LOVE
FOR DEVELOPMENT

We read this description in 1 Cor. 13:4-7:

Charity suffereth long, and is kind; charity envieth not; charity vaunteth not itself, is not puffed up, doth not behave itself unseemly, seeketh not her own, is not easily provoked, thinketh no evil; rejoiceth not in iniquity, but rejoiceth in the truth; beareth all things, believeth all things, hopeth all things, endureth all things.

This is not merely an isolated description of love, but an overwhelming contrast to Corinthian life. W. Graham Scroggie comments:

Almost all the instructions of the New Testament are suggested by some occasion, and are adapted to it. We have in this chapter, for instance, not a methodical dissertation on Christian love, but an exhibition of this grace as contrasted with extraordinary gifts which the Corinthians inordinately valued. Those traits of love are, therefore, adduced which stood opposed to the temper which the Corinthians exhibited in the use of their gifts. They were impatient, discontented, envious, inflated, selfish, indecorous, suspicious, resentful, censorious, and these things are all and always contrary to love (51:36).

How then, is love defined in this passage?

First of all we are told that:

1. Love Suffereth Long and Is Kind

The first is love's passive quality, and the second is love's active quality. Love overcomes the passions of life that make us act rashly, to move hastily. It is not given to emotional outbursts. In the face of wrongs it is quiet and passive. Complimenting this, the kindness of love is actively patient towards injurious or provoking persons. It exhibits a useful, gracious, gentle behavior in all things. A loving person will therefore render gracious well-disposed service to others, in spite of wrongs suffered.

Frederick Dale Bruner points out that 1 Corinthians 13 can only be rightly interpreted in the context of the spiritual problems abundant in the Corinthian Church.

> For example, Paul's first positive definition of Christian love is *makrothumei* (v. 4), i.e., Christian love is not so much emotional, passionate, or fiery (*thumos*) as it is the "making broad," the stretching out, the extension of "fire" (*makrothumos*). This "long-suffering" should be compared with the superscripture of the twelfth chapter where the emotionalism of heathendom is contrasted with the sober confession of the church (12:2-3). Paul would not wish for it to appear that superior Christian devotion were necessarily identical with ardent Christian expression—either vertically, toward God (12:2-3), or horizontally, toward men (13:4). Paul sees the essence of the Holy Spirit in the simple word for Christ (12:3), he sees the higher gifts of the Spirit in the cooler words of wisdom and knowledge (12:8, 28), and he sees the major characteristic of Christian love not so much in the expression as in the extension of emotion, the drawing out, taming, literally the "lengthening" (*makro-*) of emotion. In English this attribute is called patience. Each description of love in 1 Corinthians 13, when placed against the background of "Corinthianism," can be comparably highlighted (4:295).

Thus this and each quality of love has a bearing upon our attitude toward and use of the gifts of the Spirit.

Now in order to define even more closely this contrast of love for the Corinthian believers, Paul makes a number of negative statements. In order they are:

2. Love Does Not Envy

Envy can be directed towards persons. It arises from a desire for excellencies manifested in others. As W. Graham Scroggie says, "Envy was the cause of the first murder in human history, and it is the last vice to be eradicated out of the human heart" (51:39). This was the characteristic shown by the Corinthians. Ill-will rather than admiring love was the fashion of their lives. They needed a better way!

The next negative states that:

3. Love Is Not Boastful

It "vaunteth not itself." Moffatt translates this "makes no parade" (96). To play the braggard, be boastful and to show oneself off is the antithesis of love. Yet among the believers was an ostentatious display of spiritual gifts.

Everyone especially wanted to display an ability for "tongues." They wanted the applause of men, as much as the commendation of God. Like the frog in Aesop's fable, which tried to blow itself up into the size of a cow, these tried to extend the least gifts into the most important. They needed the deflation of love.

Another negative tells us that:

4. Love Is Not Arrogant

It is not "puffed up." The word is from *phusa* meaning bellows, thus literally to puff out like a pair of bellows. The connotation is that of presumptuous self-satisfaction and pride which is contemptuous of others. This inflated vanity is the opposite of love. Frederick Dale Bruner remarks:

> It is interesting to observe, for example, that the spiritual pride or inflated sense of one's own spiritual experience ("puffed up," *phusioun*) which Paul saw as the peculiar affliction of the Corinthian higher-life Christians (cf. 4:6, 18, 19; 8;1) appears in its negative in this passage: "love is . . . not *phusioutai*" (v. 4). Paul's description of love in chapter thirteen, then, is not simply poetry; it is a concrete apostolic application of truth to elements of a church in need of learning what being Christian really and not spectacularly meant (4:296).

W. Graham Scroggie tells the following story about Dr. Cairns who was the head of the Theological College in

Edinburgh. He was offered the Principalship of the University there, but declined it, preferring to serve his church in a humbler way. On public occasions, he was accustomed to stand back and let others pass him, saying, "You first, I follow" (51:41). Such is the attitude of love. However, for the Corinthians the order of the day was, "Me first." They needed to have defined for them "a more excellent way."

Following this, a negative says that:

5. Love Is Not Unseemly

To "behave unseemly" comes from an old verb *aschēmōn,* meaning "not decent." Love is not devoid of moral decency. However, according to 1 Cor. 5:1-7, this gifted congregation was and because of it they were "puffed up."

Then again, in a more common usage, the word refers to good taste, to politeness and ordinary courtesy. Of Robert Burns, the ploughman-poet, Carlisle said there was no truer gentleman in all of Europe. But the word "gentleman" simply means a gentle man, one who does all with consideration and understanding. One might say he lives by the rule of love, for love is never disorderly, or indecorous.

How unlike the Corinthian congregation who must be told, "Let all things be done decently and in order" (1 Cor. 14:40). Their services were a shame to their profession. They needed a superior standard.

Then a negative definition states that:

6. Love Is Not Selfish

It "seeketh not her own." Love is not confined to self interest, rather it is unselfish in its exhibition of life. The good of others is its standard of practice. There is no overbearing demand for personal rights in love.

The prophet of old said, "Seeketh thou great things for thyself? seek them not" (Jer. 45:5). Love has no trouble in following this command. Why? Because love has already yielded itself to God for His glory.

But the glory of the Corinthians was in themselves. Each one must have his personal boast and position and special gift. They had not learned the meaning of love which lives for others. Their need was to "follow after charity" (1 Cor. 14:1).

This next negative tells us that:

7. Love Is Not Irritable

It "is not easily provoked." This is the provocation that comes from not getting one's own way. It is that temper which is incessantly angered to find the world at cross purposes with itself. Scroggie comments on this, "It is generally the self-centered people who are touchy and easily exasperated" (51:43).

Now such irritability and love are never companions. This kind of bad temper and love are never wed together. Of such dispositions Henry Drummond wrote:

> No form of vice, not worldliness, not greed of gold, not drunkenness itself, does more to unchristianize society than evil temper. For embittering life, for breaking up communities, for destroying the most sacred relationships, for devastating homes, for withering up men and women, for taking the bloom of childhood, in short, for sheer gratuitous misery-producing power this influence stands alone (10:35).

Such were the Corinthians. Like hostile children they had divided themselves into different camps (1 Cor. 1:12), and there was "strife" among them (1 Cor. 3:3). The antidote for this was for them to learn to love. They needed to rectify their relationships by love. Their need was the way of love.

Negatively, we are further told that:

8. Love Is Not Vindictive

So it "thinketh no evil." The word is from an old verb meaning to count up. It has the idea of taking account of wrongs as though in a ledger or notebook. Thus one translation has it that love "keeps no score of wrongs" (98).

Scroggie uses David as his example in this, saying:

> It is tragic to find David on his dying-bed recalling the wrongs that Joab had done him, and hearing again the curses of Shimei showered upon him as he fled from Jerusalem. He had all these things written down in his account books; but love does not keep such records (51:44).

Like David, these Corinthian believers had not learned the Godly grace of forgiving and forgetting. To them Paul must write, "In malice be ye children" (1 Cor. 14:20). They needed to learn that love which is generous in its forgetfulness.

The last negative definition states:

9. Love Is Not Malevolent

Love "rejoiceth not in iniquity." It never rejoices in the triumph of evil. G. G. Findlay says, "To 'rejoice at iniquity,' when seeing it in others, is a sign of deep debasement" (Rom. 1:32) (13:899). Love doesn't do that.

The greatest indictment of those wicked people whom God "gave up" in Romans chapter one, comes in verse 32. After the catalog of their iniquitous behavior, Paul writes, "Who knowing the judgment of God, that they which commit such things are worthy of death, not only do the same, but have pleasure in them that do them" (Rom. 1:32). They were rejoicing not only in their own iniquity, but vicariously in the wickedness of others.

The Corinthian believers needed to learn this truth. They needed to learn it in family life, at the communion table, and in the discipline of individuals within the church. They needed to be rid of malignant joy; that which comes from the triumph of evil in another person's life (1 Cor. 5:2). The only way to do so was the better way of love.

Now all of these negatives describe the love that "suffereth long and is kind." Unless these things are stripped from our very personalities, we cannot love as this passage describes love. Thus, Paul is as much telling these Corinthians of what they must divest themselves, as what they must possess in their church life.

But not only does love suffer long and remain kind, for we read:

10. Love Rejoices in Truth

This is the positive aspect of love's joy, as opposed to that which joys in iniquity. The word is a compound, composed of *sun* meaning with, and *chairō* meaning to rejoice (70:270). Love rejoices "with" truth. Whatever truth rejoices in, love does also.

Look again at this description, for there is a definite article in the original before the word "truth." G. G. Findlay says that this is personified (13:899). The joy is found in nothing less than "the Truth." Of course, we remember that it was our

Lord Jesus Christ who said, "I am the Truth" (John 14:6). And the ministry of the Holy Spirit is to cause us to confess "Jesus is Lord" (1 Cor. 12:3) and to exalt Him!

Now it takes love to truly accomplish these matters. Only love can truly rejoice together with Christ. He is the source of that love and He is the means of that love. Such love enables the church to exult in the truth of His gospel, in the work eternally accomplished as triumphant over sin and death and hell.

It would seem that the Corinthians were failing in this. Paul had to remind them what the truth of the gospel is (1 Cor. 15:1-4) and what it accomplishes in men's lives (1 Cor. 6:11). Not the gifts, but the gospel had accomplished God's grace-work in their lives. They needed to be rejoicing more in the truth, therefore, than in the gifts. Only through the love which has truth as its objective rejoicing, can this happen. They must learn to love properly, for love is a better way.

Love not only "suffereth long and is kind," and "rejoiceth in the truth," but:

11. Love Is Virtuous in "All Things"

Notice how the virtues of love tumble from the apostle's pen, "beareth all things, believeth all things, hopeth all things, endureth all things" (1 Cor. 13:7).

Love "beareth all things." Beareth is from an old verb meaning "roof." It covers and protects, keeping out resentment as a roof does the rain (47:178). Peter says, "Above all things have fervent charity among yourselves: for charity shall cover the multitude of sins" (1 Peter 4:8). Love which is not irritable and malevolent and which does not gloat over the shortcomings of others, protects—not allowing resentment to press damages. How the Corinthians needed to learn this (1 Cor. 6:1-8)!

Love "believeth all things." The word is from *pisteuō* meaning to believe in the sense of to be persuaded of, to place one's confidence in, to trust. There is, therefore, more than the idea of mere credence, there is the stronger thought of reliance upon. It is a word loved by the Gospel writers, for example, John uses it ninety-nine times (68:116)!

W. Graham Scroggie says of this word:

This does not mean that love is blind and credulous, that it is easily deceived; but it does mean that it is not suspicious; that it is entirely alien to the spirit of the cynic, the pessimist, the anonymous slanderer, the secret detractor (51:46).

So love takes the kindest view, seeks the maximum good, and makes all possible allowances for the individual in which it believes.

Such love does the maximum good to others. As Henry Drummond remarks:

> You will find, if you think for a moment, that the people who influence you are people who believe in you. In an atmosphere of suspicion men shrivel up; but in that atmosphere they expand, and find encouragement and educative fellowship (10:39).

Oh how these Corinthians, with their divisions, suspicions, envyings and strifes (1 Cor. 3:3-4), needed such love in their midst.

Love "hopeth all things." Hope is one of the final triumvirate of verse 13. The word denotes a favorable and confident expectation. It describes the happy anticipation of good. Sometimes it is translated "trust," in our Authorized Version, as in 2 Cor. 1:10 which speaks of God, "who delivered us from so great a death, and doth deliver: in whom we trust[1] that he will yet deliver us."

This kind of hope refuses to despair. It has the quality of being able to look on the bright side of things in the most difficult of circumstance. Hope sees the sovereign hand of God behind every trial, every problem, every dark circumstance. There may not be an answer to the temporal, "Why," but there is a realization that God has an eternal reason for every thread in the tapestry of life. Had the Corinthians had such love, they would not have had the hopelessness that 1 Corinthians 15 was written to dispel.

Love "endureth all things." The word is *hupomenei,* a compound composed of *menō* meaning "to abide," and hence to endure; and *hupo* meaning "under." It thus means to abide

---

[1] "We trust," is *ēlpikamen;* the first person, plural, perfect, indicative, active of *elpizō;* "hope" in 1 Cor. 13:7.

under, with the significance of bearing up courageously. This causes love to persevere when others give up.

Like a stout-hearted soldier, the person with this quality will "endure hardness" (2 Tim. 2:3). This causes Scroggie to write:

> Love holds its ground in the day of defeat. At midnight it keeps its face to the dawn. When others faint and give way, love holds on.
>
> The best of all other efforts grows weary in its labors to get God's will done on earth as it is done in heaven, but love persists in spite of all delays (51:49).

Because the Corinthians needed this quality, Paul exhorted in his closing remarks, "Watch ye, stand fast in the faith, quit you like men, be strong. Let all your things be done with charity" (1 Cor. 16:13-14). Such love "endureth all things."

We have learned thus far that "gifts need love for profit" and that "temperament needs love for development." Now Paul adds another section to this explanation of "a more excellent way." He tells us that:

C. TIME NEEDS LOVE FOR MATURING

In the church, there are three periods in which love is seen as a timeless treasure to enable the church to mature. The first period concerns:

1. The Childhood of the Church

What a shock this was to the Corinthian believers. To them the gifts of the Spirit were the important thing. Being endowed to speak in tongues, or to perform miracles, or whatever the manifestation of the Spirit, took precedence among them. But love as relegated to a position of unimportance.

How it must have amazed them to hear Paul say, "Charity never faileth: but whether there be prophecies, they shall fail; whether there be tongues, they shall cease; whether there be knowledge, it shall vanish away" (1 Cor. 13:8). Prophecies shall be made idle. Tongues shall cause themselves to cease. Knowledge shall become inoperative. But love never fails! The word for "faileth" is *piptei,* denoting failing in the sense of cessation, of dropping out of existence. It is the word used in Luke 16:17 to describe the unfailing detail of God's Word. There we read, "It is easier for heaven and earth to pass, than one tittle of the law to fail." There is contrast here to the *charismata* of chapters 12 and 14. They are to cease, each at a determined point, but love is incessant and never will cease.

Though not realized by those in Corinth, love was the greatest treasure the early church could possibly possess. They were like children who had not yet learned the exhibition of love in their personal lives. Selfishness was their rule of conduct. Self-adulation was their confession. The gifts, and not their use in love was their self-concern. Blindness to the more excellent way of love was their plague. They could never sing the maturity song of A. B. Simpson:

> Once it was the blessing, Now it is the Lord;
> Once it was the feeling, Now it is His Word;
> Once His gifts I wanted, Now the Giver own;
> Once I sought for healing, Now Himself alone.
>
> All in all forever, Jesus will I sing;
> Everything in Jesus, And Jesus everything (103).

Therefore the childhood of this church was marked by self-interest, self-indulgence and self-love. They were so soon removed from the eleventh commandment, that it was as if Christ had never said:

> A new commandment I give unto you, That ye love one another; as I have loved you, that ye also love one another. By this shall all men know that ye are my disciples, if ye have love one to another (John 13:34-35).

No wonder Paul called the attention of these believers to a better way.

The second period Paul deals with might be broadly termed:

2. The Maturity of the Church

Paul writes:

> For we know in part, and we prophesy in part. But when that which is perfect is come, then that which is in part shall be done away. When I was a child, I spake as a child, I understood as a child, I thought as a child; but when I became a man, I put away childish things (1 Cor. 13:9-11).

Childhood must give way to adulthood. Thus, as time passed and events unfolded, the fragmentary gave way to the complete. All the partial knowledge of God's eternal revelation and the partial utterances of the prophets and the partial messages to the church through supernatural language facility gave way to the perfect Word of God.

The church grew up and all the things of childhood were laid aside. Gifts temporary and necessary to church childhood were superseded by the fulness of God's revelation. But one thing was still as necessary as ever—love! "Charity never faileth" (1 Cor. 13:8). The church still needs to, "Follow after charity" (1 Cor. 14:1).

How tragic, therefore, when the church begins to seek after the signs of immaturity, rather than the seal of maturity. When people pattern themselves after the self-seeking children of Corinth rather than the full-fledged adulthood of love, it is a catastrophe of regression. Well says James W. Bryant:

> The crisis that the presence of the tongues movement has brought to the evangelical church today is a crisis of love. This is the greatest challenge the evangelical church has faced in modern times (5:70).

Will we be able to meet such a challenge among our churches? We will if the emphasis is upon the "more excellent way" of 1 Corinthians 13 rather than upon the infantile among the gifts of the Spirit.

The third period of church life concerns:

3. The Consummation of the Church

Paul continues in 1 Cor. 13:12, "For now we see through a glass, darkly; but then face to face: now I know in part; but then shall I know even as also I am known." W. A. Criswell comments:

> We see now as in an esoptron, a polished piece of bronze metal that reflects the image so imperfectly. The ancients had no splendid mirrors of silver-lined glass as we possess today. Their looking glasses were wavy, indistinct, shadowy. Thus they say "as in an ainigma," "as in an enigma," "as in an obscure thing." But someday, some glorious day, we shall see and know and understand fully and completely, even as God knows all things (7:233).

Surely love cannot be the greatest treasure on that day of consummation, when we meet Christ? Will not He be the greatest Jewel of all? Ah yes! But "God is love," and He is the object of our love. Now we endure as seeing Him who is invisible, but then we will see Him face to face. Here we love Him by faith, but there by sight.

This great hope of love may be fulfilled by way of death. Should the Lord tarry each member of the body will go home through the valley. So we sing:

> Some day the silver cord will break,
> And I no more as now shall sing;
> But oh, the joy when I shall wake
> Within the palace of the King!
>
> And I shall see Him face to face,
> And tell the story—Saved by grace;
> And I shall see Him face to face,
> And tell the story—Saved by grace (101).

For the Christian, death is but love's highway to His presence!

Again, the fulfillment of hope's love may be by rapture. Someday the church will be called to God's presence. As it is written, "Enoch walked with God: and he was not; for God took him" (Gen. 5:24)—just so it is written that one glorious day God will take home His bride, the Church.

> For the Lord himself shall descend from heaven with a shout, with the voice of the archangel, and with the trump of God: and the dead in Christ shall rise first: Then we which are alive and remain shall be caught up together with them in the clouds, to meet the Lord in the air: and so shall we ever be with the Lord (1 Thess. 4:16-17).

O glorious day! The heartbeat of love longs for it. The poet rapturously expresses that longing:

> Face to face with Christ my Savior,
> Face to face—what will it be
> When with rapture I behold Him,
> Jesus Christ Who died for me?
>
> Only faintly now I see Him,
> With the darkling veil between;
> But a blessed day is coming,
> When His glory shall be seen.

What rejoicing in His presence,
When are banished grief and pain;
When the crooked ways are straightened,
And the dark things shall be plain.

Face to face! O blissful moment!
Face to face—to see and know;
Face to face with my Redeemer,
Jesus Christ Who loves me so.

Face to face I shall behold Him,
Far beyond the starry sky;
Face to face in all His glory,
I shall see Him by and by (100)!

Forever with the Lord!

The very atmosphere of heaven will be that of love. Thus Paul concludes his exposition of the more excellent way with the words, "And now abideth faith, hope, charity, these three; but the greatest of these is charity" (1 Cor. 13:13). Whether past, present or future—love abides. It is the greatest treasure we possess, and the one which enables us to relate to one another, to the world around us, and especially to Him.

At the consummation, faith will give way to sight and hope will be swallowed up in fulfillment, but love will abide as long as God abides. Love is "the greatest," for love is an attribute of God. Thus, the mightiest demonstration of His presence in the church is the practice of love and not of the gifts. Placing the emphasis on love rather than upon the gifts is, therefore, "a more excellent way" of church administration. "He that hath an ear, let him hear what the Spirit saith unto the churches" (Rev. 3:22).

BIBLIOGRAPHY

BOOKS

1. Bagster, Samuel and Sons, *The Analytical Greek Lexicon.* London: Samuel Bagster and Sons Limited, n.d.
2. Benson, John L., *The Holy Spirit—Help for Today.* Denver, Colo.: Baptist Publications, Inc., 1968.
3. Bruce, F. F., "The Book of Acts." *The New International Commentary on the New Testament.* Grand Rapids, Mich.: Wm. B. Eerdmans Publishing Co., 1960.
4. Bruner, Frederick Dale, *A Theology of the Holy Spirit.* Grand Rapids, Mich.: Wm. B. Eerdmans Publishing Co., 1970.
5. Bryant, James W. *The Doctrine of the Holy Spirit in the New Testament.* Dallas, Tex.: Crescendo Book Publications, 1973, Vol. 2, No. 2.
6. Clemens, David A., *Steps to Maturity.* Upper Darby, Pa.: Bible Club Movement, Inc., 1975, Vol. I.
7. Criswell, W. A., *The Holy Spirit in Today's World.* Grand Rapids, Mich.: Zondervan Publishing House, 1967.
8. Denney, James, "St. Paul's Epistle to the Romans." *The Expositor's Greek Testament.* 5 Vols. Grand Rapids, Mich.: Wm. B. Eerdmans Publishing Company, 1956, Vol. 2.
9. Dillow, Joseph, *Speaking in Tongues: Seven Crucial Questions.* Grand Rapids, Mich.: Zondervan Publishing House, 1976.
10. Drummond, Henry, *The Greatest Thing in the World.* Westwood, N.J.: Fleming H. Revell Co., n.d.
11. Engstrom, Ted W., *The Making of a Christian Leader.* Grand Rapids, Mich.: Zondervan Publishing House, 1977.
12. Fife, Eric S., *The Holy Spirit.* Grand Rapids, Mich.: Zondervan Publishing House, 1978.
13. Findlay, G. G., "St. Paul's First Epistle to the Corinthians." *The Expositor's Greek Testament.* 5 Vols. Grand Rapids, Mich.: Wm. B. Eerdmans Publishing Co., 1956, Vol. 2.
14. Fitch, William, *The Ministry of the Holy Spirit.* Grand Rapids, Mich.: Zondervan Publishing House, 1974.

15. Flynn, Leslie B., *Nineteen Gifts of the Spirit.* Wheaton, Ill.: Victor Books, 1974.
16. Gardiner, George E., *The Corinthian Catastrophe.* Grand Rapids, Mich.: Kregel Publications, 1975.
17. Gee, Donald, *Now That You've Been Baptized in the Spirit.* Springfield, Mo.: Gospel Publishing House, 1972.
18. Getz, Gene A., *Building Up One Another.* Wheaton, Ill.: Victor Books, 1976.
19. Gordon, A. J., *The Ministry of the Spirit.* Philadelphia, Pa.: The Judson Press, 1949.
20. Green, Hollis L., *Why Churches Die.* Minneapolis, Minn.: Bethany Fellowship, 1972.
21. Hagin, Kenneth E., *Concerning Spiritual Gifts.* Tulsa, Okla.: Kenneth Hagin Ministries, Inc., 1974.
22. Hughes, Philip E., "The Second Epistle to the Corinthians." *The New International Commentary on the New Testament.* 13 Vols. Grand Rapids, Mich.: Wm. B. Eerdmans Publishing Co., 1979, Vol. 8.
23. Hummel, Charles E., *Fire in the Fireplace.* Downers Grove, Ill.: InterVarsity Press, 1978.
24. Ironside, H. A., *The Mission of and Praying in the Holy Spirit.* (2 Vols. in 1). New York, N.Y.: Loizeaux Brothers, Inc., 1950, Vol. 2.
25. Kinghorn, Kenneth Cain, *Gifts of the Spirit.* Nashville, Tenn.: Abingdon Press, 1976.
26. Kittel, Gerherd, *Theological Dictionary of the New Testament.* 9 Vols. Grand Rapids, Mich.: Wm. B. Eerdmans Publishing Co., 1964, Vol. 2.
27. _____, *Theological Dictionary of the New Testament.* 9 Vols. Grand Rapids, Mich.: Wm. B. Eerdmans Publishing Co., 1965, Vol. 3.
28. _____, *Theological Dictionary of the New Testament.* 9 Vols. Grand Rapids, Mich.: Wm. B. Eerdmans Publishing Co., 1967, Vol. 5.
29. _____, *Theological Dictionary of the New Testament.* 9 Vols. Grand Rapids, Mich.: Wm. B. Eerdmans Publishing Co., 1974, Vol. 9.
30. Lambert, J. C., "Apostle." *International Standard Bible Encyclopaedia.* Chicago: Howard-Severance Co., 1937.
31. LeTourneau, R. G., *Mover of Man and Mountains.* Chicago: Moody Press, 1972.
32. MacArthur, John F., Jr., *The Charismatics.* Grand Rapids, Mich.: Zondervan Publishing House, 1979.

33. Macaulay, J. D., *Life in the Spirit*. Grand Rapids, Mich.: Wm. B. Eerdmans Publishing Co., 1955.
34. Mains, David R., *Full Circle*. Waco, Tex.: Word Books, 1971.
35. McRae, William J., *The Dynamics of Spiritual Gifts*. Grand Rapids, Mich.: Zondervan Publishing House, 1976.
36. Merrett, Donald C., "The Gifts of the Holy Spirit." *The Biblical Faith of Baptists*. Des Plaines, Ill.: Regular Baptist Press, 1966, Book 2.
37. Miller, Basil, *George Mueller: The Man of Faith*. Grand Rapids, Mich.: Zondervan Publishing House, 1941.
38. Morgan, G. Campbell, *The Acts of the Apostles*. Westwood, N.J.: Fleming H. Revell, 1924.
39. Morris, Leon, *Commentary on First Corinthians*. London: Tyndale Press, 1958.
40. Nolen, William A., *Healing: A Doctor in Search of a Miracle*. New York, N.Y.: Random House Publishers, 1974.
41. O'Connor, Elizabeth, *Eighth Day of Creation*. Waco, Tex.: Word Publishing Co., 1971.
42. Owen, John, *The Holy Spirit*. Grand Rapids, Mich.: Sovereign Grace Publishers, 1971.
43. Pache, René, *The Person and Work of the Holy Spirit*. Chicago: Moody Press, 1957.
44. Pentecost, J. Dwight, *The Divine Comforter*. Chicago: Moody Press, 1970.
45. _____, *Will Man Survive?* Chicago: Moody Press, 1971.
46. Pierce, Samuel Eyles, *The Gospel of the Spirit*. Grand Rapids, Mich.: Wm. B. Eerdmans Publishing Co., 1955.
47. Robertson, A. T., *Word Pictures in the New Testament*. 6 Vols. Nashville, Tenn.: Broadman Press, 1931, Vol. 4.
48. Ryrie, Charles Caldwell, *The Holy Spirit*. Chicago: Moody Press, 1979.
49. Sanders, J. Oswald, *The Holy Spirit and His Gifts*. Grand Rapids, Mich.: Zondervan Publishing House, 1979.
50. Sanderson, John W., *The Fruit of the Spirit*. Grand Rapids, Mich.: Zondervan Publishing House, 1972.
51. Scroggie, W. Graham, *The Love Life*. Reprint. Grand Rapids, Mich.: Kregel Publications, 1980.
52. Shaw, George, *The Spirit in Redemption*. New York, N.Y.: Christian Alliance Publishing Co., 1910.
53. Simpson, A. B., *The Holy Spirit*. 2 Vols. Harrisburg, Pa.: Christian Publications, Inc., 1896, Vol. 2.
54. Smith, Oswald J., *The Enduement of Power*. London: Marshall, Morgan & Scott, Ltd., 1946.

55. Spurgeon, C. H., *Metropolitan Tabernacle Pulpit.* 56 Vols. Pasadena, Tex.: Pilgrim Publications, 1970, Vol. 13.
56. _____, *Metropolitan Tabernacle Pulpit.* 56 Vols. Pasadena, Tex.: Pilgrim Publications, 1971, Vol. 17.
57. _____, *Metropolitan Tabernacle Pulpit.* 56 Vols. Pasadena, Tex.: Pilgrim Publications, 1977, Vol. 46.
58. Stott, John R. W., *Baptism and Fullness.* London: Inter-Varsity, 1964.
59. Stover, Gerald L., *The Power for Christian Living.* (Adult Student), Denver, Colo.: Baptist Publications, 1962.
60. Sweeting, William J., *The Power for Christian Living.* (Adult Teacher), Denver, Colo.: Baptist Publications, 1962.
61. Tasker, R. V. G., *Tyndale New Testament Commentaries - 2 Corinthians.* London: The Tyndale Press, 1959.
62. Thayer, J. H., *Greek-English Lexicon of the New Testament.* New York: American Book, 1889.
63. Thomson, James G. S. S., *Baker's Dictionary of Theology.* Grand Rapids, Mich.: Baker Book House, 1960.
64. Trench, Richard Chenevix, *Notes on the Miracles of Our Lord.* London: Kegan Paul, Trench, Trubner, & Co. Ltd., 1908.
65. Unger, Merrill F., *The Baptism & Gifts of the Holy Spirit.* Chicago: Moody Press, 1978.
66. Vincent, Marvin R., *Word Studies in the New Testament.* 4 Vols. Grand Rapids, Mich.: Wm. B. Eerdmans Publishing Co., 1975, Vol. 1.
67. _____, *Word Studies in the New Testament.* 4 Vols. Grand Rapids, Mich.: Wm. B. Eerdmans Publishing Co., 1975. Vol. 3.
68. Vine, W. E., *An Expository Dictionary of New Testament Words.* (4 Vols. in 1). Old Tappan, N.J.: Fleming H. Revell Co., 1966, Vol. 1.
69. _____, *An Expository Dictionary of New Testament Words.* (4 Vols. in 1). Old Tappan, N.J.: Fleming H. Revell Co., 1966, Vol. 2.
70. _____, *An Expository Dictionary of New Testament Words.* (4 Vols. in 1). Old Tappan, N.J.: Fleming H. Revell Co., 1966, Vol. 3.
71. _____, *An Expository Dictionary of New Testament Words.* (4 Vols. in 1). Old Tappan, N.J.: Fleming H. Revell Co., 1966, Vol. 4.
72. Wagner, C. Peter, *Your Spiritual Gifts Can Help Your Church Grow.* Glendale, Calif.: Regal Books Division, G/L Publications, 1979.

73. Walvoord, John F., *The Holy Spirit*. Grand Rapids, Mich.: Zondervan Publishing House, 1978.
74. _____, *The Holy Spirit at Work Today*. Chicago: Moody Press, 1973.
75. Warfield, B. B., *Counterfeit Miracles*. Carlisle, Pa.: Banner of Truth, 1918.
76. Webb, Allan Becher, *The Presence and Office of the Holy Spirit*. London: Skeffington & Son, 1883.
77. Williams, J. Rodman, *The Era of the Spirit*. Plainfield, N.J.: Logos International, 1971.

BOOKLETS

78. Coy, Larry, *The Gifts of the Holy Spirit*. Victorious Ventures, Inc., 1975.
79. Scroggie, W. Graham, *Speaking With Tongues: What Saith the Scriptures?* New York: The Book Stall, 1919.
80. Sugden, Howard F., *The Signs of an Apostle*. Lansing, Mich.: South Baptist Church, 1973.
81. Tozer, A. W., *How to be Filled With the Holy Spirit*. Harrisburg, Pa.: Christian Publications, Inc., n.d.
82. Zodhiates, Spiros, *Healing and Miracles: Are They for Today?* Chattanooga, Tenn.: AMG Publishers, 1979.

PERIODICALS

83. Benn, Gerry, "Biblical Reasons Why I Am Not a Charismatic." *Truth Aflame*. London Baptist Seminary, June 1979.
84. Chandler, Russell, "Fanning the Charismatic Fire." *Christianity Today*. November 24, 1967.
85. Lindsell, Harold, "Tests for the Tongues Movement." *Christianity Today*. December 8, 1972.
86. McAlister, R. E., "Salvation and the Baptism of the Holy Spirit." *The Pentecostal Testimony*. Special Edition.
87. McClelland, James, "Protest." *The Revivalist*. February 1977.
88. Mooneyham, W. Stanley, "Revival and Miracles - What About Indonesia?" *Christian Heritage*. November 1972.
89. Paxton, Geoffrey J., "The Current Religious Scene and the Bible." *Present Truth*. February 1974.
90. Pickford, J. H., "Baptists and the Charismatic Movement." *Evangelical Baptist*. December 1969.
91. Plowman, Edward E. & Wagner, John, "Jesus '79: Pentecost Rallies Spread a Grassroots Unity." *Christianity Today*. June 29, 1979.
92. Torrance, Thomas F., "Protestant Sacerdotalism." *Present Truth*. April 1975.

93. Welch, Wilbert, "The One Who Works in You." *Moody Monthly*. September 1967.

UNPUBLISHED MATERIALS

94. Booth, John Louis, "The Purpose of Miracles." Doctor's dissertation, Dallas Theological Seminary, Dallas, Tex., 1965. (Quoted by Joseph Dillow in *Speaking in Tongues.*).

BIBLES AND TRANSLATIONS OR VERSIONS

95. *American Standard Version.* New York: Thomas Nelson & Sons, 1929.
96. Moffatt, James, *A New Translation of the New Testament.* London: Hodder and Stoughton, 1949.
97. Scofield, C. I., *The Scofield Reference Bible.* New York: Oxford University Press, 1945.
98. *The New English Bible.* Oxford: Oxford University Press/ Cambridge University Press, 1961.
99. *The New International Version.* Grand Rapids, Mich.: Zondervan Bible Publishers, 1973.

POETRY

100. Breck, Carrie E., "Face to Face." *Worship and Service Hymnal.* Chicago: Hope Publishing Co., 1971.
101. Crosby, Fanny J., "Saved By Grace." *Worship and Service Hymnal.* Chicago: Hope Publishing Co., 1971.
102. Robinson, Robert, "Come, Thou Fount." *Worship and Service Hymnal.* Chicago: Hope Publishing Co., 1971.
103. Simpson, A. B., "Once It Was the Blessing." *Sacred Songs & Solos.* London and Edinburgh: Marshall, Morgan & Scott, Ltd., n.d.

INDEX OF SCRIPTURE TEXTS

INDEX OF NAMES

INDEX OF SUBJECT MATTER

ANOTHER BIBLICAL EXPOSITION
from the pen of
RONALD E. BAXTER

CHARISMATIC GIFT OF TONGUES

"In the midst of a great deal of confusion arising out of the present discussion concerning the doctrine of the Holy Spirit and its meaning for contemporary man, Dr. R. E. Baxter speaks particularly to the issue of the gift of tongues with a voice of biblical authority and with skill exegetes the Word of God.

"The careful distinction which the author draws between the baptism of the Spirit and His filling, between the gift of the Holy Spirit and His gifts to the church, and his extensive study of the theme of the gift of tongues combine to make this volume one which merits the attention of Christians everywhere, especially those whose lives have been touched by the modern charismatic movement."

—Dr. Roy W. Lawson

"Truths here are taught with clarity, problems are faced with courage, and one feels that here is a valuable contribution to an important area of biblical truth. The perusal of this volume will be of immense profit."

—Dr. Howard Sugden

"A thorough piece of work . . . well written and reveals much research. His approach is novel."

—Martin O. Wedge

Another KREGEL PUBLICATION